T0377666

TAKING COMMAND

America's Unsung Military Leaders, Innovators, and Difference Makers Since World War II

THOMAS D. PHILLIPS

STACKPOLE BOOKS

Essex, Connecticut

STACKPOLE BOOKS

An imprint of The Globe Pequot Publishing Group, Inc.
64 South Main Street
Essex, CT 06426
www.globepequot.com

British Library Cataloguing in Publication Information available

Library of Congress Cataloging-in-Publication Data available

ISBN 978-0-8117-7727-8 (cloth)
ISBN 978-0-8117-7728-5 (ebook)

♾™ The paper used in this publication meets the minimum requirements of American National Standard for Information Sciences—Permanence of Paper for Printed Library Materials, ANSI/NISO Z39.48-1992.

*To all those who have served our country
with honor and pride*

CONTENTS

LIST OF PHOTOS

List of Maps

PREFACE

Since the earliest days of the nation's existence, the names of a small set of exceptional military leaders have become enshrined in the collective consciousness of the American people. Their names evoke immediate recollections of specific times, places, and events. They are instantly recognizable: Washington, Scott, Grant, Pershing, MacArthur, Patton, Nimitz, and others. Their fame comes from having led the nation's military forces—most often with singular success—through the crucible of combat during perilous times. Their glory will remain for as long as America exists as a nation.

This book focuses on individuals whose achievements have sometimes equaled those of their more illustrious contemporaries. Yet, in the long stream of history, their accomplishments have somehow been overlooked; their services to the nation seldom acknowledged by the wider public. They remain in the shadows cast by the pantheon of giants.

Taking Command is not intended to rewrite or revise history. The names of these forgotten warriors are sometimes known outside military circles, although most often in a dimly lit fashion. Rather, the purpose is to shed light on these deserving leaders and, in a small way, provide balance to the historical record.

Veterans of several of the conflicts described in this book remain active in daily life, involved in and vital contributors to the nation's affairs. Therefore, I have written about the wars and the main events associated with them in detail that extends beyond a simple recap. To do anything less would, it seemed to me, shortchange the men and women who served "up close and personal" and experienced the events firsthand. I hope I have struck the right balance.

In the Vietnam chapter I have included a separate section on the Tet Offensive. Tet was such a seminal event that no discussion of the war, or understanding of it, could be complete without an explanation. The actions of several of the "forgotten leaders" revolve around the Tet occurrence. Their roles are more fully appreciated by a description of the campaign and the events that defined it.

Throughout the book, I have in places included a "Special Mention" category to capture instances of exceptional leadership during unique circumstances.

Additionally, I have noted examples of leaders whose major renown is associated with a specific war but who also rendered exemplary though largely forgotten service in a different conflict. General Norman Schwarzkopf is a case in point. Known for having led American and coalition forces to victory in the Gulf War, Schwarzkopf is less well recalled for his contributions during the invasion of Grenada.

I began this project several years ago by soliciting comments from the military history departments at the United States Military Academy, the United States Naval Academy, the United States Air Force Academy, the Virginia Military Institute, The Citadel, and the University of Nebraska–Lincoln. Sources at each of these institutions provided insights and avenues for inquiry. Within this group, I am especially grateful to Douglas Kennedy at the United States Air Force Academy and Jourdan Travis Moger at the United States Naval Academy for their assistance early in the process. I have particularly valued the contributions of Dr. Peter Maslowski, professor emeritus at the University of Nebraska–Lincoln, and his connection with this endeavor over the later stages.

As was to be expected considering the different experiences, interests, and areas of expertise brought to the project by the historians who contributed to it, there was nothing approaching a unanimous recommendation for any "forgotten leader" in any war. That result also accurately reflects the breadth of opinion regarding a most subjective, and at times highly controversial, issue.

Ultimately, the choices were mine alone.

Separate, special thanks must go to the many individuals who so generously contributed their unique expertise regarding specific battles, campaigns, and personalities described in this book. I am especially beholden to Dr. Thomas Berg, University of Nebraska–Lincoln, for providing the opportunity to partake of an extended program on the Cold

War. I am also particularly grateful to Brigadier General Raymond C. Franck Jr. (USAF—ret.), one of the military's finest historians, for his comprehensive review of the manuscript draft and for his wise counsel regarding its contents.

Space limitations in a work of this scope preclude the listing of a bibliography in the traditional sense. Where appropriate, I have instead compiled individual biographical lists, each focusing on a specific leader. These lists may be seen as recommended readings for those interested in further adding to their understanding of the individuals who led forces during this extraordinary period in the nation's history.

Similarly, traditional footnoting would have required numbering every third or fourth sentence and added further scores of pages to the text. Therefore—as have Robert Leckie (*The Wars of America*) and others who have written in this genre—in the interests of space and readability I have confined reference notes to directly quoted material.

Setting the Stage

The era covered in the pages that follow witnessed the most dynamic evolution of technology in military history. The C-47s and C-54s that sustained the Berlin Airlift (often called the "first battle of the Cold War") had carrying capacities of three and ten tons, respectively. The C-17s and C-5As of more recent years routinely handle loads of 85 and 140 tons—and can haul them across oceans. The Korean War saw the first combat between jet aircraft with American F-86 Sabres dueling Russian-built MiG-15s. Guided munitions made their appearance in the Vietnam conflict, delivered with a degree of precision that has seen continued refinement in later years. Intervention in Panama saw the first, brief introduction of Stealth aircraft, foreshadowing their extensive use in the Gulf War.

Compared to their World War II counterparts, today's tanks, submarines, aircraft carriers, and ancillary equipment represent orders-of-magnitude advances in characteristics such as speed, range, and lethality. The reach of long-range bombers spans continents. Land- and sea-based missiles share that capability, thus holding at-risk targets thousands of miles away, reachable in flight times measured in minutes. Drones and satellites have become integral components in the arsenals of modern militaries. Joining them in the foreseeable future, if not already present in the militaries of some nations, are weapons and equipment with science-fiction-like capabilities, such as hypersonic reprogrammable missiles.

"Information warfare" has become an essential topic when military conversations turn to subjects such as operational capability and technology-related acquisitions. By the third decade of the 21st century, the United States had developed the capability to deliver munitions with such extraordinary accuracy that it can employ missiles fitted with blades to, for example, attack individuals in vehicles. The missile warheads contain no explosive devices, thus greatly limiting collateral damage. As weapons systems acquire increasing proportions of automatic functions, features such as identification, tracking, and targeting, and the components that animate them, assume critical importance.

Sometimes lost in the glare of publicity surrounding combat narratives and descriptions of new and exotic weapon systems have been the quieter but equally significant advances in key support areas. Though not the central theme of this book, these considerations warrant mention in order to provide context to the milieu in which each of the "forgotten leaders" operated.

Improvements in battlefield medical care provide a fitting illustration. Korea saw the introduction of helicopter evacuation of wounded soldiers and the siting of MASH facilities close to the line of battle. Frozen blood products as well as antiseptic- and antibiotic-impregnated dressings for burn care were inaugurated in Vietnam. PTSD was first formally treated as a combat-related injury in that conflict as well.

The combination of improved handling of wounded soldiers and the quality of care they receive has markedly improved survival statistics. Even as late as Vietnam, it was not unusual for lengthy delays to elapse before wounded soldiers were returned to the United States. In contrast, the typical time for the Iraq War was four days. The fatality rate for battlefield casualties in World War II hovered around 50 percent. In Vietnam, the survival rate increased to 86.5 percent. The figures for Iraq and Afghanistan have been 90.2 and 91.5 percent, respectively. Equally noteworthy is that the survivability rate for the most critically wounded has been improved threefold.

During the period from the Cold War to the Global War on Terrorism (GWOT), America's military leaders have had to adjust to diverse circumstances both geographically and sociologically. From "Frozen Chosin" in Korea to 120-degree temperatures in Baghdad, Vietnam's triple-canopy jungle to trackless stretches of Iraqi desert, they have waged major battles in cities big and small and intense firefights in hamlets and rural areas. They have fought division-sized formations of modern armies, small squads of irregular militia, and individual terrorists bent on martyrdom.

From the outset of the Cold War to the present day, nearly 101,000 American servicemen and women have lost their lives in combat-related circumstances. Of that number, slightly more than 87,000 have been killed in action. An additional 300,000 have been wounded.

United States Military Casualties of War

	Killed in Action	Other Fatalities	Total Deaths	Wounded in Action
Cold War/ Ancillary GWOT Other Actions/ Incidents[1]	502	391	893	1,001
Korea	33,686	2,830	36,516	92,134[2]
Vietnam	47,424	10,785	58,209	153,303[3]
Grenada	18	1	19	119
Panama	23	17	40	324
Gulf War	149	145	294	849
Afghanistan[4]	1,833	385	2,218	20,093
Iraq[4]	3,481	937	4,418	31,994

1. Cold War and other /incidents include:
   Greek Civil War, Chinese Civil War, Berlin Airlift, USSR Cold War, China Cold War, Lebanon Crisis, Bay of Pigs, Cuban Missile Crisis, Dominican Republic, USS *Liberty* incident, Iran hostage rescue attempt, El Salvador, Beirut, Persian Gulf escorts, Libya, Operation Provide Comfort, Somalia, Haiti, Colombia, Bosnia-Herzegovina, Kosovo, ISIS, Yemen.
2. An additional 4,759 remain missing in action.
3. An additional 1,587 remain missing in action.
4. Figures are as of February 2021.

The United States military began this era as a segregated institution. Desegregation of the armed forces by President Harry S. Truman in 1948 was the first of several impactful changes that shaped the nation's present-day forces. Few of the world's military establishments mirror the societies from which they are drawn as closely as America's. Thus, these later changes—women in combat and others—also have ripple effects through the larger populations from which America's warriors are drawn.

Accommodating these policy adjustments has not always been easy, but introducing them, institutionalizing them, has been met with general success. That they have is a tribute to the institution as a whole, and most specifically to the skill and dedication of the officers and noncommissioned officers who implemented the changes.

As significant as the technological advances noted earlier were to the warfighting prowess of U.S. forces, they have been matched in importance by a series of structural changes that have shaped and refocused the nation's military establishment.

The United States fought World War II and the wars that preceded it using two independent lines of command. On matters concerning the Army and the Air Force (which was organizationally aligned in the Army establishment), the president/commander in chief worked through the Department of War, as the Department of the Army was then titled. On naval matters, the president's route was directly to the Department of the Navy.

Drawing on lessons from World War II, President Truman signed into law the National Security Act of 1947. Enacted on September 18 of that year, the provisions sought to achieve greater unification of the services, reduce wasteful spending, and address concerns regarding interservice rivalry. Often called one of the most important pieces of Cold War legislation, the law established a Department of Defense responsible for "coordinating and supervising all agencies and functions of government directly related to national security and the United States Armed Forces" (Public Law 235 of July 26, 1947, 61 STAT 496).

Other parts of the law designated the Air Force as a separate service; dissolved the Department of War, in its place creating a new entity that would eventually be titled the Department of Defense; and formally established the Departments of the Army, Navy, and Air Force. The act also designated the secretary of defense as the principal military advisor to the president (although initially the powers of the office were somewhat limited) and protected the Marine Corps as an independent service within the Department of the Navy.

In 1949, an amendment to the act increased the authority of the secretary of defense and removed the three service secretaries—Army, Navy, and Air Force—from cabinet-level rank. The title National Military Establishment, as the overall structure was labeled in the 1947 legislation, was revised to Department of Defense. An additional amendment in 1958 further streamlined channels of authority by removing the military departments from the operational chain of command.

In 1986, the Goldwater-Nichols Act incorporated several important modifications. Goldwater-Nichols came as a response to persisting problems of interservice rivalry in Vietnam, the failure of the Iranian hostage rescue mission in 1980, and the military's less-than-stellar operational performance in Grenada in 1983. The sweeping changes of Goldwater-Nichols were the most consequential modifications to the nation's military establishment introduced since the original 1947 legislation. The Goldwater-Nichols provisions remain essentially intact in the present day.

The legislation removed the Joint Chiefs of Staff from operational command authority, specifying that the warfighting chain of command would run from the president through the secretary of defense directly to the combatant commanders in the field. At the same time, the power of the chairman of the Joint Chiefs of Staff was enhanced. The chairman was designated as the principal military advisor to the president, the secretary of defense, and the National Security Agency. The chairman was additionally tasked with overseeing policy and formulating strategy, but would not exercise command authority over any of the services, whose roles were specifically defined. Military departments were charged with organizing, training, and equipping forces for use by the combatant commanders. A less visible provision, but one with far-reaching implications, required that promotion to senior rank—admiral or general—would require experience in a joint service organization and completion of joint professional military education schooling.

During the years since its passage, Goldwater-Nichols has generally received good reviews. Though procurement issues have not by any means been eliminated, organizational changes prompted by the law have led to a fuller consideration of the views of each of the services. Discussions and formulation of doctrine and strategy, while often still difficult and contentious, are markedly improved over the two lines of authority situation that existed through World War II. Interoperability of weapon systems and components between services draws more attention and emphasis than in the past. Improvements in these areas have at times contributed to economy-of-scale savings in purchases of equipment and materiel.

Most important, though, has been the very clear improvement in the nation's warfighting capability fostered by the legislation. Pre-Goldwater-

Nichols operations in Grenada were less than satisfactory. Among several problems, commanders experienced severe difficulties in coordinating the employment of forces from different services. Communications issues between them would at times have been almost laughable had lives not been at stake.

Grenada took place in 1983. Goldwater-Nichols was enacted in 1986. Operation Just Cause (Panama) occurred three years later—and met with extraordinary success. Soon after Just Cause, the military's performance in the Gulf War further validated the results.

The most recent change to the nation's military structure took place on December 20, 2020, with the establishment of the United States Space Command as a separate command within the Department of the Air Force.

As noted at the outset, the period from the onset of the Cold War to the present day has been the most vibrant ever in American military affairs. The changes that have taken place over those seven-plus decades have been dynamic, enormous in number, and significant in scope and impact. They have touched every aspect of the U.S. military establishment and have tested America's military leadership in both peace and war.

CHAPTER ONE

The Cold War

THE PATH TO WAR

For a period of more than 40 years, the United States and the Soviet Union threatened each other with nuclear annihilation. The confrontation touched the entire planet. Though conflict came terrifyingly close at times, the two superpowers never directly fought each other in a shooting war. Both, however, engaged in proxy wars supporting client states in places like Korea, Vietnam, Angola, and Afghanistan. Elsewhere across the globe, with varying degrees of success, indigenous forces allied to the West combated communist-inspired uprisings in Malaya, Hong Kong, the Philippines, China, and Nicaragua.

In essence, the Cold War was a clash between worldviews, between civilizations—and each side viewed it as such. Pitted against American free-market capitalism was the centrally controlled command economy of Soviet communism. The contest shaped world politics for decades, driving the foreign policies of both nations and propelling a nuclear arms race, massive military establishments, and intense technological, political, and economic competition. Eventually, two enormous military alliances—the North Atlantic Treaty Organization and the Warsaw Pact—stood face-to-face across the continent of Europe and by extension elsewhere throughout the world.

The causes cited for the Cold War are almost as numerous as the legions of scholars who have analyzed and written about it over the years. Some trace its antecedents all the way back to the closing days of World War I. When the tsarist regime collapsed and the Kerensky government was subsequently overthrown in March 1918, Lenin accepted German peace terms (the Treaty of Brest-Litovsk) and withdrew Russia from the war on the side of the Allies. Relatively small numbers of British and American forces were sent to Russia ostensibly to protect supplies intended for tsarist and Kerensky forces that had been dispatched prior to the Soviet takeover. The new communist government regarded the Western actions as interference in Russian affairs and accused the Allies of tacitly supporting "White Russian" and other forces that opposed the new regime.

Relations remained frosty for many years—the United States did not accord formal diplomatic recognition to the Soviet Union until 1933. As conditions in Europe deteriorated in the 1930s and Nazi Germany became increasingly bellicose, Soviet leader Joseph Stalin was for a time apparently amenable to supporting Britain and France in opposition to German incursions. However, when the Western Allies took no action after several German territorial moves and at Munich formally acquiesced to the Nazi takeover of the Sudetenland, Stalin's support began to cool. In early 1939, Germany took over the rest of Czechoslovakia. Britain and France warned that any further move against Poland would be regarded as an act of war. By then, however, it was too late—Stalin had moved on.

From the middle of the decade, Stalin had been providing Germany with strategic resources—such as crude oil, rubber, and manganese—and allowing the German army and air force to train in secret on Russian soil in violation of the Versailles Treaty.

A week before Hitler launched the attack on Poland that started World War II, Russia signed a nonaggression pact with Germany (the Molotov-Ribbentrop Pact) that promised the continued flow of raw materials to the Third Reich. In a secret protocol, the two nations agreed to partition Poland: the western half would go to Germany; Russia would occupy the eastern portion. Two weeks after the Wehrmacht struck in the west, Russian forces moved into eastern Poland. Russia also invaded Finland; demanded and received extensive portions of Rumania; and annexed the Baltic countries of Lithuania, Latvia, and Estonia. Germany and Russia had essentially divided the continent of Europe between them. This duplicity was not lost on the Western Allies. Stalin's pact with Germany would remain intact until Hitler shattered it by invading Russia on June 22, 1941.

Despite cooperation between the major allies—Russia, Great Britain, and the United States—strains were evident during the course of the conflict. Foremost among them was Russia's insistence on a "second front" in Europe to relieve the enormous pressure on the Red Army. At the Tehran Conference in 1943, Stalin accused the Western Allies of delaying a cross-channel invasion and was adamant that an attack be made quickly.

Throughout the war the United States provided massive amounts of war-fighting material to the Soviet Union through the Lend-Lease program. Though the goods and equipment contributed substantially to Russia's capability to withstand the Wehrmacht, Soviet leaders were far more influenced by the 22–28 million Russians killed during the course of the war. Russia's historical experience had caused the nation to view security in terms of space. Once again, Eastern Europe had formed an invasion route into Mother Russia.

A hint of the approach that would later guide Russia's postwar actions occurred during the Warsaw Uprising in August 1944. As the Red Army advanced toward the city, the Polish underground rose up in an attempt to rid themselves of the Nazi yoke. Stalin denied aid to the insurgents, holding his forces outside the city while preventing the United States and Great Britain from coming to their assistance. Apparently seeing the uprising as an opportunity to weaken opposition and ease the way for his own subsequent occupation of Poland, Stalin stood by as the Polish underground army fought for 63 days until it was crushed by the Nazis and the city was destroyed.

When the "Big Three" Allied leaders—Stalin, Roosevelt, and Churchill—met at Yalta in February 1945, they attempted to define the postwar framework. Although there was modest agreement in some areas, they were unable to resolve differences regarding the occupation of Germany, reparations, and loans.

The conference saw extended debate regarding the composition of Poland's postwar status. During the war, two Polish governments in exile had evolved. One was a communist regime supported by Stalin. The other, favored by Roosevelt and Churchill and based in London, was democratic in principle. While Roosevelt and Churchill pushed for self-determination for Poland and other nations of Eastern Europe, they were confronted by the reality that hundreds of thousands of Russian troops occupied the territory and that the Soviets exercised de facto control over that entire half of the continent. In the end, the two Western leaders were forced to accept a rather vague and toothless "Declaration of Liberated Europe" proclamation that promised self-determination after the war was over. As events would reveal, obsessed with security concerns and in a dominant "boots on the ground" position, Stalin would never allow the provisions of the declaration to be carried out.

At Potsdam in July and August 1945, immediately following the end of the war, the leaders—the Western Allies now represented by Truman and Attlee (who replaced Churchill during the course of the meeting) discussed zones of occupation and the future development of Germany and Eastern Europe. Again, the differences proved irreconcilable. The Allies wished to rebuild Europe, particularly Germany, to enable it to become a democratic hub of economic and political affairs. Stalin's aim was control and domination; he eventually built a system of satellite states subservient to and dependent upon the Soviet Union.

In the coming months the separation between the powers widened. When the United States created the World Bank and International Monetary Fund to help spur recovery, the Soviet Union declined admission. On June 5, 1947, the United States announced the Marshall Plan, offering economic assistance to all European countries willing to participate. Stalin's view, though, was of a bipolar world. The USSR refused to join, and at his behest, the satellite states declined also.

In February 1948, a brutal Soviet coup d'état in Czechoslovakia brought further hardening of positions. In June of that year, Russia cut off surface-road access to Berlin, denying food, water, and supplies to American, British, and French sectors of the occupied city. The Allied response, the Berlin Airlift, was the first major confrontation in the shadow war that would last generations. Many more would follow, among them the Berlin Crisis, the Berlin Wall, Checkpoint Charlie, the Cuban Missile Crisis, and various proxy wars around the world. All were overshadowed by the looming presence of nuclear weapons.

Debates concerning causes of the war and factors that contributed to it have persisted over the years. John Lewis Gaddis, the great historian of the Cold War, acknowledges extraordinary circumstances and faults on both sides, but places considerable responsibility on Stalin.

"Geography, demography, and tradition contributed to the outcome but did not define it. It took men, responding unpredictably to circumstances, to forge the chain of causation; and it took Stalin in particular, responding predictably to his own authoritarianism, paranoia, and narcissistic predisposition, to lock it in place."

Forgotten Leader: William H. Tunner

The Miracle from the Sky

In China, Germany, and Korea, Tunner led three of the most consequential airlifts in military history. The success of the Berlin Airlift gave America and its allies "the first victory of the Cold War" and may have saved Europe. U.S. AIR FORCE—AIR FORCE HISTORY OFFICE

For America and its allies, the Berlin Airlift was the first victory of the Cold War. For 15 months the future of Europe had teetered on the brink. With the citizens of Berlin threatened by a blockade that shut off all access to the city by road, rail, and river, the stakes were enormous not only for them but indeed for the entire continent. In the early days of the crisis, General Lucius D. Clay, commander of the Office of the Military Government and military governor of Germany, stated, "[If] Berlin falls, West Germany will be next. If we withdraw, our position in Europe is threatened and [the Soviet Union] will run rampant."

On June 24, 1948, the Soviet Union blocked all land and water approaches to Berlin. The Soviet action was the culmination of a series of disputes that had fractured the Allied powers' war-winning alliance. Quarrels precipitated by currency reforms and a score of issues big and small shattered hopes for an enduring peace.

Surrounded by more than a million and a half Soviet troops, the Western Allies responded to the provocation with what some would later label a miracle: an unprecedented airlift that supplied the world's fifth largest city—2.5 million people at the time—as well as occupation troops and several thousand other foreign nationals, with all of their daily needs. Everything was flown in: food, medical supplies, construction equipment, fodder for cattle, provisions for the animals in the city zoo—*everything*.

It would turn out to be the greatest humanitarian aviation event in history.

Through three 20-mile-wide air corridors, planes flew around the clock. Eventually, operations became so proficient that the tonnage exceeded the amount that Berlin had received before the blockade began.

When the Russians finally opened the barriers and Operation Vittles (as the American portion of the airlift was labeled) ended, more than 124 million air miles had been flown and 2.3 million tons of supplies had been delivered. And, with all that the outcome portended for the future of Europe, the city had been saved. In a turbulent, threatening international climate, humanitarian relief delivered by air had helped preserve the peace. Seldom has America's "soft power" been so superbly employed.

The architect of the miracle in the skies above Berlin was Air Force Major General William H. Tunner.

Berlin in the summer of 1948 was a scene from the *Inferno*. Twenty percent of its buildings were totally demolished. Seventy percent were shattered, minimally usable for shelter. Though damaged, the remaining 10 percent were, with work, suitable for occupation. Hospitals had been destroyed, and more than half the city's industrial base had been blown up or removed to the Soviet Union by Russian occupiers. (Troops from the Western Allies—the United States, Great Britain, and France—were not allowed to enter Berlin until eight weeks after Germany's surrender.) None of Berlin's 87 sewer systems was functional. Almost all of the city's electricity was generated in the Russian zone. Plots inside the city could produce only 2 percent of the food its population needed to survive. For the rest, inhabitants were dependent upon produce imported across areas controlled by the Russians.

In April, in response to a series of earlier threats and provocations, General Clay had ordered supplies for Western Allies' military garrison to be delivered by air. Later called the "little lift," the effort was placed under then-Lieutenant General Curtis E. LeMay, newly assigned as commander, United States Air Forces in Europe. Using available C-47 aircraft with a

BRITISH BASES
1. Schleswigland
2. Lübeck
3. Fuhlsbüttel
4. Finkenwerder (flying boat base) (closed December 15)
5. Fassberg
6. Celle
7. Wunstorf

AMERICAN BASES
8. Rhein-Main
9. Wiesbaden

Berlin Air Corridors and Primary Airlift Bases

A. Tegel Airfield
   Tegel was constructed over a three-month period with material and equipment flown into the city piece by piece. Until it closed in November 2020, Tegel served as Berlin's primary international airfield.
B. Gatow Airfield
C. Tempelhof Airfield

I. Havel River
   Until the river and the lakes it fed froze over, British Short Sunderland flying boats used sites on the river near Gatow to fly salt and other supplies into Berlin.
2. Spree River

Berlin Aerodromes

three-ton load capacity, the "little lift" sustained the 6,500 members of the American garrison through the late spring and early summer. Clearly, however, if a total blockade was imposed, additional planes and personnel would be required. Though the small garrison was kept supplied, the operation was not particularly smooth or without problems. LeMay and his staff were bomber and fighter experts—indeed much of the Air Force's postwar inventory comprised those types of aircraft. Experience in conducting air-lift on a major scale—such as would be necessary to provision an entire city—was lacking.

It appears from Russian documents released in recent years that in the spring of 1948, Soviet Premier Joseph Stalin decided that a blockade of West Berlin would inexorably bring the entire city under Russian control. Increasing pressure was applied, building throughout April and into May with incidents near the air corridor, disputes about communications equip-ment, and periodic disruption of air traffic. As events transpired, it was the introduction of a new currency aimed at stabilizing the monetary system in the western zone—the Russians had undermined the existing currency by printing unrestricted amounts—that precipitated Stalin's action.

On June 24, concurrent with large military maneuvers around the city, the Russians severed land and water routes into the city. The following day, Soviet officials announced that they would no longer supply food to Ger-man citizens living in the city's western zones. Electrical power was shut off the same day. Later assessments generally conclude that Stalin proba-bly did not want war. More likely, he anticipated that the blockade would humiliate the Western Allies and force them to negotiate on his terms.

As the siege began, General Clay and his staff were fairly confident that the Allied military garrison could be supported by an "air bridge" to the encircled city. All 2.5 million citizens living in the western zone were an entirely different matter. Certainly the needs of the city could be met only for a few days under existing conditions. The Air Force had only two squadrons of C-47 aircraft that could be used as cargo carriers. Indeed, the Air Force had only 104 cargo planes available in all of Europe. The RAF was similarly strapped (only 25 cargo planes), and the French had only a handful of carriers of assorted types.

Still, authorities at the highest levels of British and American govern-ments—President Harry S. Truman was directly involved—determined to hold the city and, if possible, supply it through the air. A joint planning team was established and met for the first time on June 30.

Perhaps equally as important, Major General William H. Tunner was appointed to lead the airlift effort. Tunner was acknowledged as the Air Force's (if not the world's) preeminent air transport specialist, having guided the monumental airlift effort in the China-Burma-India Theater in World War II. His leadership of the flights from India to China over the

Himalayas—"The Hump"—provisioned Chinese and Western armies holding back the Japanese.

Meanwhile, calls went out for additional C-47s and C-54s, a four-engine aircraft with a cargo-carrying capacity of 10 tons. The British began augmenting their aircraft—primarily Avro Yorks with a smattering of Lancasters and other types as well. RAF Short Sunderland flying boats soon joined the operation. Their presence was vital. Their interiors had been treated with anticorrosion chemicals, and they were the only Allied aircraft capable of carrying salt to the city.

At the same time, Air Force B-29 bombers were sent to Great Britain. It is now generally concluded that the threat of nuclear weapons likely dissuaded Stalin from attempting to take Berlin by force. Instead, he would try to starve it into submission.

Food commodities had been stockpiled in anticipation of a crisis, but the amounts varied widely: two and a half weeks for milk, meat, and potatoes; three and a half for flour; about eleven for sugar.

Early estimates of requirements for food-related substances to feed the city at minimum levels amounted to more than 1,500 tons each day. But far more would be needed: coal, liquid fuel, medical supplies, tools, building material, newsprint, among almost countless other items large and small. Perhaps, it was thought, about 3,500 tons each day would be needed to sustain the city at near subsistence levels. Soon after, that figure was determined to be insufficient. In actuality, something closer to 4,500 would be needed to save Berlin. Whatever the final tonnage turned out to be, it clearly exceeded the present capacity of the air assets on hand. Planners knew there might be operational and technical problems in addition to overriding political issues. For example, once allied aircraft were over the city, they would have to share airspace with several Russian airfields in near proximity. The flight patterns of some of those aerodromes intersected with airlift routes into Tempelhof and Gatow, the two existing airfields in the western zone.

As the program was being organized, Tunner worked for a time from his office in Washington, DC, where he was deputy commander, Military Air Transport Service. When Tunner arrived on July 28, he brought with him enormous energy, unprecedented expertise in air logistics, and a conviction that Berlin was a "battle" the Allies could not afford to lose. He also demanded perfection, saying that he wanted to make the airlift "as inflexibly systematic as a metronome." Indeed, like a metronome operating around the clock, aircraft flew 200 miles an hour, positioned three minutes apart over entrance and egress corridors devised by Tunner.

Two weeks into his tour, an incident later termed "Dark Friday" showed Tunner at his decisive best and prompted a revision of procedures that would sustain the remainder of the airlift. On August 13, horrific weather generated a series of incidents: one crash, several missed approaches, and a dangerous stacking problem above the city. Tunner, personally flying that day, radioed all aircraft to return to their bases. Henceforth, any aircraft that missed an approach would be sent back through a central corridor—there would be no more stacking. Like a conveyor belt, aircraft would fly at the same speed with three minutes of separation along two eastbound corridors. Those who missed landings would fly back to the west through the designated space to their point of origin, then pick up their place in the corridor pattern and be rerouted back east to Berlin.

Tunner's innovation, one of many that would follow, made an enormous difference. Where stacked aircraft could take as many as 90 minutes to land, Tunner's system sent the planes straight in, one behind the other, at three-minute intervals, achieving 30 landings in the same 90-minute time period. Other changes followed. Ground-controlled approach capabilities were substantially improved. All flights were conducted on instrument flight rules. Once on the ground in Berlin, pilots would remain in their aircraft. No time would be wasted—weather and other flight information would be sent to pilots in their cockpits. Lunches and snacks were provided at planeside by mobile snack bars. Eventually, turnaround time—landing, unloading, and takeoff time—was reduced to 25–30 minutes.

While the bulk of the airlift was handled by American and RAF planes and crews, Tunner also integrated a modest number of civilian contract carriers (altogether, 25 private charters would be used) as well as French, Australian, New Zealand, and South African units into the effort. U.S. Navy crews, aircraft, and maintenance technicians were also employed in a major way. Coordination issues with different aircraft types and load capacities as well as air traffic control and dispatching questions were addressed by the establishment of a Combined Airlift Task Force commanded by Tunner with headquarters in Wiesbaden.

For the first six months of Operation Vittles, two Berlin airfields supported the lift: Gatow in the British sector, and Tempelhof in the American zone. At the end of the year, Gatow became the world's busiest airport. Operations went on around the clock, with landings every three minutes and a ton of freight handled every 53 seconds. Workers hurried to begin unloading as soon as chocks were placed under an aircraft's wheels.

In December, Tegel in the French section was also opened to airlift traffic. Construction of Tegel was a story in itself. All the heavy equipment necessary to build the aerodrome had to be flown in. None of the existing aircraft was large enough to carry, for example, an intact road grader, cement layer, or water truck. Equipment of that sort was disassembled, flown in piece by piece, reassembled, and quickly put to work. (A new power plant was constructed using the same method.) Tegel was completed in three months. For many years, it served as Berlin's central air terminal. Meanwhile, amid ongoing operations, runways and support facilities at Gatow and Tempelhof were repaired and expanded. Massive underground fuel tanks were constructed at Gatow to store fuel offloaded from arriving aircraft.

To maintain aircraft engaged in almost continuous operations, Tunner established additional repair facilities at Burtonwood, Great Britain, and manned it with some of the Air Force's best technicians brought in from maintenance centers in the United States. Locally, Tunner began using former Luftwaffe maintainers—highly skilled and motivated by paychecks and extra rations. Rather quickly, maintenance and local periodic inspection times were cut in half.

American C-54s and British Avro Yorks continued to handle the largest portion of the airlift traffic. However, both air forces integrated the few available larger aircraft into the flow when possible. The United States began using C-82 transports (though only five were available), and in August began employing one C-74 Globemaster.

As work went on, with experience and the influx of additional planes and crews, daily tonnages increased markedly. In December, British crews made their 50,000th landing at Gatow and delivered their 100,000th ton of cargo. At Tempelhof, the Americans broke the 100,000-ton threshold in September. By the end of 1948, Tunner had nearly 10,000 officers and men devoted to airlift operations. Concurrently, Tunner established a tour length and crew-rotation schedule to improve safety and minimize fatigue.

As the lift went on, improvements were made in packaging and insights gained regarding weight and space requirements for various foodstuffs. Interesting lessons were learned in unusual areas. In all of West Berlin only 3,000 cows had survived the war. In order for each to produce five liters of milk each day, 800 tons of food had to be flown in daily to preserve Berlin's cattle. Food for the animals at the Berlin Zoo also had to be delivered.

For Tunner and other airlift authorities, balancing requirements would by necessity be a major focus throughout the crisis. Each day Berlin needed more than 1,500 tons of food to survive. The city's public services needed 2,500 tons of coal. During winter months, an additional 550 tons of coal was needed to heat residences. Newspaper production was eventually suspended. Rolls of newsprint weighed four tons each; food was given priority. Medical supplies were also given precedence. Each month the city needed 20 tons of plaster of paris, thousands of yards of X-ray film, massive amounts of ether, and about 1,300 gallons of medicinal alcohol.

Despite herculean efforts, for the first few weeks of the lift—the period prior to Tunner's presence on scene—Berliners were receiving only about 40 percent of the food and supplies they had been consuming before the blockade began . . . and winter was coming.

Tunner was relentless in ramping up the tonnage delivered to the city. Instrument instruction was emphasized at stateside bases, reducing training time for newly arriving crews. At the height of the lift, more than 45,000 Berliners were engaged in off-loading aircraft, maintenance, runway repair, and other airlift-related activities.

Routes and corridors had been regularized early on. Airlift flights were flown from Rhein-Main and Wiesbaden in the American Zone and from six bases in the British sector, which served as the terminus for the northern and central routes—the two shortest air corridors.

By September and October, the goal of 4,500 tons per day was being consistently met. By then, Tunner had standardized the U.S. fleet, using C-54s except in emergencies. With a 10-ton cargo capacity, the Skymasters were bringing in more than 5,000 tons daily. British aircraft added another 1,500. In peak conditions, 800 aircraft landed daily at the three airfields. C-47s were unloaded in three and a half minutes. C-54s took seven and a half. Eventually, 312 C-54s out of the Air Force's total inventory of 441 were devoted to airlift activities. On February 18, 1949, the one millionth ton of cargo was delivered to Berlin.

A 52-day supply of prestocked coal allowed authorities to increase the daily food ration. Greater quantities of milk and sugar were especially well received, and an additional 250 calories per day improved nutrition in general. A special effort on September 18, 1948—in celebration of the Air Force's birthday—brought nearly 7,000 tons of food and supplies to the city. At Christmas, authorities made sure that each child in Berlin received chocolate to eat. For Berliners, many of whom bordered on malnutrition, huddled in bomb-ravaged buildings, and coped with a four-hour

A C-54 Skymaster on final approach at Tempelhof airfield is cheered on by an awaiting crowd. In what was to become the world's greatest humanitarian airlift, Tunner's planes sustained the 2.5 million Berliners surrounded by a million and a half Soviet troops.
U.S. AIR FORCE—AIR FORCE HISTORY OFFICE

allotment of electricity each day, even the smallest gesture was regarded as a special blessing.

In January 1949 Tunner introduced a complete integration of British and American operations to include air traffic control, communications, and installation facilities. April of that year saw a Tunner-orchestrated airlift extravaganza. In an event that became known as the Easter Parade, pre-positioned supplies and competition between units resulted in delivery of an amazing 12,900 tons of cargo. Innovations and refined procedures were introduced throughout the course of the lift. Tonnage figures rose consistently, eventually reaching an average of 8,893 tons per day. Clearly, the airlift was sustainable and working beyond all expectations.

With the advent of the Marshall Plan, industrial and economic programs were beginning to transform the western zone of Germany and indeed most of Europe not occupied by the Red Army. The blockade was becoming an embarrassment for the Soviet Union. In a communiqué to Washington, America's ambassador to the Soviet Union said, "Berlin blockade back-fired, airlift was a phenomenally practical and political success."

Eventually, Stalin acceded to the continuing futility. After dropping earlier conditions that the Western Allies not establish a West German state and that a nonaggression pact be negotiated between the adversaries, he agreed to end the siege of Berlin. On May 12, 1949, the Soviets formally lifted the blockade.

The airlift did not end immediately. Threats of a renewed blockade persisted for some time. The military government of the western zone agreed to keep the airlift in place until a four- to five-month stockpile of essential supplies was built up. If Berlin was again placed under siege, those provisions would carry the city until another full airlift could be put in place.

On September 30, 1949, a U.S. Air Force C-54 from Rhein-Main Air Force Base flew the last official mission. The cargo was symbolic: the Sky-master carried a load of coal. After 15 months, the airlift was over.

The final landing brought the count of airlift miles flown to nearly 124,401,000 miles. The effort had not been without cost. There were 101 fatalities during the course of the airlift—included among them were 31 American and 40 British personnel. Several occurred prior to Tunner's arrival. Ironically, many were sustained in ground incidents at the three aerodromes. Altogether, the Americans lost 17 aircraft and the British 8.

As many historians have noted, the Berlin Airlift was the first victory of the Cold War. Though no shots were exchanged, the lift was very much a military operation. Success preserved the democratic enclave of West Berlin, and the aftermath helped shape postwar Europe. Several factors contributed to the victory: the political will of Western leaders such as Harry Truman, the courage of the Berliners themselves, the professionalism of the aircrews, the dedication of the thousands of support personnel, and—in a major way—the masterful guidance of William H. Tunner.

Before and After

Tunner was the ideal choice to command the Berlin Airlift; indeed, he may have been the only person with the requisite experience, intelligence, and drive to carry it off. Tunner's baptism under fire in the airlift world took place in the China-Burma-India Theater during World War II.

In March 1942 the Japanese occupied Burma, closing the Burma Road, the single route across the Himalaya Mountains. By halting traffic on the road, the Japanese shut off the flow of supplies to American and Chinese forces in western China. There, on the Chinese mainland, Allied armies sought to hold off more than a million battle-tested troops of the Japanese Imperial Army.

An "air bridge" was soon established to transport supplies over a 500-mile route across the world's highest mountain chain. For the remainder of the war, "The Hump," as it soon became known, was a vital source of supplies for the embattled Allies. Though Air Transport Command steadily increased monthly tonnage figures from 2,500 early on to 10,000 a year or so later, the months prior to Tunner's arrival were fraught with hardship and perilous to aircrews. In January 1944, every 200 trips over the three-and-a-half-hour mission resulted in the loss of an aircraft. Every 1,000 hours flown to China cost the lives of three American airmen.

Tunner arrived on September 3, 1944. His mission was twofold: increase the tonnage of materials flown to China and reduce the horrific accident rate. Tunner brought with him a hand-picked staff and made immediate changes. An extensive, rigorous checklist procedure for Hump pilots was put in place. Aircraft maintenance was revamped. Each Hump base specialized in one type of aircraft repair. Specialized crews were trained to perform specific maintenance functions.

The change reduced inspection time by a quarter; aircraft utilization rates skyrocketed.

Quarters for crews and support personnel were abysmal when Tunner arrived. Immediate modifications improved living conditions while innovative programs instilled unit pride. Tunner was the first—or most certainly one of the first—to devise a mobile PX operation and place it on the flight line. As he would later in Berlin, Tunner revamped the crew rotation policy to improve stability and continuity of operations. Eventually, he lobbied for, and began to receive, the military's C-54 aircraft. Safe to fly and with a large cargo capability, the C-54 would also become Tunner's aircraft of choice in Berlin. Soon after he arrived, his staff developed a second route into China called the "Low Hump" and widened airlift corridors from 50 to 200 miles.

The results were quick and extraordinary. Accident rates dropped, morale improved, and tonnage increased astronomically. On October 12, 1944—a month after Tunner's arrival—Hump tonnage exceeded 24,000 tons, over 20 times the amount airlifted less than two years earlier. Before Tunner returned to the United States on March 16, 1945, accident rates had been cut by 75 percent despite a doubling of hours flown.

Before

Born July 14, 1906, at Elizabeth, New Jersey, Tunner graduated from West Point in 1928 and chose aviation as his branch of service. He received his pilot's wings at Kelly Field, Texas, the following year. Tunner's early service—before his wartime assignment channeled him into airlift—was typical of that of many of his contemporaries. He was first assigned to a bomber unit at Rockwell Field, California, where he concurrently gained his first bit of experience with transport aircraft (a Fokker tri-motor). After a short time as an instructor pilot at Randolph Field, Texas, he moved to staff duties before being transferred to the Canal Zone as an observation pilot. In Panama, he held down staff and operations duties in addition to flying. In 1937, back in the States at Lawton Field, Georgia, Tunner served as adjutant while continuing to fly observation aircraft.

After attending an Air Corps Tactical School short course in 1939, Tunner was given his first command. It was a small one, a recruiting billet in Memphis, Tennessee. As war approached, Tunner, now a major, was assigned to the Personnel Division of the Office of the Chief of the Air Corps in Washington, DC.

In June 1941, Tunner became a key figure in creating the Air Transport Command. Only the second member assigned to the fledgling organization, he had advanced by the end of the year from adjutant to personnel officer to executive officer. By March 1, 1942, he was a full colonel.

As the military expanded and the war assumed global proportions, the mission of the Transport Command changed significantly. Originally envisioned as an organization whose main purpose was to shuttle newly built aircraft from factories to bases across the country, necessity drove it toward a far larger and more consequential role—supporting allied military operations worldwide.

The delivery of men, weapons, supplies, and equipment through the air to combat zones around the globe would become the mission the new command was most remembered for. However, the delivery of aircraft from factories to bases remained an important part of the organization's charter. In April 1942, Tunner adopted a plan devised by Nancy Harkness Love, his executive troubleshooter, and established what was initially known as the Ferrying Command. As the organization's first commander, Tunner launched the Women's Auxiliary Ferrying Squadron (WAFS), using highly qualified women pilots to move planes from factories to airfields where they were turned over to military units. In August 1943 the WAFS program merged with Jacqueline Cochrane's Women's Flying Detachment to become the renowned Women's Air Force Service Pilots (WASPs).

Tunner was promoted to brigadier general on June 30, 1943. The following year, he was chosen to command the supply mission from India to China. After a quick inspection trip in mid-1944, he wrapped up his duties in Washington, DC, and returned to the CBI Theater to take charge of "The Hump" mission on September 4, 1944.

Fortunately for the Air Force, Tunner was retained in airlift-related duties following the war. On January 1, 1946, he was named inspector general of the Air Transport Command before assuming a series of air division commands. He received his second star in July of that year.

In September 1947, the Air Force became a separate military service. Concurrently, the Military Air Transport Service was formed by combining the Air Force's Air Transport Command with the Navy's Naval Air Transport Service. In March 1948 Tunner was named deputy commander of the new unit. He was serving in those duties when Air Force Chief of Staff General Hoyt Vandenberg—reacting to the inadequate and somewhat haphazard operations employed to address the five-week-old crisis in Berlin—appointed him to run the airlift.

After

Berlin demonstrated the utility of having a military air arm capable of transporting men and materiel for long distances on short notice. If there was any remaining need to reinforce that lesson, the conflict in Korea provided it only a few months later. Within days after the war began, Tunner flew to Tokyo to take over a newly formed organization—the Combat Cargo Command. The new command quickly began providing support for General Douglas MacArthur's Inchon landing and for the paratroop drops that followed. (MacArthur awarded him the Distinguished Service Cross on the spot.) In the four and a half months that Tunner commanded the provisional unit, the Combat Cargo Command flew 32,632 sorties, delivered 136,170 tons of cargo, carried 155,294 troops, and evacuated 72,760 casualties sustained by the United Nations forces. Though his time in Korea was relatively brief, Tunner pioneered the use of helicopters in airlift operations.

When U.S. Marines made their gallant fighting withdrawal from the Chosin Reservoir, Tunner's crews dropped bridge sections and bridging equipment to help the Marines walk out together as their commander, Major General Oliver P. Smith, had vowed.

In January 1951 Tunner returned from Korea to assume duties as deputy commander of the Air Materiel Command. In 1953, now a lieutenant general, he returned to Europe, this time as commander, United States Air Forces in Europe. He held that job for four years during the height of the buildup of NATO air forces. A Pentagon posting followed as deputy chief of staff for Operations at Headquarters, U.S. Air Force. July 1958 brought Tunner's final assignment. It was one to which he was indeed well suited: commander, Military Air Transport Service (MATS).

The commander, MATS, position provided an ideal forum for his articulate, impassioned support for increased airlift capabilities. Tunner became a particularly strong advocate for the development and deployment of the C-141 Starlifter as the primary jet transport for the Air Force.

Tunner's tenure at MATS came at a critical juncture for the future of military airlift. The senior Air Force hierarchy at the time was dominated by "bomber generals" who viewed the command's primary role as supporting strategic bomber deployments and assisting Strategic Air Command to reestablish its forces in the early stages of a nuclear conflict. Opposing that view were numerous political and military leaders (primarily Army) who saw the need for worldwide deployments of air and ground forces in all types of conflict. Tunner was firmly on the side of "flexible response" advocates, but he recognized that the Air Force's existing inventory of aircraft was woefully inadequate to carry out that mission.

On March 8, 1960, congressional hearings regarding national airlift opened in Washington, DC. Chaired by Representative L. Mendel Rivers (D-SC), the hearings provided a forum for members of the so-called Congressional Reform Movement who favored additional funding for non-nuclear forces to give the United States more diplomatic and military flexibility. In addition to Rivers, the Reform Movement's influential members included Representative Carl Vinson (D-GA), chairman of the House Armed Services Committee; Senator Dennis Chavez (D-NM), chairman of the Senate Appropriations Committee; and several others, including Lyndon Johnson and John F. Kennedy. Opposed by members of the administration who favored precedence for nuclear forces, early witnesses testified to the need for airlift planners to give equal priority to the requirements of limited war. Army Chief of Staff General Lyman L. Lemnitzer told the committee that the Army had a firm requirement for the capability to move two infantry divisions (25,000 soldiers and 40,000 tons of cargo) by air to any point on the planet within four weeks. Follow-on Air Force witnesses testified that the service's existing inventory, both by type and numbers, was vastly inadequate to handle that mission.

With the hearings underway, Tunner sought to provide the committee with a real-world example of the existing shortfalls in military airlift. With Lemnitzer's concurrence, Tunner arranged a large-scale exercise in which thousands of Army personnel would be flown from 14 U.S. bases to Puerto Rico. For two weeks beginning in March, a mishmash of 477 planes of various types—C-124s, C-118s, C-121s, and a few C-133s—all that Tunner could lay his hands on, airlifted Army troops and support equipment to the Caribbean. To support the effort, the entire airlift system shifted to 84-hour work weeks, and some personnel pulled sustained-duty periods of 35 hours or more. After two weeks, the effort could no longer be sustained. Though 29,000 troops and 16,000 tons of cargo were airlifted, MATS personnel and their aircraft were on the verge of breakdowns, and maintainers were running out of spare parts.

Tunner did a masterful job of educating opinion makers during the course of the exercise. Planeloads of generals, representatives, and newsmen were flown in as observers. Tunner thoroughly and fairly portrayed the shortfalls and work-arounds that had been necessary to sustain the effort—which in any event would have been inadequate in a real-world crisis. Troops did not arrive fully prepared for combat, and in some cases ammunition and gas masks had been left behind to lighten loads. Making the airlifted forces combat ready would have required several more days and at least 300 more sorties.

Tunner's effort succeeded brilliantly. One of his subordinates said that the exercise was "the most spectacularly successful failure in the history of military training."

Tunner was one of the finest speakers at the hearings, recapping lessons learned, shortfalls, and requirements. The hearings turned out to be a triumph for military airlift. Out of the committee's recommendations would eventually emerge the C-141, additional numbers of C-130s, and cargo versions of the KC-135 tankers. Those programs set the stage for the C-5As and C-17s that would follow in the years ahead, giving the United States an unprecedented capability to quickly move people and equipment around the globe. Tunner's role in all of this was transformational: strategic airlift would alter the elements of national defense.

Tunner left a substantial legacy. When he retired from the Air Force on May 31, 1960, he had successfully organized and commanded the three largest airlifts—"The Hump," Berlin, and Korea—that had yet been undertaken. All were extraordinary achievements. Berlin, though, was a masterpiece that saved a city and perhaps much more.

General Tunner died on April 6, 1983, and was buried at Arlington National Cemetery.

Forgotten Leader: Bernard A. Schriever

The Ace in the Hole

Schriever's foresight and superb leadership of some of the nation's brightest minds enabled the United States to rapidly develop a range of missiles that provided deterrence during the Cuban Missile Crisis and throughout the Cold War. U.S. AIR FORCE— AIR FORCE HISTORY OFFICE

In October 1962, sirens sounded on U.S. Air Force Strategic Air Command bases around the globe. The klaxons placed SAC forces on DEFCON (Defense Condition) 2—the highest level ever employed. As the world held its breath, America's military forces stood at the ready on military installations throughout the world. SAC's B-52 bombers flew airborne alert. Missile crews waited at their consoles. The United States and the Soviet Union stood at the brink of nuclear war.

The Cuban Missile Crisis—the name given to perhaps the most fearful period the world had yet experienced—was fomented by the Soviet Union's introduction of well-tested R-12 and R-14 medium-range, nuclear-tipped missiles into Cuba. At best a portion of SAC's bomber force would have been degraded had the missiles achieved full operational capability. Reaction time to missiles fired only 90 miles from American shores was minimal if not nonexistent. Much of the United States and sizable portions of Canada were within range of the missiles and held hostage by the threat posed by them.

While the threat posed by Soviet missiles in Cuba was particularly acute, the entire years-long underlying tone of the Cold War was one of menace—consistent apprehension fraught with varying degrees of danger. Cuba, though the most intense and dangerous, was but one of many confrontations that disturbed the peace during this unique era in world history.

An earlier extended period that threatened to tip the balance occurred at the beginning of the missile age when the Soviet Union decided to focus on missiles as its primary strategic weapon. If left unchecked, the USSR's quest for nuclear superiority would have exposed the United States to attack with limited prospects for reprisal. At the minimum, the resulting nuclear overbalance would have made military blackmail a tempting prospect for Soviet leaders, opening the door for interdiction and adventures worldwide.

Both episodes—the long-term underlying threat and the brief, intense crisis that developed from events in Cuba—directly affected the security or survival of the United States. In each instance the outcomes were favorable to the United States. The Russians did not achieve superiority or the capability to attack without risking a catastrophic counterstrike. In Cuba, Soviet Premier Nikita Khrushchev withdrew Russian missiles in the face of overwhelming U.S. offensive capability.

In each instance, the individual most responsible for creating the weapon systems and hardware that enabled the United States to prevail was Air Force General Bernard A. Schriever.

CUBAN MISSILE CRISIS MISSILE SITES

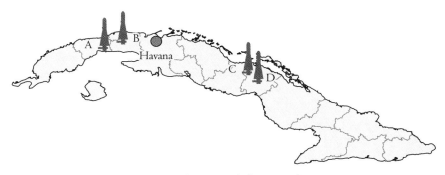

A. San Cristobal Missile Site SS-4 medium-range ballistic missiles
B. Guanajay Missile Site SS-5 intermediate-range ballistic missiles
C. Sagua La Grande SS-4 medium-range ballistic missiles
D. Remedios SS-5 intermediate-range ballistic missiles

SS-4 medium-range ballistic missiles had a range of 1,290 miles.
SS-5 intermediate-range ballistic missiles had a range of 2,300 miles.
Both missiles were capable of carrying warheads of more than two megatons.
The coverage area of the SS-4 held the United States from Chicago eastward at risk.
The coverage area of the SS-5 included almost all of the continental United States and
large portions of Canada.

Cuban Missile Crisis—Missile Sites

CUBAN MISSILE CRISIS
SURFACE TO AIR MISSILE SITES AND MIG FIGHTER BASES

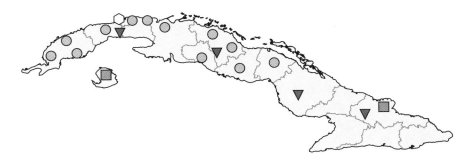

● SURFACE-TO-AIR MISSILE SITE	▼ MIG FIGHTER BASE	
■ SUSPECTED MISSILE SITE	⬡ HAVANA	

Cuban Missile Crisis—SAM Sites and MiG Fighter Bases

The vision that guided the United States in its quest for the ultimate weapon can be traced to a specific event, a meeting of the Air Force Scientific Advisory Board held at Maxwell AFB, Alabama, in 1953. Sitting in the audience that day was then-Colonel Bernard Schriever, who was at Maxwell by virtue of his research and development duties at the Pentagon. During the course of the meeting, Schriever heard board member John von Neumann, a Hungarian-born mathematical genius, and Edward Teller, a world-renowned physicist, describe how within a few years the United States could build a hydrogen weapon that would weigh less than a ton yet have the destructive capacity of at least 80 of the bombs that had destroyed Hiroshima.

Schriever grasped the implications. In its quest to field a weapon against which there was no defense—that is, a bomb carried by a ballistic missile with intercontinental range—the United States faced a major problem to that point: the enormous weight of the warhead. Schriever realized that if von Neumann and Teller were correct, it would be possible to construct an enormously destructive weapon, put it on a missile, and hold any military target in Russia at risk. Not only would such a warhead blunt the Soviet's drive for nuclear superiority, it also held the promise of being something more—it might be a system that would deter a nuclear holocaust.

After confirming with von Neumann and others the feasibility of constructing a suitably lightweight warhead, Schriever set out in 1954 to build the set of systems that could enforce peace—at least at the nuclear level—with the Soviet Union.

For the United States, Schriever's involvement could not have been more timely. In a meeting of the Politburo in 1953, the Soviet Union had already made the decision to develop and employ missiles—not a large fleet of long-range bombers—as the nation's strategic offensive weapon of choice. Testing of an intermediate-range missile, the stepping stone to a weapon with intercontinental range, began as early as March of that year.

Schriever, ably assisted by a few key players on the Air Staff and in the office of the Secretary of the Air Force, began assembling the team that would drive the United States into the missile age. A high-level group, initially labeled the Strategic Missile Evaluation Committee, was formed with Schriever as point man. As the organization took form, it became clear that a more formal permanent structure would be required to institutionalize the program and move it forward. It was decided to create a separate organization within the Air Force's Air Research and Development Command (ARDC). The new unit ostensibly fell under the purview of the

ARDC vice commander, but, given the unit's sole responsibility to lead the nation's Intercontinental Ballistic Missile (ICBM) program, by unanimous agreement throughout the Air Force hierarchy, both military and civilian, the leader would be then-Brigadier General Bernard Schriever.

The tasking document specified that Schriever would remain with the program for its duration until the program was substantially completed. Schriever was personally selected as "a brigadier general of unusual competence to work directly with the contractors in supply of top level support and technical supervision." He was to assemble a "systems management group with the highest competence." Indeed, the cadre that was eventually put together may have been the most formidable in the country. Placement within the R&D structure would allow Schriever to draw on the full resources of that organization as well.

Schriever accepted the job only with the promise that he would be allowed to run it without interference from the Pentagon. It was well that he demanded that autonomy. Early on, he discovered that on one relatively small initiative, as many as 42 approvals would normally have been required before proceeding. With the Russian tests now an established fact, time was becoming urgent and a fast-track approach was essential.

Schriever had taken the first step in what would eventually be a nine-year journey through design, development, testing, and fielding the Atlas and Titan II liquid-fueled ICBMs, and the Thor intermediate-range missile (IRBM). Finally, just weeks before the Cuban Missile Crisis brought the world to the brink of war, he oversaw the placement in silos of the first 10 solid-fuel Minuteman missiles.

For an extended period of time, there were threats posed by the Army, led by Major General John B. Medaris, to take over the nation's missile program. Arguing that missiles were a form of extended artillery and that the Army had better expertise (in the persons of Wernher von Braun and other German scientists), Medaris sought to capture the program and its funding. Eventually, the agreement was settled by President Dwight D. Eisenhower, who placed the space exploration portion (von Braun's primary interest) of the nation's missile program with a new civilian organization, the National Aeronautics and Space Administration. Schriever's program and his role in it were left essentially intact.

Early on, there were difficult contract disputes to sort out. Convair, as per previous development models, was designated to act as prime contractor for the entire system. Schriever wanted the company to manufacture only the fuel tank and certain other sections of the body of the missile.

He preferred that the remainder of the missile be built elsewhere (concurrently) to speed the process. Convair would then assemble the missile when all the components were ready. For a time, even Schriever's immediate boss, Major General Thomas Power, commander of ARDC, was opposed to Schriever's management approach. However, generals higher up in the Air Force chain—General Thomas White, Air Force chief of staff, and General Nathan Twining, chairman of the Joint Chiefs of Staff—favored Schriever's method. With a few modifications, Schriever's management scheme—drawing ideas from several sources with the company finding the best solution getting the contract—became the blueprint for the Atlas program and for others that would follow.

Eventually, even General Power was won over. On Schriever's next performance report, Power wrote that "[Schriever] has excellent staying qualities when things get rough. Professionally, he is characterized by his thoroughness. He has a brilliant mind and can be depended on for outstanding work. He is highly respected by his associates, both senior and junior. His management ability has been demonstrated in the organization and operation of the highly classified special project for which he has been handpicked."

By the mid-1950s the Cold War was becoming colder and the potential threat posed by Russian adversaries in rocketry increasingly apparent. In March 1954, President Eisenhower asked that a study be made of the potential for a "nuclear Pearl Harbor" strike against the United States. The investigating panel that was formed to study the issue became known as the Killian Committee (named after James Killian, the president of MIT who chaired the task force). The panel's report, delivered in February 1955, was in many ways unprecedented. The committee's recommendation, sent to the president and the National Security Council (NSC), warned of the ominous consequences if the Soviet Union achieved ICBM capability before the United States. The panel urged the NSC to formally endorse the ICBM project—the first time a request of that kind had been proposed. In very strong terms, Killian's group called for the administration to make the ICBM a "nationally supported effort of the highest priority."

Soon after, formal briefings were presented to Eisenhower and the NSC staff. The briefing, which would become somewhat famous in its own right, had three presenters. Trevor Gardner, special assistant to the secretary of the Air Force for Research and Development (and a dedicated advocate of the missile program), spoke first. Gardner described ICBMs as an irrevocable change in the world's power equation if the USSR won the race to deploy an operational system. Gardner stressed that a missile launched from the USSR would impact on American soil in 30 minutes.

John von Neumann, chairman of the Scientific Advisory Board and a key member of a host of other scientific panels (and already legendary as having a mind second only to Einstein's) followed with technical details superbly cast in laymen's terms. Von Neumann embellished Gardner's account regarding an incoming missile's 30-minute flight time, noting that the actual warning time when the missile would be detected by U.S. sensors would be no more than 15 minutes. He noted that there was no foreseeable defense.

Schriever took the podium as the final speaker. He described the organization that was being established to run the program and told the president it was being managed with wartime urgency.

The outcome was all that Schriever and his colleagues could have hoped for. Eisenhower signed off on the program, designated the ICBM project a "research and development program of the highest priority above all others," ordering the effort to be pushed forward with "maximum urgency." Later, the Thor IRBM missile was placed under the same umbrella, though "not without resulting friction from the Army, which was fielding the Jupiter missile at the time."

The national decision to press ahead with an accelerated program made Schriever's already hectic pace even more daunting. In addition to the design and engineering work, infrastructure had to be built at Patrick AFB, Florida, to test missiles under development. Not long after, at Schriever's instigation, Camp Cooke, a little-used Army post in a somewhat isolated portion of California, was turned over to the Air Force. Renamed Vandenberg AFB, the location was ideal for operational testing and for training missile crews in live-fire practices. It would also prove to be almost perfect for launching satellites into polar orbit.

In August 1954, Schriever had moved his organization, then labeled Western Development Division, into an abandoned schoolhouse at a vacant Roman Catholic boys' school in a suburb of Los Angeles. Later renamed the Air Force Ballistic Missile Division and relocated under the Research and Development Command, the unit would guide the nation's move into the missile age. By the end of 1957, the Thor IRBM was nearing deployment, having been tested for a year. The Atlas ICBM had been in operational testing since midyear. Manufacturing had begun on the Titan, initially intended as a backup/safeguard missile in the event problems developed with Atlas. Planning for the first photo-reconnaissance satellite of its kind was underway. The two ICBM programs engaged 17 contractors, 200 subcontractors, and thousands of individual suppliers at locations spread across the continent. The Atlas alone consisted of 40,000 parts.

Handling the entire series of the world's most complex design and engineering programs evidenced Schriever's leadership and management genius. One of his extraordinary gifts was the ability to choose the right people and position them in key management roles. For the Atlas program, the choice was particularly inspired. Simon Ramo (later the "R" in TRW), would serve as chief engineer and scientist. Ramo was responsible for guiding work on almost everything except the H-bomb itself—that work was handled at Los Alamos. Ramo's purview included guidance and control mechanisms, warheads/reentry vehicles, and a myriad of other components. All were built concurrently by contractors or subcontractors chartered and managed by Schriever and Ramo.

Schriever's other choices for leadership roles were equally inspired. The role in developing the Minuteman, the nation's first solid-fuel missile, was given to Ed Hall, a brilliant Air Force lieutenant colonel who became known as the "guru for Air Force rocketry." Colonel Vince Ford, a Schriever protégé—Schriever had restored Ford to active duty though he was technically disqualified as a result of a youthful flying accident—was employed in the beginning as executive assistant in research and development activities for the secretary of the Air Force. Ford orchestrated the steps that led to the briefings given to President Eisenhower and the NSC. Dean Wooldridge (later the "W" in TRW), a world-class physicist with a PhD from Cal Tech, would also play a key role in the ICBM program. Benjamin Bellis, later a three-star Air Force general, devised a procedure called "configuration control" to identify, record, integrate, and phase in changes to the thousands of parts that occurred through the production process. Lieutenant Colonel Benjamin P. "Pete" Blasingame, a PhD engineer from MIT, would develop a turbofan engine, a version of which still propels the Air Force's largest transports.

In addition to selecting the right people, a second component of Schriever's management style was a system for keeping track of the enormous number of projects that fell under his purview. The key feature was a monthly briefing that became known as "Black Friday." Placed under the direction of Air Force Lieutenant Colonel Charles Getz, an officer with a background in statistical analysis and degrees in economics and industrial management, the system provided a reporting mechanism for every detail of every program for which Schriever was responsible. Getz facilitated the presentations and ruthlessly held briefers to time and reporting requirements. Schriever chaired the meetings, insisting that they focus on problems, not just on status reporting or "good news." His assumption was that if problems were solved and the program moved forward even though impediments remained, good news would inevitably occur. Schriever's guidance to briefers and program managers was succinctly expressed: "I will not fire you for giving me bad news. I will fire you if you don't give me bad news."

Although there were severe growing pains and multiple test failures with all systems, each of the enormously complex programs moved inexorably forward. As General Power wrote in Schriever's efficiency report "[Schriever had] excellent staying power when things got rough."

The Atlas—75 feet long, 10 feet in diameter, 243,000 pounds with a range of 6,330 miles—came first. Titan—90 feet long, more sophisticated, with two stages, capable of carrying a monstrous nine-megaton warhead— came next. The Minuteman eventually followed with a solid-fuel propulsion system rather than the volatile kerosene and liquid oxygen mixture that drove the Atlas and Titan.

Schriever had started Ed Hall on Minuteman development while work on the liquid-fueled missiles was ongoing. The Minuteman was smaller and simpler in construction, less costly, and could be produced by the hundreds. For the Air Force, and the nation, the Minuteman had many virtues: it was reliable; it could be stored for long periods; the launch time was near-simultaneous (less than one minute); and the missile was highly accurate. The Minuteman would be the largest rocket program ever undertaken by the United States. Eventually, 1,000 of the various system types would be deployed. Approved in February 1958, the first missiles were in place during the Cuban Missile Crisis.

When Chairman Khrushchev introduced Russian IRBMs into Cuba, the Soviet Union possessed about 20 ICBMs of uncertain reliability, 58 Bison bombers whose limited range would have forced a one-way mission, and 60 or so slower turboprop bombers. Facing Russia at the time, fully deployed, were 96 Atlas, 54 Titan, and 10 Minuteman missiles, 48 more Polaris missiles on Navy submarines, as well as 1,742 Strategic Air Command B-47, B-52, and B-58 bombers. There were as well, under dual control, 60 Thor missiles in Great Britain, 30 in Italy, and 16 in Turkey. Confronted with the U.S.'s overwhelming superiority, Khrushchev backed down.

It had been nine years from the time in March 1953 when Schriever had glimpsed the vision of an American ICBM at the meeting of the Air

Force Scientific Board and the Cuban Missile Crisis in October 1962. During that time, under Schriever's leadership, the United States had designed, developed, tested, and deployed two generations of ICBMs. The first 10 second-generation Minutemen were in silos at Malmstrom AFB, Montana. They were, as several pundits would later label them, "America's ace in the hole." The United States had won the missile race.

There were notable milestones along the way. In 1958, President Eisenhower's Christmas message was beamed to the world from a satellite lifted into orbit by one of Schriever's Atlas missiles. On April 18, 1960, the first successful photo reconnaissance satellite lifted off in polar orbit from Vandenberg AFB—confirming Schriever's prescience in selecting the site—and in a single mission photographed more of the Soviet Union than all of the U-2 flights combined. In the long run, the work produced by Schriever's program would have effects far outside the military sphere. The first astronauts rode into space on missiles developed for the military. In the Mercury Program, John Glenn was lifted into orbit on an Atlas. Titan II served as the lifting body for the Gemini series. American astronauts returned safely home in capsules that were modified versions of the reentry vehicles developed for the H-bomb.

The United States came to owe a considerable debt to "Bernie" Schriever and the marvelous team he had assembled. Perhaps their greatest achievement was to keep the peace—to buy time until the Soviet Union collapsed of its own internal contradictions. They had created weapon systems of enormous power that in all probably would—thankfully—never be used. So visible was the strength projected by the U.S. arsenal that no Soviet leader could miscalculate the capability of the United States to retaliate in a way that would utterly devastate the Soviet Union. Thus, thanks in large measure to Schriever and his group, which had become known as "Bernie's colonels," America's ICBMs achieved their ultimate purpose: to deter nuclear war.

The officer to whom the nation's primary debt was owed stood six feet, two inches tall. Movie-star handsome—some associates commented on a passing resemblance to actor James Stewart—at 180 pounds he was slender and athletic. In demeanor, he was reserved, pleasant and courteous to staff and friends, but not much given to small talk. His engineering background and his many years of experience in research and development enabled him to interchange easily and credibly with scientific and technical experts from inside and outside the military. Many were world-renowned—John von

Neumann, Edward Teller, Theodore von Karman, Simon Ramo, and many others. Schriever knew them all, worked directly with most of them, and used their talents for the nation's benefits.

Schriever was revered by his staff, not only because of his professional competence and managerial genius but also because of his moral fiber. As a junior colonel, his responsibilities in research and development sometimes brought him in conflict with General Curtis E. LeMay during LeMay's tenure as commander in chief (CINC), Strategic Air Command, and vice chief of staff of the Air Force. LeMay was a legendary though autocratic figure with a towering reputation earned from his service in World War II. In the military vernacular, LeMay was an officer "who took no prisoners." Still, as a junior officer, Schriever clashed with LeMay on several occasions, openly opposing him on issues ranging from aircraft engines to bomber attack profiles, strategic aircraft development, and missile programs. Schriever's opinions were delivered calmly and with respectful professionalism, but it was clear, as several contemporaries noted, that "he was not afraid of anything."

Before and After

Schriever was born in Bremen, Germany, in 1910. His father was an engineering officer on a German ship that was interred in New York harbor as World War I approached. His mother was able to secure passage for herself and her two sons and joined her husband in 1917, not long before the United States entered the war. The family soon moved to a German-speaking community in Texas before eventually settling in San Antonio. Schriever's father was killed in an accident in 1918, leaving his family impoverished. For a time Schriever and his brother were placed in an orphanage until his mother found a housekeeping position that provided sufficient income to reassemble the family. A year later they moved into a small house on the outskirts of Breckenridge Park. The house bounded the park's golf course, a circumstance that had important consequences for Schriever's life.

After a time, Schriever's mother opened a small refreshment stand on the adjacent course to supplement the family's income. Schriever helped at the stand and in the meantime became a superb player in a sport that became his passion. Within a few years he would become captain of the Texas A&M golf team, Texas State Amateur Champion, and twice San Antonio City Champion. Golf would later serve him well, easing social interchanges and conversations with military leaders, scientists, and captains of industry.

Schriever received his citizenship at age 13, in 1923. After graduating from Texas A&M in 1930 with a bachelor of science degree in engineering, he was accepted the following year into the Army Air Corps flight training program. After completing primary training at Randolph Field and follow-on training at Kelly Field, he received his pilot's wings on June 29, 1933.

Schriever's first posting as an aviator took him to March Field, California. His assignment as a member of the 9th Bombardment Squadron would come to define Schriever's life and his service to the nation. At March Field, Schriever worked for then-Lieutenant Colonel Henry H. "Hap" Arnold. Arnold—a future five-star general—was a visionary who saw the importance of science and technology to the future of the Air Force and, ultimately, to the security of the nation. Indeed, it was Arnold who would later establish the Air Force Scientific Advisory Board—the group whose session at Maxwell AFB led to Schriever's involvement with the nation's missile program.

Arnold recognized special qualities in his young subordinate and would later, as Air Corps chief of staff, earmark him for key duties in research and development. Also at March Field were Carl "Tooey" Spaatz, who later became the first chief of staff of the United States Air Force, and Ira Eaker, who would command bomber forces in Europe and the Mediterranean. March Field was a perfect storm of influential, prescient officers, all of whom got to know Bernard Schriever and to appreciate his rare combination of talents.

Schriever was at March Field during the ill-conceived experiment during which the Air Corps flew the nation's mail. Schriever's routes took him from Salt Lake City to Boise and from Salt Lake City to Cheyenne. Though Schriever's personal experience was favorable—he flew his routes safely and successfully—the overall experiment was a fiasco. Lives were lost, schedules were not met, and the whole episode revealed the poor state of the nation's air arm. The one favorable outcome was that the results were so obvious that by necessity improvements began to be made. For Schriever, the lesson was clear: in wartime a nation that did not keep pace technologically was doomed to defeat.

After a brief interlude away from active duty (he had not yet received a regular commission), he was recalled to service as an officer in charge of a Civilian Conservation Corps (CCC) camp. The posting turned out to be a marvelous learning experience for a young officer. In an unusual environment—CCC members were civilians and subject to military discipline—he learned the importance of choosing good leaders who could get the job done and enforce standards through the influence of their own example and personality. He devised a "kangaroo court approach" aimed at airing problems in an open forum. The threads of his future management style—studying a task, choosing the best people, addressing problems willingly, and openly supporting people confident and courageous enough to bring bad news to him—were developed at the CCC camp. Schriever was also very concerned with morale. He ran a "happy camp," providing multiple activities for the young people assigned to him, and sought out excellent cooks to prepare the camp's meals. When he left the camp in the summer of 1936, the young men took up a collection to buy him a target pistol and a wristwatch, both of which he treasured for years to come.

Schriever then served for a year as aide-de-camp to Brigadier General George H. Brett, commander of air units in the Panama Canal Zone. Still not having received a regular commission and vulnerable for deactivation at a time he was about to be married, he left the service to fly for National Airlines, piloting a route from Seattle to Billings, Montana. In March 1938 Hap Arnold flew to Seattle to specifically request that Schriever take a competitive exam for a regular commission. In addition to valuing Schriever's exemplary skills, Arnold foresaw the importance of creating an "all-weather" air force and realized that civilian airline pilots such as Schriever provided a repository of experience in that area.

Schriever's tenure as an airline pilot was short-lived. As urged by Arnold, he took the competitive examination for regular officer status, passed it with high marks, and was sworn in on October 1, 1938, at Hamilton Field, California. His assignment there in a bomb squadron was also of brief duration. Later that fall he was posted to Wright Field (now Wright-Patterson AFB) at Dayton, Ohio. At Wright Field he flew for nine months as a test pilot in the Flight Test Section before entering the difficult, prestigious Air Corps Engineering School in July 1940.

Schriever graduated from the school with a "Superior" rating in July of the following year. Though war seemed imminent and experienced pilots were at a premium, Arnold and others saw his unique potential and sent him to Stanford University for a master's degree in advanced aeronautical engineering studies.

In June 1942, with the war now six months old, Schriever graduated from Stanford. He was immediately sent to Australia to serve at the headquarters of the U.S. Army Air Services, Southwest Pacific Area. Except for a two-week interval, he would be "in theater" for the next three years and three months.

His 39 months in the combat zone saw him fill a variety of positions of ever-increasing scope and responsibility. Schriever joined the 19th Bombardment Group at the time the unit was preparing to support General Douglas MacArthur's push into New Guinea. Schriever was assigned as engineering officer, placed in charge of the group's maintenance function. He fixed the unit's B-17 bombers but also insisted on being put on the roster to fly combat missions. By war's end, he had flown 63 missions in the "Flying Fortress."

A few months later, at the direction of General George Kenney, MacArthur's senior airman, Schriever was transferred to the 5th Air Force Service Command as chief of the Maintenance and Engineering Division. Increased responsibilities soon followed. First came assignment as chief of staff of the 5th Air Force Service Command, where he was tasked with accelerating the pace at which crated bombers were assembled and put into the fight. Schriever did it faster than it had ever been done before. On his forthcoming performance report, his supervisor wrote, "This is the most capable officer known to me." Schriever received an accelerated promotion to colonel.

Schriever was then made chief of staff of the Far East Service Command, a larger organization that combined the two major air forces in the Pacific region. September 1944 brought a difficult, critical posting as officer in charge of the Advance Echelon of the Far East Service Command. As MacArthur carried out his island-hopping campaign, Schriever's mission was essentially that of a troubleshooter, moving from place to place across the Pacific, improvising resolutions on the spot to supply problems, and overseeing the construction of new airfields and depots as air units moved in concert with MacArthur's infantry.

Finally, in September 1945, Schriever returned home to a Pentagon assignment in the Air Staff's Research and Development Division. Within days of his arrival, he was summoned by Hap Arnold and given the task of cultivating relations with the civilian scientific community. A new office—the Scientific Liaison Board—was created for him within the R&D Division. As events would show, the position provided nearly ideal preparation for the duties and responsibilities that would later befall him. His interactions immersed him in a variety of disciplines and gave him a realistic conception of what was feasible in the future. Unlike many warfighters, his focus shifted to the years ahead.

After attending National War College in 1950, Schriever returned to the Pentagon as assistant for evaluation and later as assistant for development planning. It was in those duties that circumstances brought him in contact—and occasional confrontation—with Curtis LeMay. The first major occurrence concerned plans for a nuclear-powered bomber. LeMay insisted on supersonic capability for the imagined weapon. Schriever's research confirmed that while a subsonic system might be feasible, the heat generated by a reactor powerful enough to propel supersonic flight would melt any material currently known or foreseeable. LeMay was adamant. Schriever, though, had exhaustively scoured the scientific and engineering communities and knew his conclusion was accurate, although most assuredly not the one LeMay wanted or expected to hear. Schriever told LeMay, "If you can find someone who is knowledgeable, a scientist or an engineer who understands all the technology that is involved in supersonic flight in a nuclear power plant, I will stand corrected." The atomic plane was never built.

Among other things, the two of them also had disagreements concerning bomber attack profiles, refueling techniques, and engines. LeMay was a strong advocate of a proposed high-flying, supersonic manned bomber. Schriever's studies led him to conclude that Soviet advances in radar, surface-to-air missiles, and latest-generation fighter capability would make successful penetration of Soviet airspace from high altitude increasingly problematic. Much better, he thought, to go in low, "under the radar." As events played out, one of the early acts of the Kennedy administration was to cancel the XB-70 program, the developmental high-altitude, supersonic bomber. Low-altitude, "under-the-radar" attack remains the preferred approach for Strategic Air Command bombers not cloaked in radar-shielding stealth technology.

The months ahead would bring contradictory views on refueling technology and discussions concerning the relative utility of a "probe-and-drogue" technique (better suited for refueling multiple aircraft at the same time and particularly well suited for fighter aircraft) and various versions of the flying boom (preferred by LeMay for fueling SAC bombers). SAC would continue to use the flying boom for its bomber force. Years later, the huge KC-10 tankers would be equipped with the probe-and-drogue system that enabled the tanker to refuel all Air Force and Navy aircraft in the U.S. inventory, as well as NATO and Allied fighters.

The two also disagreed on issues associated with new engine technology. Schriever's scientist, Pete Blasingame, developed a turbofan engine that would greatly improve thrust and fuel efficiency. Large airplanes would need fewer engines and could operate from shorter runways. The engines initially developed for a prospective future bomber were never "sold" to SAC, perhaps because they were maximally efficient at low levels and LeMay was bitterly opposed to that attack profile. The engines developed by Schriever and Blasingame would later be used in the Air Force's C-141 and C-5A transports.

Though some of LeMay's early objections may be attributable to his fear that money spent on missiles would deflect funds from his bomber force, it should be noted that he and Schriever were not always at loggerheads. When the development of the Minuteman missile was at a key decision point, LeMay spoke strongly in its favor, perhaps seeing Minuteman as the "ultimate weapon"—accurate, reliable, fast-firing, capable of being produced in large numbers—a system that would fit his concept of deterring the Soviet Union or destroying it if war ever came.

In April 1961, the Air Materiel Command was divided into two new organizations: the Air Force Logistics Command and the Air Force Systems Command. Schriever was placed in command of the latter. The scope of the new organization was extraordinary: Systems Command was given responsibility for research, development, and initial production of all the Air Force's weapons—aircraft, missiles, and other systems. In July 1961 he received his fourth star. In 1963, anticipating that his days in uniform were coming to a close, Schriever directed Project Forest, perhaps the most comprehensive long-range assessment of military science and associated technology ever conducted.

Though the nation's missile programs were progressing under Schriever's guidance, he did not get along well with Robert S. McNamara, the new secretary of defense. Schriever believed McNamara and his "whiz kids" packaged preconceived notions in statistical wrappings that were void of military experience and the realities of combat. Increasingly frustrated, he retired on April 16, 1966—two years prior to his mandatory retirement date—at Andrews AFB, Maryland.

At periodic reunions of the "Bernie's Colonels" group following his retirement, he was repeatedly recognized as the father of the modern, high-tech Air Force. In the end, Schriever and the men who in the early days had gone through the anguish of watching rockets blow up on test projects took special relish seeing them lift off into space, knowing that the machines they had devised did more than just secure the peace—they also opened space for American exploration.

Through the decade of the 1970s, Schriever's "disciples" moved into senior positions in space operations and management. Satellites that preserved the peace by not only photographing the adversary's movements and capabilities but also listening in on their conversations were designed and launched under their guidance. Eventually, Defense Support Program satellites capable of detecting Soviet missiles at the moment of launch were put into monitoring orbits, providing another layer of certainty that the United States would not be taken by surprise. GPS satellites soon followed.

Among the many honors that came to Schriever in his later years was the Smithsonian National Air and Space Museum Trophy for Lifetime Achievement. On June 5, 1998, Falcon AFB, Colorado—the center for control of U.S. satellites—was renamed Schriever AFB. It was the first time that the Air Force had named an installation for a living person.

The significance of those honors has been validated by the test of time. Had the Soviet Union fielded a fleet of ICBMs prior to the United States, the consequences would have been most uncertain. At the minimum, American credibility among allies and adversaries alike would have been shattered. SAC's bomber force would have been held at risk, as indeed the entire nation would have been threatened with destruction within 15 minutes with limited means of retaliation.

Thus, Schriever left a legacy with a vital but seemingly implausible contradiction. The weapons he created with such power and precision were never fired in anger. The fact of having them—and having them first—kept the nation and the world free of nuclear conflict.

Aerospace historian G. Harry Stine described Schriever's personal character best of all. Stine said Schriever was "known as a man with complete integrity and sound judgment, neither rebel nor conformist . . . he could stimulate action and get things done. And he had a rare understanding of the intricacies and internal politics of the aerospace industry."

For the United States and the free world, Schriever was the right man at the right time and place.

Bernard Schriever died January 20, 2005, at age 84. He was buried at Arlington National Cemetery, not far—at his request—from his friend and mentor Hap Arnold. The inscription on his tombstone reads, "Father of the Air Force's Ballistic Missile and Space Program."

CHAPTER TWO

Korea

THE PATH TO WAR

Japan's surrender on September 2, 1945, ended that nation's brutal 35-year occupation of Korea. Conditions on the peninsula, however, remained unsettled in the aftermath. During the closing days of the war, the United States and the Soviet Union had agreed that the Soviets would be responsible for taking the surrender of the Japanese troops north of the 38th parallel—the dividing line that roughly bisects the Korean landmass as it projects north to south from the Asian mainland. Japanese troops south of the parallel would surrender to American forces. From the American perspective, that agreement was intended as a temporary administrative arrangement to facilitate the surrender process and a restoration of sovereignty to a unified Korea. Instead, the 38th parallel was to become the de facto boundary between separate nations. In the face of a United Nations decision to oversee elections throughout Korea in 1947—an action, it was believed, that would result in reunification—the Soviet Union blocked the plebiscite in the North and installed Kim Il Sung as the leader of a communist state, the Democratic People's Republic of Korea.

South of the parallel, the United States supported Syngman Rhee, the elected leader of the newly formed Republic of Korea (ROK). Both leaders were autocratic, dedicated nationalists who aspired to reunite the nation, although under markedly different political visions. Almost immediately, threats began being hurled back and forth, and periodic skirmishes erupted along the parallel. In 1949, as per a United Nations agreement, both the Soviet Union and the United States withdrew combat forces from the peninsula, although both retained advisory and training cadres.

The withdrawal of Russian and American combat units further reduced restraints on aggressive actions on both sides of the boundary. Belligerent statements and threats of invasion by both the North and the South grew in frequency and intensity. In one week alone, March 3–10, 1950, there were 18 incidents along the parallel and 29 attacks by communist operatives throughout South Korea.

On June 25, 1950, after yet another series of contentious interchanges—and after being assured of political and military support from the Soviet Union and the People's Republic of China—North Korea launched a surprise attack. In the aftermath, some observers conjectured that Kim Il Sung's decision might have been influenced by a statement made by U.S. Secretary of State Dean Acheson that could be interpreted as implying that Korea was outside of America's defense perimeter. Whatever the combination of factors that led to it, early weeks of unfettered success appeared to validate Kim's decision to invade. The poorly trained and ill-equipped South Korean Army proved no match for Kim's forces, thousands of whom were battle-trained veterans, having fought with Mao's forces during the Chinese Civil War. Striking with overwhelming superiority in artillery and armor, North Korean formations pushed forward almost unchecked in a drive that would eventually carry all the way to the southern tip of the peninsula.

In response, the United States called for an immediate meeting of the United Nations Security Council—a move abetted by a major diplomatic faux pas by the Soviet Union, which had earlier walked out in protest of the UN organization's failure to seat representatives of the People's Republic of China. Absent the threat of a Soviet veto, the Security Council passed a resolution condemning the North's aggression and demanding the withdrawal of its forces. To supplement South Korean formations, combatant units from 15 nations, the largest contingent consisting of American personnel, were sent to repel the North's onslaught. Another 41 nations contributed material aid of various kinds.

American President Harry S. Truman, wary of the further spread of communism and of a possibly imminent threat to nearby Japan, cited a National Security Council memorandum (NSC-68) as rationale for injecting American forces into the conflict. NSC-68 called for the use of military force to contain the spread of communism.

The president used the provisions of NSC-68 to buttress his decision to employ U.S. combat forces without the explicit approval of Congress. Though not unprecedented in itself, the Korean "police action" would be the largest commitment of American forces without a formal declaration of war until the Vietnam conflict a decade later and the Gulf War 40 years later.

The passage of time has not diminished the historical significance of the Korean War. The conflict expanded the Cold War, making it a global endeavor—until then the focal point had almost exclusively focused on events in Europe. Korea created the concept of limited war—the implicit understanding that the superpowers, sometimes using proxies, would contest a war without escalating the conflict to the nuclear threshold.

While conflict was indeed limited in the sense of weapons employment and the tacit agreement to restrict fighting to the Korean Peninsula and the airspace above it, the term is not in any way descriptive of the scale or intensity of the fighting, the number of combatants involved, or the extent of the casualties inflicted on the civilian populations or on the soldiers, sailors, and airmen on all sides who fought in the conflict. As many as two and a half to three million civilians in North and South Korea were killed, wounded, or went missing during the course of the war. Chinese forces alone are believed to have sustained 600,000 casualties (out of perhaps as many as three million military and civilian personnel who were deployed to Korea at some point during the war). While the ground war seesawed up and down the peninsula, the war in the air was never a stalemate. American and allied airpower controlled the skies and subjected Chinese and North Korean forces to punishing aerial attacks.

The Korean War was a watershed event in the wider Cold War context. The direct intervention of thousands of Chinese troops in support of North Korea, as well as tacit and material assistance from the Soviet Union, made it the first armed conflict between major belligerents during that tenuous era. Convinced of the inherently aggressive nature of a worldwide communist movement, the United States and its allies adopted a policy of containment, seeking to bottle up communist bloc nations until they would eventually fall from their own internal contradictions. President Truman's response to the invasion and his success in making it a United Nations war surprised and chastened Soviet leader Joseph Stalin. The commitment of American forces validated claims that the United States would act to defend democratic nations against communist insurgent movements.

For the United States, the war, while not unifying the Korean Peninsula, prevented it from being overrun by communist forces and markedly enhanced the security of Japan. In the larger sense, the conflict preserved and promoted the notion of collective action by Western and other "free world" allies. More than 70 years later, American troops remain in South Korea.

Forgotten Leader: Walton "Johnny" Walker

"There Will Be No More Retreating"

Walker's inspired defense of the Pusan Perimeter bought time for allied forces to reach the peninsula and set the stage for the landing at Inchon. Later, he skillfully led the withdrawal from the North after the Chinese massively intervened. Walker has been cited as "the most forgotten general in America's most forgotten war." U.S. ARMY— U.S. ARMY HISTORY AND EDUCATION CENTER

When measured over the entirety of his long career, Walton Walker was by most assessments a good, but not necessarily a great, general. Competent and brusque, his service during World War II had been solid and reliable. During that conflict, Walker was best recalled for his aggressive nature and for his acquired reputation as George S. Patton's favorite general.

As with many senior officers, the degree to which those who served under him embraced his leadership varied somewhat according to circumstances. In fairness, it must be said that in the early days in Korea, popularity could not have been his remotest consideration. Time after time Walker had to throw his battered, exhausted soldiers against numerically superior forces in a desperate, but ultimately successful, attempt to buy time for the arrival of additional units and for the landing at Inchon, which reversed the initial tide of the war.

At the time of his death in a jeep accident, and out of favor with his boss, General Douglas MacArthur, he may well have been about to be removed from command. For three months, though, at the beginning of the conflict in Korea, "Johnny" Walker's generalship bordered on genius. Initially outmanned and outgunned, his defensive stand on the Pusan Perimeter prevented U.S. and UN forces from being pushed off the Korean Peninsula, if not annihilated completely. Under enormous pressure, Walker shifted his sparse forces to cover threatened breakthroughs while integrating newly assigned troops, often green and marginally trained, into a desperately held but coherent defensive line. From July 1950 until the breakout following the September 15 Inchon landing, Walker's troops, abetted by his astute use of terrain, intelligence intercepts, naval gunfire, and allied airpower, held back North Korean advances that threatened to turn Pusan into a latter-day Dunkirk.

Walton Walker had arrived in Japan and taken command of the Eighth Army in September 1948. From the outset, it was clear that he was not a "MacArthur man." During World War II, he had fought in the "wrong" theater, which in MacArthur's eyes made him an adversary: generals in the European Theater had gotten troops and supplies that MacArthur believed should have rightfully been assigned to him. Walker was also a friend of people who provoked MacArthur's suspicions—George Marshall and Dwight Eisenhower foremost among them.

At the time, the Eighth was essentially a constabulary force composed of the 7th, 24th, and 25th Infantry Divisions and the 1st Cavalry Division. With an area of responsibility encompassing the Japan home islands, the

Eighth had been in Japan since the end of World War II, assigned to police the terms of surrender.

In addition to that role, the position placed two additional responsibilities on Walker. His units served as administrators for the military government, and he was responsible for training the army of occupation. Walker was known as an exceptional trainer of troops. But in Japan he faced a daunting task. The Eighth Army was in appalling condition. Walker had four undermanned divisions with outdated and poorly maintained weapons. The soldiers were physically unfit and ill-equipped to a surprising degree. The unit had grown soft in occupation duty and was poorly prepared for combat.

Though sorely constrained by congressionally mandated budget cuts, manpower shortfalls, and the Army establishment's overriding emphasis on Europe, Walker enthusiastically launched into the task of "training up" the Eighth Army in the summer of 1949. Exercises were conducted at battalion level, but time allowed little in the way of preparations involving regiments and divisions. Though progress was being made, the Eighth was far from ready to confront a veteran, well-equipped adversary.

On June 25, 1950, North Korean Army forces swept across the 38th parallel, the artificial boundary separating North and South Korea. More than 100,000 troops—many of them veterans of the Chinese Civil War—liberally supplied with Russian tanks and artillery, quickly drove into South Korea, overwhelming poorly trained and ill-equipped Republic of Korea (ROK) units completely devoid of armor, large guns, and antitank weapons. The 500 U.S. advisers in Korea were carried along with the surging tide.

Internationally, the political implications were obvious from the outset. Militarily, given the size, scope, and initial success of the attack, the situation immediately assumed crisis proportions.

Two days after the attack, the South Korean government evacuated Seoul, the capital city. Within five days, South Korean military forces, which had numbered about 100,000 at the time of the invasion, were reduced through casualties, capture, and desertion to considerably less than half that number. Much of their sparse, antiquated equipment was abandoned as well.

Abetted by United Nations Resolution 83, recommending that member states provide military assistance, President Harry S. Truman committed U.S. naval and air forces to assist South Korea on June 27. A decision to put troops on the ground followed soon after. Truman justified the action

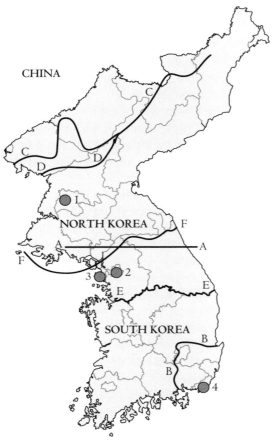

1. PYONGYANG
2. SEOUL
3. INCHON
4. PUSAN

A. 38th parallel
B. Pusan Perimeter: Sep 7, 1950
C. Farthest advance by U.S./UN forces: Oct 27, 1950
D. Front line as Chinese attacked: Nov 25, 1950
E. Farthest line of retreat by U.S./UN forces: Jan 15, 1951
F. Eventual armistice line

Korean War—Initial Stages

both as a lesson drawn from the failure of appeasement in World War II and (although not explicitly stated at the time) as a measure needed to carry out the nation's policy of containing communism on a global basis. (National Security Report 68, the foundation for the policy, was not declassified until 1975.)

Truman was convinced that the fall of South Korea would embolden leaders of the communist bloc. Over time, nations closer to American shores would be placed in jeopardy as smaller countries would be unable to withstand the growing threat. Concerned about the implications of a communist victory in Korea, Truman wrote: "If we had not pressured the United Nations to back up the free Republic of Korea, Western Europe would have gone into the hands of the communists."

As the North Korean attack rolled southward down the peninsula, efforts began in earnest to cobble together a defensive force. The nearest American military establishment, the Far East Command led by General MacArthur, was headquartered in Japan. The major U.S. ground component, the Eighth Army, was commanded by Johnny Walker.

Walker had inherited a hollow force, spoiled by occupation duty. Although World War II had been over for only three years when he took command, only 10 percent of his soldiers were combat veterans. Other obstacles would complicate his efforts once his force was deployed. In budget moves, Congress had stripped the Eighth Army of its corps artillery and corps headquarters, hindering Walker's ability to handle his units in the field.

On July 7 Walker flew to Korea to assess the situation. He found conditions worse than he had expected. There were obvious problems with commanders, tactical failures, and critical shortages of almost everything. The troops he encountered—both South Korean and American—were badly led, poorly trained, and ill-equipped to confront veteran troops and Russian tanks.

It was also obvious that the Korean landscape would not offer an easy place to fight. The South, the scene of initial combat, is cut by three mountain ranges. A narrow plain extends along the east coast, with a few scattered quasi-level areas elsewhere. Only about 15 percent of the land is arable. Large segments of the peninsula's forest cover had been cut down. Several major rivers cut across the country before emptying into the Yellow Sea and Korea Strait. One river, the Naktong, would play a vital role during the initial phase of the war. Walker would use it as an essential part of his defensive barrier.

Seen through the veils of history, the initial U.S./UN response was woefully inadequate. MacArthur deployed a small, 540-man contingent, labeled Task Force Smith after its commander, Lieutenant Colonel Charles B. Smith, with instructions to engage the enemy as far north as possible and stop or delay their advance. Smith's soldiers carried only

120 rounds of ammunition per man, and the small force, deficient in antitank weaponry, was generally incapable of defeating the Russian T-34s that soon came rumbling toward it. Smith and his men landed at Pusan on June 28 and moved north as quickly as possible. On July 5, near Osan, 20 or so miles south of Seoul, they made contact for the first time. As Smith pushed forward, his small force, part of the 1st Battalion, 21st Infantry, 24th Infantry Division, met a column of eight T-34s with a supporting force of perhaps as many as 5,000 infantry. Despite the disparity in manpower and equipment, Smith deployed his men to receive the attack that came at him down the highway from Suwon to Osan, succeeding momentarily in holding up the North Korean advance. Rather quickly, though, the task force was enveloped and overwhelmed, losing 163 men killed, wounded, or captured. Smith ordered a retreat to the south, which was accomplished in considerable disorder. Task Force Smith's story would be repeated several times by other units in other locations during the early days of the war.

On July 13 Walker, "a squat, plump, square-jawed Texan who looked more like a small town businessman than an Army commander," was placed in command of all U.S. Army troops in Korea. That same day, he called his subordinates together. Meeting with them for the first time in the war zone, he painted a bleak but temporary picture, associating the situation in Korea with the early days of World War II. He acknowledged that, at present, the UN forces did not have the capability to stop the North Korean advance. The allies, he told them, had to slow down the assault until the help that was on its way got to Korea. Eventually, he said, the allies would prevail. For a while, though, it would be necessary to trade time for space.

Four days later, on July 17, Walker also assumed operational command of the ROK Army forces. Command of all UN ground forces would soon follow.

Walker established his initial headquarters (Eighth U.S. Army in Korea—EUSAK) at Taegu, about 60 miles north of Pusan, a place he had to hold at all costs. On the extreme southern tip of the peninsula, Pusan was the only available deepwater port in South Korea. Walker had gained notoriety in World War II as Patton's most aggressive corps commander. In Korea, he would be forced into a much different type of battle—a defensive struggle aimed at giving UN forces time to gather the men, materiel, and supplies necessary to turn back the North Korean attack. It was immediately obvious that Taejon—a city astride a vital junction—would play an important role in the campaign that would follow. If Taejon fell, the Allies would have to move back to the Naktong River—a move that would place them deep in the toe of the Korean Peninsula.

Events, though, rather quickly spiraled downward. Beginning with Task Force Smith's debacle, American and UN forces met with a crushing string of losses as the North Korean Army drove southward. On July 28, the North Koreans pushed the 24th Infantry Division out of Taejon, capturing division commander Major General William Dean in the process. Five days later, the 1st Cavalry lost Yongdong. Small counterattacks failed, often yielding bitter lessons regarding the caliber and tenacity of North Korean troops.

As the losses continued and the North Koreans moved farther south, Walker took extraordinary measures to stem the tide. He was, quite frankly, running out of real estate. To concede further ground would result in insufficient depth to maintain and maneuver a reserve force or to properly mass units for a counterattack.

To hold the perimeter, Walker could employ five battered ROK divisions, the understrength U.S. 24th and 25th Infantry Divisions, the 1st Cavalry Division, and a portion of the 2nd Infantry Division. Reinforcements were arriving through the Pusan harbor—the 5th Regimental Combat Team, the 1st Marine Provisional Brigade, and the 27th British Infantry Brigade being among the first ashore. After 120 miles of retreat, constantly shuttling regiments, battalions, and companies, Walker bought his last remaining amount of time by falling back behind the Naktong River barrier.

Squeezed into the southeast corner of Korea, the resulting area, quickly named and indelibly etched in military annals as the "Pusan Perimeter," was a horseshoe-shaped configuration 100 miles long and 50 miles deep. The Naktong formed the western boundary of the perimeter. The northern edge was shaped by a mountain line; the east by the Sea of Japan and the south by the Tsushima Strait. Naval fire support off both coasts anchored each end of Walker's line. Led by the U.S. Fifth Air Force, allied airpower provided air supremacy, destroying follow-on North Korean forces and devastating supply lines. Command of the air by Air Force, Navy, and Marine aircraft allowed Walker to shift forces in daylight over rail connections between Pusan and areas under threat. The compact battlefield enabled him to exploit his superior mobility and firepower, advantages that were further leveraged by intelligence intercepts from code breakers who decrypted North Korean ciphers and provided information on enemy intentions and capabilities.

Using the Naktong as a shield, still sometimes having to ration his artillery to five rounds per day, Walker held on. With conditions especially grave, Walker issued what soon gained notoriety as the "stand or die" option.

"We are fighting a battle against time," he told his soldiers. "There will be no more retreating, withdrawal or readjustment of lines or any other term you may choose. There is no line behind us to which we can retreat . . . there will be no Dunkirk, there will be no Bataan. A retreat to Pusan would be one of the worst butcheries in history. We must fight until the end. . . We must fight as a team. If some of us must die, we will die fighting together. . . . I want everyone to understand that we are going to hold this line. We are going to win."

August was marked by days of desperate fighting. Finally, though, shortly after mid-month, American and South Korean troops claimed their first major victory, prevailing in bitter combat that saved Taegu. On August 17, Walker—now a bit better equipped with antitank weapons and other ordnance, launched a limited counterattack. The area—a long, narrow valley in proximity to Taegu and the Naktong River with rugged hills along both sides—was called the "Bowling Alley" by allied troops. Difficult fighting and, for one of the first times, exemplary performance by a ROK division pushed the North Koreans back. Taegu was saved.

Despite heavy losses, the North Koreans continued to hammer at Walker's line with 15 divisions, sending six against the western flank and four against the northern portion of the line. Though the North Korean Army had been heavily reduced through air strikes and naval gunfire, Kim Il-sung continued to feed new units into the battle. In late August, three fresh divisions struck in the center and at other points along the UN perimeter.

Walker met the threat by adapting a novel "mobile defense" strategy. Strapped initially for manpower, Walker invented the approach on the fly. Allocating a small portion of his defenders to hold a series of forward strongpoints, he kept the bulk of his forces in reserve for use in plugging gaps and as counterattack elements. Walker's creation was at the time nowhere found in Army manuals or tactical doctrine. Existing doctrine provided for "positional defense," with most units posted along a continuous line of fixed positions backed at key points by small, mobile forces. A positional defense assumed six to eight miles across each division front. By contrast, Walker's divisions along the Naktong had to hold as many as 25 to 35 miles of frontage.

The shifting conditions and degrees of threat required a different form of leadership. Walker crafted his forces, placing them in terrain for which they were best suited. He then devoted his personal attention to points where critical battles might occur. He would, in fact, command by exception—the occasions and timing of his interventions would be driven by the extent of the threat and the immediacy of the crisis.

Spending most of his days moving from unit to unit via a specially modified jeep or flying over enemy lines in an L-19 Bird Dog aircraft, Walker cobbled together a series of improvised counterattack units made up of troops drawn from relatively quiet sections and newly arrived formations. Over time, these "fire fighters"—the 5th Regimental Combat Team and 1st Marines were among the units most often called upon—would play important roles in the outcome.

Between August 5 and 24 the North Koreans launched fiercely sustained assaults that struck heavily against four separate but converging areas. When one attack near the west coast threatened to roll up Walker's left flank, he hurriedly shifted his "fire fighters" to close the breach. On one occasion, Walker shifted an entire division more than 100 miles in less than 24 hours.

Soon after that attack began, another North Korean thrust threatened to envelop Taegu from both the north and the south while at the same time placing the vital railroad to Pusan in grave danger. Walker adroitly shifted forces to close the "Naktong Bulge," clearing it by August 17.

The crisis had not slackened, however. Elsewhere, north of Taegu, two North Korean divisions forced their way across the Naktong, collapsing a portion of the perimeter. Abandoning his headquarters at Taegu, Walker shifted the British brigade and the ROK 1st Division to meet the advance.

Perhaps seeking a decision before UN forces could be brought to the peninsula in more substantial numbers, the North Koreans continued the series of massive, rolling assaults first initiated in early August. On August 27, Walker beat back simultaneous attacks at five locations that threatened to overwhelm the line so thinly held by UN forces. Local breakthroughs occurred in places, jeopardizing for a time the entire perimeter. Walker again shuffled his units, already stretched to the maximum, and held on.

In the early days of September, in a desperate two-week battle—one of the most ferocious of the entire war—a small contingent of Army and Marine units with an engineer battalion thrown in, somehow, almost miraculously, saved the vital town of Yongsan. If Yongsan had fallen, the road to Miryang, 12 miles away, would have been exposed. And afterward, Miryang, then Pusan. Beyond Pusan, the war was lost. Yongsan, like so many of the struggles along the perimeter, was enormously consequential though little remembered except by the soldiers and Marines who fought there and accomplished so much with so little. Even after Yongsan, with the road to Miryang blocked, heavy fighting along the Naktong persisted—and would do so until Inchon changed the war. The North Korean tide crested on September 12, defeated by Walker's switching of units, allied air and naval dominance, and the availability at long last of additional numbers of U.S. medium tanks newly arrived on the peninsula.

The peaking of the North Korean surge coincided with the event that brought the initial turning point in the war. Although the Joint Chiefs of Staff, worried by considerations of tidal fluctuations and defensive emplacements, were reluctant in their support, General MacArthur secured agreement to conduct an amphibious landing at Inchon, the port of Seoul, 10 miles west of the capital city.

On September 15, an invasion force numbering 50,000 soldiers and Marines waded ashore 150 miles north of where Walker was holding the line around Pusan. The surprise attack succeeded almost beyond expectations, threatening to trap the bulk of the North Korean forces engaged far to the south. Walker, though his defenses had been further stripped by the removal of the 1st Marines and other formations—withdrawn to take part in the landings at Inchon—planned a breakout in the south to complement the strike at Inchon.

At first in some places the breakout did not achieve the speed Walker anticipated. Though Inchon threatened to entrap them, North Korean units stayed in place for a few days in their heavily fortified positions, resisting attempts by UN forces to push them aside and move north. Nor was Walker always satisfied with the support he was receiving from his own headquarters. Though resistance at Inchon had not been heavy, Major General Ned Almond, commander of the X Corps invading force, had been given, and had used, an immense amount of ammunition. Walker was heard to say, "They expended more ammunition to kill a handful of green troops . . . than I've been given to defeat ninety percent of the North Korean Army." Then, too, X Corps had taken almost all of the bridging equipment, leaving little for Walker to use in spanning the Naktong and other streams before he could unleash the Eighth Army and head north.

Once on the move, though, as many have commented, the breakout after Inchon placed Walker in his element. Like his heady days in Europe leading Patton's aggressive, fast-moving forces, Walker's soldiers struck hard at the retreating North Koreans, prompting signs of disintegration in some units. One of Walker's tank units traveled 106 miles in a single day.

Walker had been opposed to the choice of Inchon as a landing spot. He thought the invasion should take place farther south so the troops who broke out from the perimeter had less distance to travel before linking up with the units that had conducted the invasion. Most of all, Walker's concern was about numbers. While he was fighting to keep allied units from being driven out of Korea, two American divisions and considerable amounts of his supporting air and naval units were taken from him for six crucial weeks as preparations for Inchon were being made.

Many senior naval officers also objected to the choice of Inchon, but Walker's opposition surely increased MacArthur's existing distaste for him. As with many things, Inchon was a test of loyalty for MacArthur. MacArthur's deputy, the sycophant Ned Arnold, passed it with flying colors. Walker did not.

The movement of UN forces inland from Inchon and north from the Pusan Perimeter brought the first of several controversial decisions associated with the war. Instead of sending his forces immediately across the peninsula to more completely cut off the escape route of North Korean Army units fleeing north, MacArthur chose to focus first on clearing Seoul and restoring the South Korean government in the capital city.

To a lesser degree, Walker was subjected to somewhat similar criticism for allegedly placing more emphasis on linking up with the Inchon forces than in destroying North Korean units as they streamed north in disarray. Although desperate to avoid the closing trap, many North Korean units, for various reasons, did not begin withdrawing from the south in a major way until a few days after the Inchon landing. As they hurried away toward the 38th parallel and beyond, many formations lost unit integrity and collapsed into small, individual pockets of fleeing soldiers, some of whom merged into the countryside and adopted guerilla warfare tactics.

Against crumbling opposition, Walker sent ROK forces up the east coast while the 1st Cavalry Division and units drove northwest, taking the key junction of Taejon. On September 27, his units linked up with the 7th Infantry Division, part of the Inchon invasion force, just north of Osan, about 20 miles south of Seoul.

Notwithstanding the misgivings associated with MacArthur's decision to capture Seoul vice blocking the escape path of the North Korean Army, the toll exacted on the North Koreans was extremely heavy. It is believed that in battles around the Pusan Perimeter, perhaps as many as 14 North Korean divisions were all but annihilated. Of the initial invading force of

100,000 or more, perhaps only 20,000 to 30,000 eventually made it back to North Korea.

Walker's forces had paid a high price as well. From early July until the initial breakout after September 15, the Eighth Army's casualties totaled 4,280 killed in action, 12,377 wounded, 2,107 missing, and 401 confirmed captured.

As the remnants of the North Korean Army fled north, another strategic decision whose consequences remain with us today confronted political leaders. The initial UN mandate provided for the use of force to clear South Korea of the invaders. Now, rather unexpectedly, the opportunity presented itself to go further—to occupy some or all of North Korea and punish the regime that had precipitated the war.

Walker favored digging in about 100 miles north, across the narrow part of the peninsula, leaving the remaining two-thirds of the country—mostly sparsely settled wilderness—untouched. A line drawn there would be easy to defend and supply and would expose any attack on it to UN airpower.

On October 7, as urged by the Truman administration, the UN voted in support of a resolution calling for the UN forces to carry the war into North Korea. For Walker, and indeed for the entire UN military effort, the war was about to enter a new phase. Though for a time the military campaign went well, Walker would be burdened by an increasingly strained relationship with MacArthur and by a bizarre organizational arrangement that defied all military logic.

When X Corps—the force that landed at Inchon—linked up with the Eighth Army, X Corps should rightfully have come under control of Walker and the Eighth Army. Instead, the Commander of X Corps, Major General Edward Almond, a favorite of MacArthur, continued to report directly to Far Eastern Command headquarters. Incongruously, Almond was also MacArthur's chief of staff. Thus, Almond, one of the most controversial and widely despised officers in U.S. military history, had direct access to MacArthur, while Walker, the organization's senior field commander, had to report through X Corps. Walker, the three-star, took orders from Almond, the two-star.

The command arrangement had other ripple effects as well. Although Almond was a two-star, he was deft at implying that he was the de facto five-star speaking on behalf of MacArthur and not for himself. The structure hindered Walker's attempts to procure the capable field officers he wanted and so desperately needed. When troopships arrived in Japan, records were screened, and the best officers went to Ned Almond at MacArthur's headquarters.

Walker was sometimes later criticized for having a somewhat disorganized and ineffective staff. That may indeed be true—or at least partially true. If so, it is likely that the situation was exacerbated by the fact that many of the most qualified staff officers were being siphoned off for duty elsewhere.

Almond did not hesitate to restrict and filter Walker's communications to headquarters. That MacArthur, an urbane and aristocratic figure, never had an easy relationship with the blunt, taciturn Walker, made an already uncomfortable situation all the more difficult.

While policymakers in Washington debated the efficacy of fighting a limited war or striving for all-out victory, UN forces crossed the 38th parallel and moved mostly unchecked into North Korea. By this time, a sizable portion of the North Korean Army, which initially numbered about 135,000 troops, had been utterly destroyed. Pyongyang, the North Korean capital, was captured on October 20. On October 24 Walker moved his headquarters into a complex evacuated by North Korean leader Kim Il Sung.

From the time UN forces first crossed the 38th parallel, China, most often in the person of Premier Chou En-Lai, had warned the UN not to move against North Korean territory. Now, with UN forces continuing to advance toward the Yalu River, China's border with North Korea, the warnings became more frequent and ominous. In October, the presence of Chinese troops was noted for the first time. Though evidence continued to mount that Chinese Army units were present in sizable numbers, the UN push continued, and MacArthur commented that the troops would be "home for Christmas," a remark that, among other things, caused some allied governments to withhold plans to send forces to Korea.

Walker was reluctant to push on, momentarily delaying his offensive operations until he had replenished supplies and alleviated his shortages of manpower. His halt, though brief, was not looked on favorably at MacArthur's headquarters. MacArthur and Almond minimized the threat of Chinese intervention and ordered the advance to continue along both coasts.

For a considerable time, Walker had harbored doubts about the all-out push to the north. His concerns were not yet shared at MacArthur's headquarters in Tokyo or at the Pentagon in Washington. Reports, though, began to paint an ominous picture—already perhaps as many as 300,000 Chinese troops had pushed into Korea. By this time, Walker's logistical weaknesses were becoming apparent. Supplies had been exhausted during the long, sustained advance. If a heavy attack occurred, he would not have enough left to defeat it.

Also of concern was a major consideration affecting any drive to the north. The plan was for Walker and the Eighth Army to move up the west coast while Almond and X Corps would advance along the east side of the peninsula. The problem lay in the middle, where the Taebaek mountain range separated the two forces. Indeed, moving at night and hiding by day, the Chinese would use the mountains to infiltrate thousands of troops, where they were poised on the flanks of the two armies.

Though MacArthur's advance was delayed somewhat by periodic spoiling attacks, some units—like the 7th Regiment of the ROK 6th division—reached the Yalu. Then, on October 25, as units of Walker's Eighth Army moved up the west coast of the Korean Peninsula, they were suddenly and massively attacked by Chinese forces numbering in the tens of thousands. The Chinese First Phase Offense struck elements of the American First Cavalry Division and several units of South Korean infantry. Surprise was complete. For a time the entire ROK II Corps was near collapse, and the Eighth Army's right flank was in danger. North of Pyongyang, near the town of Unsan, ROK forces were routed and an Eighth Cavalry regiment was engulfed from three sides. Fighting in that sector was continuous, eventually forcing the Americans to flee into the hills, severing them from substantive support. As the fighting continued, the Eighth Cavalry's Third Battalion was totally cut off and fought a desperate battle for survival as Walker struggled to restore his front.

Then the inexplicable happened. In early November, as suddenly as the enemy forces had appeared, they withdrew, disappearing into the mountains and other hiding places. The move, intended as a deception, enabled the attackers to replenish their tenuous supply line. In the days ahead, it almost seemed as if the entire episode was dismissed or forgotten. Though by this time there was no mistaking the identity of the attackers—they were Chinese—MacArthur believed that UN forces could detect major troop movements across the Yalu and ordered the advances along both the east and west coasts of Korea to continue.

Under pressure to resume the drive to the north, Walker got permission to momentarily delay his advance. His supply situation was indeed in extremis; one of his corps commanders had only one day of ammunition, a day and a half of fuel, and three, possibly four, days of food rations remaining.

Walker believed circumstances dictated a withdrawal to the narrow waist of Korea. It was an approach also advocated by senior British and French officers. MacArthur disagreed, favoring instead a resumption of the offensive. Walker's seven divisions, tanks, and artillery would require four thousand tons a day to support a major campaign. He was getting only half of that.

Meanwhile, the danger posed by the Korean landscape grew ever more threatening as the UN armies drove farther north toward the Yalu. The Taebaek Mountains thrust like a spear down the middle of the peninsula, making contact between the two wings almost impossible. Now, in mid-November, gaps that would eventually grow to 70 miles or more separated Walker's forces from Arnold's. Travel by road over treacherous mountain trails was even longer.

Walker had mostly solved his logistics problems early in the month. On November 10, MacArthur ordered Walker and Almond to continue their drives to the north. Their routes would take them directly into the path of an enormous army, hidden from sight, and bent on their annihilation.

On November 19, one of Almond's spearheads, a unit of the 7th U.S. division, reached a village on the Yalu. The news was greeted ecstatically by MacArthur's headquarters and the Pentagon, both of whom had apparently forgotten the fate of the ROK unit that had touched the Yalu in the west a few days earlier.

With a plan apparently personally devised by Mao Tse-tung, the Chinese had prepared a trap. As anticipated by Mao, MacArthur's order for an all-out advance on November 24 played right into it. After first temporarily ceasing offensive operations and withdrawing from the battlefield—a move that was misinterpreted by most allied planners—Mao had continued to mass thousands of troops and hide them in the rugged mountains that formed the spine of North Korea.

MacArthur visited Walker on the morning of November 24, expressing confidence and reiterating that the troops would be eating Christmas dinner at home. Walker was far less sure. His almost daily overflights and jeep travels had left him with grave trepidations regarding Chinese capabilities and intentions. When MacArthur left Walker's headquarters brimming with confidence, Walker, who almost never used profanity, cursed out loud—"Bullshit"—startling his staff. Soon after, he made one of the most momentous decisions of the war. He ordered that instructions be relayed to the commander of the 21st Infantry, the unit leading the attack, that "if he smells Chinese chow, pull back immediately."

With those words, Walker changed MacArthur's directions for an all-out attack into orders for a reconnaissance in force. It was the type of decision that every commander, every officer, hopes to never be confronted with. As General Matthew Ridgway described it, the greatest challenge a combat commander faces is his choice between an irrational order and the safety of his men. Walker had made his choice and was prepared to accept the consequences.

On November 25, as Walker cautiously pushed toward the Yalu, the Chinese launched a massive attack against the Eighth Army's right flank where it brushed against the mountain chain. Labeled the Second Phase Offensive, waves of Chinese infantry struck UN forces along the Chong-chon River about 50 miles south of the Yalu. The assault quickly collapsed three ROK divisions and uncovered the entire right flank of Walker's army. Eventually, four massive Chinese armies would assault Walker's forces. By the following day, the survival of the Eighth Army was in doubt.

By the 28th, MacArthur realized that the situation was of crisis propor-tions. Faced with obvious disaster, Walker received headquarters' approval to withdraw south to avoid being outflanked. Given the circumstances, his fighting retreat was well handled. The 24th and 25th Infantry Divisions fell back in reasonably good order, while the 2nd Armored suffered more severely and some units lost cohesion early in the retreat. Fighting delay-ing actions in the face of numerical superiority, Walker had successfully extracted the bulk of his forces by early December and withdrawn them to the vicinity of Pyongyang. His first inclination had been to try to hold a line north of the city. But, soon after, additional ROK divisions were shat-tered and the U.S. 2nd Armored Division was ambushed and caught in a cauldron. As conditions deteriorated, Walker was constantly on the move, spending hours every day in the air over the front or taking his jeep to observe conditions along it. Pyongyang, he was now certain, could not be held. He would have to continue the retreat southward. He made plans to withdraw, fight delaying actions, and destroy anything of military value to the Chinese and North Koreans.

Walker evacuated Pyongyang then fell back to the Imjin River, destroy-ing bridges, trestles, and supply dumps. Soon after, he placed almost all of the Eighth Army south of the 38th parallel and, after a retreat of 120 miles, stabilized a line south of Seoul.

Walker's correct appreciation of Chinese strength and intentions and his skill as a tactician during the withdrawal had saved the central core of the Eighth Army. His well-handled but speedy withdrawal in late November and early December had led some less well-informed outsiders to interpret the retreat as flight by a panicked army. Others, conversant with the situa-tion, thought Walker's performance was superb and that only great leaders achieve a high degree of success while operating on the defensive. Of

Walker's actions during this time, British historian Callum McDonald said, "It is difficult to believe that any other general could have done better."

Rumors of his prospective dismissal by MacArthur around this time are difficult to substantiate. On one occasion, MacArthur spoke openly to a group of subordinates about his misgivings concerning Walker's leadership. Publicly, though, MacArthur lauded his well-conducted retreat and later spoke highly of his tenacity and fighting spirit.

Like his mentor, George Patton, Walker had a jeep specially modified for his use—the vehicle was equipped with a platform and traverse bar that allowed him to stand while the jeep was moving and wide fenders to prevent him from being splattered with mud.

On the morning of December 23 Walker set out on a planned visit to several units. At one stop the plan for him was to make an award presentation. The occasion would have special meaning for him: Walker's son, Sam, was to receive a second Silver Star.

Though the roads were covered with ice, Walker's jeep, as usual, was traveling at high speed. Midway through the journey, Walker and his party in the jeep met a long line of 6th ROK division trucks traveling toward them from the north. As the convoy moved past them on the opposite side of the road, a ROK weapons carrier vehicle pulled out of line and attempted to pass the trucks in front of it. The ROK vehicle struck Walker's jeep, which rolled over but in the icy conditions continued to slide down the road. Walker was pinned beneath it and killed instantly.

Before and After

Walton Walker was born December 3, 1889, in Belton, a small town on the plains of central Texas. Cut by streams and rolling hills, the landscape complemented Walker's abiding interest in the outdoors. Encouraged by his father, he grew up to become an avid hunter and horseman. "A short, chunky nice looking fellow," Walker was known for his tenacity and unflagging energy.

After attending Virginia Military Institute for one year as preparation for an anticipated United States Military Academy appointment, Walker entered West Point in 1908. He graduated with the class of 1912 ranked 73rd in a class of 96.

Walker heard guns fired in anger for the first time while accompanying the Vera Cruz expedition as a young lieutenant in 1914. Two years later, while patrolling the American border, he became a tentmate and close friend of Dwight Eisenhower. Those duties were preliminary to an extended period on the front lines during World War I. Serving with the 5th Infantry Division, he led a machine-gun battalion through heavy fighting at St. Mihiel and during the Meuse-Argonne campaign. He was awarded the Silver Star (the first of three he would earn during his career) for gallantry in action and was appointed temporary colonel during the occupation duty that followed the signing of the armistice.

Following his postwar reversion to his permanent rank of captain, an eclectic series of moves followed his return from Europe in 1919. Interspersed among them were tours as instructor at West Point; the Infantry School at Fort Benning, Georgia; and the Coast Artillery School at Fort Monroe, Virginia. Three years (1930–33) at Tsientsin, China, with the 15th Infantry further broadened his background, as did subsequent attendance at the Army War College. Sometime during this period, he acquired his nickname "Johnny Walker" after the brand of Scotch whisky. Later, Walker acquired another sobriquet—"Bulldog"—for his tenacity and aggressiveness.

A particularly notable posting followed his graduation from the war college. At Fort Vancouver, Washington, Walker served in executive officer duties with the 5th Infantry Brigade. His performance impressed the Fifth's commander, an officer already held in awe by the army establishment: George C. Marshall. Walker's next series of assignments read like building blocks in preparation for his wartime responsibilities: 1937–40, War Plans Division with further duties as executive officer; April 1940 (colonel), commander of the 36th Infantry, Camp Polk, Louisiana; July 1941 (brigadier general), commander, 3rd Armored Brigade. The following year would bring his promotion to major general along with command of the 3rd Armored Division.

Early in the war, Walker's friend George Patton had established the Desert Training Center, an immense area of 55,000 square miles covering parts of California, Nevada, and Arizona, that allowed units to simulate operations by large formations. Walker succeeded Patton at the training center, expanding it considerably and improving its facilities. After a brief sabbatical to North Africa to assess training, strategy, and tactics and to study German methods, Walker returned to the United States to resume command of IV Corps (later redesignated XX Corps), consisting of the 26th, 40th, 75th, 83rd, and 98th Infantry Divisions and the 12th and 20th Armored Divisions. He was in those duties until February 1944, when he took the corps to the United Kingdom to prepare for the forthcoming invasion of Europe.

Walker unexpectedly saw action on D-Day when he flew to the beachhead to temporarily take command of XIX Corps when its commander became ill. Although in France only briefly, he earned a second oak leaf cluster for his Silver Star by personally leading an attack near St. Lo.

With the Allies having established a foothold on the continent, July 1944 saw the activation of George Patton's Third Army. Walker's XX Corps came ashore across Utah Beach on July 23. With the capture of Metz and other victories, Walker's corps established a reputation as the fast-moving spearhead of Patton's drive across France. Walker's slashing attacks and the prohibition against mentioning unit designations in news releases caused the XX Corps to be referred to, sometimes by friends and foes alike, as the "Ghost Corps."

When the Third Army was diverted north to help contain the "Battle of the Bulge" attack, Walker's corps covered the entire front formerly held by the Third Army. As the Third Army continued to hammer the Wehrmacht, XX Corps crossed the Moselle, broke through the Siegfried Line, and liberated Buchenwald and Ohrdorf concentration camps. In the closing days of the war, the corps swung south and east, reaching Linz, Austria, at the time of Germany's surrender. Walker was promoted to lieutenant general on April 27.

The close personal connection between Walker and Patton was evidenced when Patton was injured in a vehicle accident while on occupation duty a few months after the war ended. Eisenhower chose Walker to accompany Patton's wife Beatrice when she flew to Germany to attend her husband at the U.S. Army hospital in Heidelberg.

Postwar duties subsequently took Walker to Chicago, where for three years he served as commander of the recently reactivated Fifth Army. In September 1948 Walker was posted to Japan as commander, Eighth Army, relieving Lieutenant General Robert Eichelberger. Korea followed.

Although believed by some to be under somewhat of a cloud at the time of his accident, Walker was posthumously promoted within a month of his death to four-star general.

His funeral at Arlington National Cemetery was notable for those who came to honor him. Among the 25 who served as honorary pallbearers were George C. Marshall, Dwight Eisenhower, and Omar Bradley.

Walker's inspired defense on the Pusan Perimeter gave UN forces time to gather men and equipment and muster the political will to turn back the first military aggression of the Cold War. His legacy is held in high esteem in the Republic of Korea, where he is regarded as having saved the nation.

David Halberstam wrote, "If American military history has short-changed any of the nation's wars in the past century, it is Korea, and if any aspect of that war has been overlooked, it is the series of smaller battles fought along the Naktong in July, August, and September 1950, and if any one commander has not been given the credit he deserves, it is surely Walton Walker."

Walker's pilot, Mike Lynch, said, "He was the forgotten commander of the forgotten war."

Forgotten Leader: Oliver Prince ("O. P.") Smith

"Retreat, hell, we're simply advancing
in a different direction."

Along a single narrow road closed in by mountains and outnumbered by as much as twelve to one, Smith led the miraculous fighting withdrawal of U.S. and allied forces from the Chosin Reservoir to safety at the port of Hungnam. Against overwhelming odds and bitter cold, Smith's masterful leadership secured the safe withdrawal of the force's casualties, armor, and equipment. During the perilous journey he brought with him the bodies of the Marines killed in action. U.S. MARINE CORPS— U.S. MARINE CORPS HISTORY DIVISION

Noted author David Halberstam spoke for many military historians when he wrote, "The Marine breakout from the Chosin Reservoir is one of the great moments in American military history, not just Marine history, but military history."

Among several other scholars, American military historian/author Thomas E. Ricks rates United States Marine General O. P. Smith as the most underrated general in American history. Quiet, reserved, scholarly—his subordinates labeled him "The Professor"—Smith led the nearly miraculous withdrawal of the First Marine division and other associated units from the vicinity of the Chosin Reservoir to safety at the port of Hungnam.

Surrounded by forces that sometimes outnumbered his by twelve to one, battling minus-30-degree cold, under almost continuous fire along the single road to deliverance, Smith overcame all that. And more: the numbers, the cold, the impassable road were all visible obstacles. Less obvious was a command structure that must surely rank as one of the most ill-conceived in American military history. That he accomplished it all while bringing out his wounded and dead and saving his equipment—tanks, trucks, jeeps, ambulances, artillery—adds additional luster to an already monumental achievement.

In the context of the war in Korea, the name of United States Marine Major General Oliver Prince ("O. P.") Smith surfaces first in a major way with the landings at Inchon on September 15, 1950. As commander of the 1st Marine Division, Smith led the forces that made the successful landing, quickly took Kimpo Airfield, and fought house to house in capturing Seoul, the capital city of the beleaguered South Korean nation.

Though Smith was one of the world's foremost experts on amphibious warfare—and would lead the landing force—he was seldom consulted during the preparations for the attack. Experiences at Inchon would foreshadow later difficulties with the command hierarchy and his personal interactions with U.S. Army Major General Edward M. Almond, his superior in the convoluted chain of command. Issues with Almond surfaced almost immediately. Almond, who had never led, much less observed, an amphibious assault, casually dismissed the complexity of the operation. Though only two months older than Smith, Almond persisted in calling him "son" in front of subordinates. Those who knew and worked with Smith universally described his "quiet, reserved" personality and almost invariably remarked on his consummate professionalism. Though Almond's conduct and later his obvious lack of competence undoubtedly galled him, Smith never responded in a harsh manner or openly criticized him.

As the war progressed, Smith's issues with Almond would mirror those of his colleague, Eighth Army Commander Walton Walker, as the two of them led the United Nations forces that advanced north on opposite sides of the Korean Peninsula.

Smith had watched the Inchon landing from the deck of the USS *Mount McKinley*, MacArthur's command ship for the invasion. The 1st Marines were well chosen to spearhead the assault. His four regiments were well trained and were composed of sizable numbers of World War II veterans. By the next day, the 16th, Smith was ashore with his 13,000 Marines. Kimpo Airfield lay 10 miles to the east. Smith had orders from MacArthur to take it as quickly as possible. He did so, ahead of schedule, securing the aerodrome by mid-morning of September 18. His Marines then continued the drive toward Seoul, another six miles inland. MacArthur's controversial decision to take the city instead of bypassing it and cutting off North Korean formations fleeing from Walker's troops pushing up from the south was apparently driven by a promise he had made to South Korean President Syngman Rhee to return the capital to him by the end of September.

The attack on the city began on September 22. After crossing the Han River, Smith brought the 1st Marines to the outskirts of Seoul. With his regiments positioned line abreast—5th, 7th, 1st—he struck the city. Substantive resistance ended on September 26. When his Marines took the capitol building, they presented Smith with the North Korean flag that had flown from one of the building's flagpoles. It was done as a gesture of respect to him. It was not appreciated by Almond or his staff at X Corps. On the 29th, Smith was one of only four Marine officers amid a mass of Army generals and other dignitaries invited to attend the ceremony in which Seoul was returned to the government of South Korea.

The momentous decision of the United States and the United Nations to cross the 38th parallel followed soon after. MacArthur's plan took the Eighth Army under Walker up the west coast. Almond's X Corps, of which Smith and his Marines were the tip of the spear, would move north along the opposite coast after landing at Wonsan. The 7th Infantry Division would advance farther east while the 31st Infantry would initially remain some distance to the south to help guard the tenuous supply line.

On October 26 Smith and the 1st Marines landed at Wonsan, a major port on the east coast of North Korea. The landing was unopposed. Indeed, the city was already in ROK Army hands, a circumstance brought about by MacArthur's and Almond's insistence on going ahead with the landing despite lengthy delays, logistics issues, and transportation problems.

Smith's Marines, reinforced by a British unit, the 41st Royal Marine Commandos, moved north. In addition to the 1st Marines, X Corps—altogether about 30,000 men—also included two regiments each from the

3rd and 7th Infantry Divisions. Later, a regimental combat team composed mostly of 7th Division soldiers would be split off and spread along the east bank of the Chosin Reservoir. ROK units also supplemented X Corps during the campaign. Eventually, Smith's operating area would comprise about 1,000 square miles. A considerable concentration of airpower supported the advance and would provide desperately needed assistance during the later withdrawal. The 1st Marine Air Wing and Navy aircraft from five carriers positioned off the coast (Task Force 77) provided interdiction and critical close air support, sometimes flying 230 sorties a day. C-119 "Flying Boxcars" from the United States Air Force Far East Cargo Command based in Japan would eventually drop 250 tons of supplies each day to resupply X Corps's trapped units and later sustain them as they fought their way back to the coast.

As he had instructed Walker in the west, Almond's direction to Smith was to race north as quickly as possible to the Yalu River. The early days of the advance went well. Smith and his Marines pushed forward through towns whose names would soon become familiar in Marine Corps lore: Sudong, Chinhung-ni, Kotori, Hagaru, Yudam-ni. All were along a single, mountainous track—100 miles of treacherous winding road, single-lane gravel in places—that would form the only way in and, as Smith would duly note, the only way out for the 1st Marines.

Smith, as he was known for, patrolled aggressively as his forces were on the move. The Marines began to take prisoners, many of whom talked openly, confirming Smith's judgment that large numbers of Chinese troops were present in the nearby hills. Almond and MacArthur's intelligence staff in Tokyo disagreed, believing that the captives were shattered remnants of forces in retreat.

Soon Almond would dispute Smith's insistence on building supply depots, and later airstrips, along the route. On the drive north, engineers widened and leveled the roadway to better handle the "six by" trucks that flowed in a steady stream. With the cooperation of Naval Supply troops, large supply depots were constructed at Chinhung-ni and Kotori. Another major depot would soon follow at Hagaru. Still concerned with the vulnerability of the single supply route, Smith had airstrips built at Kotori and Hagaru to accommodate the U.S. Air Force C-47s that would deliver additional supplies and transport casualties to hospital ships and medical facilities in the south. Work on the airstrip at Hagaru went on around the clock. Completed in a remarkably brief period of time, the strip provided essential services when Smith orchestrated the breakout. Eventually, the presence of the supply depots and airstrips, and Smith's foresight, would be the salvation of X Corps.

When fully revealed, the number of Chinese facing the Eighth Army and X Corps would astound MacArthur's intelligence staff. Already hidden in the mountains of North Korea or poised just across the border in Manchuria, 33 full divisions stood ready for combat. At some point on October 18 or 19, Chinese leader Mao Tse-tung ordered a major strike against Walker's Eighth Army, which by that time had advanced beyond Pyongyang. That offensive, which began on October 25 and lasted into early November—after which the attacking force mysteriously disappeared—was essentially disregarded by the planners in Tokyo. Almond ordered Smith and other commanders to continue to move toward the Yalu, dismissing the building opposition now being felt all along the line. Indeed, he commented to one Army commander whose unit had been pushed off a hill by overwhelming numbers of Chinese troops: "Don't let a bunch of Chinese laundrymen stop you." Those "Chinese laundrymen" were, in fact, present in massive numbers, and a sizable portion were veterans who had fought in World War II and in the Chinese Civil War.

On the west coast near Sudong, on November 2–4, Marines and ROK forces fought the first substantial encounter of the campaign. The Marine regiment most closely engaged defeated an assault in division strength, killing more than 600 Chinese attackers. Within three weeks of the battle, the 1st Division would possess the entire Chosin Reservoir basin.

Despite evidence of thickening opposition, Almond's orders were to "barrel through" to the Manchurian border, directions that Smith regarded as unrealistic. In addition to the single, marginal road, the mountainous terrain was severe, the intense cold was debilitating to men and machines, and, despite Almond's insistence, Smith was increasingly concerned that the Chinese were present in enormous and ever-increasing numbers.

Running almost straight south to north, the Chosin Reservoir was a narrow, winding body of water about 15 miles long. Wispy, fingerlike projections extended from the main channel basin, giving it a maximum width of three to five miles in places. For Smith and his Marines, the reservoir was a key feature on the route to the Yalu. Built to provide hydroelectric power to mining operations in the north, the reservoir was frozen thick at that time of year. The village of Hagaru at the southern end was a major objective of X Corps's advance.

On November 13 the Marines began their final march to the reservoir, pushing cautiously forward with two regiments—the 5th and 7th—aligned in columns. Two days later, lead elements of the 7th reached Hagaru and prepared to move on to Yudam-ni, 14 miles farther north. Meanwhile, the 5th Marines moved along the edge of the reservoir.

In Smith's mind there was another major cause for concern. At the Funchilin Pass, between Chinhung-ni and Kotori, the only passage to the north was over a long concrete bridge that covered four large conduits that fed water from the reservoir to a nearby power plant. The bridge was in a narrow funnel—a natural chokepoint—where the road compressed, squeezed in by steep mountains that pushed against it on both sides.

Smith thought it was incongruous that the Chinese had not blown the bridge to slow or halt the Marines' advance. The more likely reason it was left intact, he believed, was that the Chinese *wanted* his force to move across it. Once on the other side, it could be destroyed, trapping the Marines north of it. As events would reveal, the Chinese had indeed prepared an ambush of extraordinary proportions. Almond had pushed his X Corps into the slender open end of a mountainous horseshoe whose sides teemed with thousands of Chinese soldiers. To the Chinese, the area was ideally suited for that purpose: they referred to it as a "preselected killing zone." As Smith had anticipated, during the retreat from the Chosin Reservoir, the Chinese would, in fact, destroy the bridge. Smith's Marines survived the trap only through foresight, marvelous feats of airlift and engineering, and the heroism of those who fought there.

As Smith's concerns grew, so did his efforts to diffuse Almond's attempts to disperse the 1st Division. He slow-walked directives that would have scattered the unit into detachments fragmented across the landscape. After receiving yet another order to advance full speed, he essentially told Almond directly that the Marines were not going anywhere until its units were consolidated. Eventually, Smith believed he had reconstituted his division to a moderately acceptable degree. He posted two regiments north of the reservoir in the area of Yudam-ni, put a battalion at Hagaru, and, at the southern tip, placed battalions at Kotori, about 11 miles south of Hagaru on the main supply route, and another 10 miles farther south at Chinhung-ni to provide additional security for the road. Though still somewhat separated, the units would be able to provide some degree of mutual support.

As the battle would later unfold, Smith had the 1st Marines and a portion of the 7th Marines at Hagaru, the 5th, 11th, and other portions of the 7th Marines at Yudam-ni. Other forces were at Kotori and a Regimental Combat Team of the 7th U.S. Army Infantry Division (not initially under

Smith's control) was positioned east of the reservoir. Smith established his headquarters at Hagaru and immediately had his engineers begin construction of an airfield. Though the need for the field was dismissed by Almond, Smith saw it as vital for bringing in ammunition and supplies, and if, as he suspected, he was cut off, the strip would be essential for flying out casualties. Almond's retort was recorded as "What casualties?"

Tensions with Almond would color every aspect of the campaign. There was an enormous gap in reality from what Smith and his commanders saw on the battlefield and the illusory picture held by MacArthur and Almond at their Tokyo headquarters. "Mercurial and flighty," Almond consistently minimized the strength of the forces arrayed against Walker's in the west and Smith's in the east and downplayed the severity of the conditions both of them faced. The Marines regarded him as unrealistic, out of touch with the realities at the front and unwilling to acknowledge the desperate nature of the situation there. They saw him as careless with the lives of his men and overly concerned with public relations. It now seems clear that Almond's actions and his disputes with Smith were precipitated by his loyalty to MacArthur and his almost fanatical belief that MacArthur was infallible. Indeed, one of his subordinates stated, "Almond's greatest weakness as a commander in Korea was his conviction that MacArthur could do no wrong."

As Smith's Marines took possession of Hagaru, he paused for a short time, over Almond's objections, to concentrate his forces, positioning them closer together and exchanging places between some Marine units and others from the U.S. Army's 7th Infantry Division. Work on the airfield continued around the clock. Smith regarded it as essential that it be made ready to handle C-47 aircraft.

Almond, meanwhile, ordered U.S. Army Major General David G. Barr to form a Regimental Combat Team and dispatch it farther east to skirt the rim of the reservoir. The force, commanded initially by Colonel Allan D. MacLean, was composed of two infantry and one artillery battalion as well as other support troops—altogether about 3,000 U.S. and ROK soldiers. The unit would be labeled Task Force MacLean.

MacArthur's—and thus, Almond's—plan was for the 1st Marines and the 7th Infantry Division to secure the reservoir and then quickly push farther north. From the Chosin, units of the X Corps would move west, toward the town of Kangye. MacArthur believed the maneuver would put the corps north of and behind the enemy forces facing the Eighth Army. Smith and others thought the notion was foolhardy. The drive would entail a move of more than 50 miles in freezing weather through the heart of the Taebaek Mountains over a road that in places was not much more than a farm path, unsuited for the movement of trucks, tanks, and armor. Worse, even if the U.S. troops reached Kangye, the force would be too thin to hold it, much less envelop the tens of thousands of Chinese troops in the region.

The push to the north had proceeded with no attempt to move in concert and little care given to exposed flanks that resulted from the independent campaigns along each coast. The Taebaek Mountains, projecting like a dagger down the spine of the peninsula, served as a barricade between the two armies, separating them and hindering contact between them.

Now, at long last, after an abysmal failure of intelligence, the Tokyo Headquarters began to give some late credence to the looming catastrophe that was about to be thrust upon them.

It was too late.

On November 25 the Chinese 13th Field Army Group struck a major portion of Walker's Eighth Army troops west of the mountain chain. The attack was skillfully handled. Surprise was complete and the ambush threw the entire Eighth Army into a full retreat. It is indicative of the caliber of leadership at the Tokyo Headquarters—and perhaps a measure of the degree to which they were stunned—that for a considerable time no one thought to inform Smith that the Army he was about to move in support of was no longer in place.

Despite the cascading disaster unfolding in the west, Almond insisted that X Corps continue the drive to the Yalu. The jump-off date was set for November 27. MacArthur and Almond had initially split the X Corps from the Eighth Army. Now Smith saw them attempting to dismember his fighting power, segmenting it into smaller, dispersed formations. Smith had struggled for several days to reverse or delay a battle plan he greatly distrusted. While he slow-walked his orders, he continued to bring his units closer together and move ahead with supply dumps and the vital airfield. It is a reflection of his concern that he took the extraordinary step of writing directly to the commandant of the Marine Corps to inform him that he regarded the operational plan as placing his Marines in mortal peril. Among other concerns, he noted that the plan left "wide gaps" in his left flank and his units were not in position to support one another.

Even before the Marines had arrived at Hagaru, Smith was convinced that the X Corps was being led into a trap. The enemy's failure to destroy the bridge at the Funchilin Pass—an action that would have stopped the Marines' advance—his aggressive patrolling, and the details provided by Chinese captives, all seemed to confirm that his men were proceeding in harm's way.

Indeed, as the 1st Division moved north, the Chinese 9th Army Group, commanded by General Sung Shi-Lun, left Manchuria. Sung led 12 full divisions, each organized with an extra battalion, altogether initially totaling about 150,000 men. Bulked up with extra infantry, mortars, and machine guns, the massive force slipped across the Yalu and moved into North Korea. The speed of the assembly and departure caused Chinese formations to leave without adequate provisions of food and winter clothing—shortages that caused intense suffering and deaths in the infantry units.

General Sung's mission was to destroy X Corps, but it was clear to all that the heart of the offensive would be directed at the 1st Marine Division. Sung posted his troops on either side of the reservoir in multidivision strength and moved other strong formations to positions to cut the road in several locations south of Hagaru. The Chinese attacks were massive in size, simultaneously striking Hagaru, Kotori, and Task Force MacLean in division-sized assaults. Ironically, perhaps, the Chinese attack at the end of November nearly coincided with the intended start date Almond had planned for his drive to the Yalu.

Smith's Marines defeated a rare daylight attack on Hagaru fortifications on November 27. It was obvious, though, from patrolling and captured prisoners that the main danger would come at night. In the dark, the Chinese could use stealth and better exploit their enormous advantage in manpower. The Americans' air superiority—which enabled them to devastate formations caught in the open—was more constrained at night.

The November 27 attack added to the urgency with which the Americans fortified their positions and made ready for nighttime actions. Their efforts were thorough—and timely.

They were outnumbered initially by about 12 to 1, and the frozen ground—rock solid from minus-20- to minus-30-degree temperatures— made fighting holes difficult to dig.

Starting on the night of November 27–28, the Chinese launched three days of intense nighttime battles and daylight probes. Except for an important hill east of Hagaru, all positions held. The Marines took casualties but inflicted enormous losses during attacks that came in repeated waves.

Task Force MacLean, the primary U.S. Army and ROK unit sent east by Almond, was less fortunate. Strung out along the rim of the reservoir, the unit immediately took heavy casualties. Eventually, as they attempted to fight their way back to Hagaru, the column was split in places and the Task Force lost unit cohesion. MacLean was killed early in the battle; his place in command was taken by Lieutenant Colonel Don Carlos Faith Jr.

Task Force Faith, as it was now called, fought its way along the narrow road that bounded the waterline. As it struggled to reach safety, the column was attacked from bordering hills and hit from front and rear in overwhelming numbers. In what eventually became a suicide job, truck drivers were targeted by Chinese riflemen, causing roadblocks as the vehicles stalled. The Chinese then killed all aboard the trucks—in many cases wounded soldiers often stacked in layers inside the truck beds. The force was destroyed piecemeal, losing wheeled vehicles and artillery. Faith was killed, and the surviving members of the task force moved ahead on foot in small, frozen, disorganized, groups. Some clusters of desperate soldiers set out directly across the ice of the frozen reservoir, where in several instances Marines from the garrison at Hagaru went out to extract them. Eventually, about 670 of the force of 3,500 survived, only about half of whom were fit for further duty.

Around Hagaru the violent attacks were nearly continuous, pushing against the Marines' desperately held perimeter. Each succeeding night saw attacks in enormous size as the Chinese struck from out of the darkness attempting to overrun artillery positions, the airfield, and command post. Though rifle companies on the front lines were reduced by one-third to one-half, the Marines held on, inflicting casualties in amounts that decimated many of the attacking units. Smith addressed the assaults with artillery barrages fired around the clock, the ammunition having been stockpiled through his foresight. While artillery held the Chinese at bay during the night, American air power rained terror on them during the day. Air Force units joined Navy and Marine squadrons in hammering Chinese positions, tearing up clusters of soldiers and punishing units caught in the open.

Control of the skies allowed Smith to adroitly shift his forces, redeploying them while reinforcing thinly held trouble spots. The attack that began on November 27 left horrific scenes across the various battlefields. Scores of Chinese dead lay strewn across the desolate, frozen landscape. Farther north at Yudam-ni, Marine units were surrounded, and one company was cut off for five days. The cost to the Chinese was enormous—at least five full battalions were destroyed. At Hagaru, the entire perimeter was under enormous pressure. East Hill, an important terrain feature at the northern portion of the line, was in Chinese hands. To the south, Kotori, commanded by legendary Marine Colonel Lewis B. "Chesty" Puller, was also under heavy assault.

As both sides recognized, Hagaru was the key. The town formed a vital junction that provided access to almost all of the American combat units. If overrun, X Corps would be severed; the northernmost units at Yudam-ni would be left isolated, separated from Kotori and other units positioned on the road farther south. In an effort to assist the defenders at Hagaru, Puller sent a force from Kotori in an attempt to fight through to the embattled garrison. Led by Lieutenant Colonel Douglas Drysdale of the Royal Marine Commando, the column—labeled Task Force Drysdale—consisted of the British unit and companies of U.S. Marines and U.S. Army soldiers. As the units moved north, the column was immediately taken under fire by a full Chinese division. Caught at a narrow defile called "Hell Fire Valley," the formation was broken in half. The lead elements managed to make it to Hagaru, providing additional, vital riflemen to augment the embattled defense. The rear portion of the column was virtually destroyed; only a few of its men returned safely to Kotori.

By November 29 the massive presence of Chinese forces and the potential for disaster could no longer be ignored at MacArthur's headquarters. In a meeting that day, Almond received MacArthur's order to withdraw. A few hours earlier, MacArthur had sent a message to Washington, DC, that shocked authorities there. The message read: "We face an entirely new war."

On November 30 Almond appointed Smith overall commander of field operations for X Corps, giving him control of the two Army infantry divisions—the 3rd and 7th—which along with his 1st Marines made up X Corps. The decision better accommodated the circumstances and the rapidly changing conditions on the battlefield. It was long overdue. As one of the Army division commanders conjectured to Smith, it may also have been expedient—setting up Smith as a scapegoat if things went seriously wrong.

The decision to withdraw X Corps did not end Smith's contretemps with Almond. Now divorced from the blind optimism of a few days before, Almond adopted a worst-case approach. Forces near Hagaru were to assemble there, where they would be flown to safety. All heavy weapons, vehicles, and supplies would be abandoned. Units already at Kotori and locations farther south would move immediately to Hungnam.

Almond's directions set the stage for one of the most momentous decisions of the war, or, indeed, any of America's wars. Smith refused to comply with the order. He would not abandon his equipment or his casualties. He would need his trucks and jeeps to carry them, and tanks and artillery to clear the path. He would fight his way out. It would, for sure, be a fighting withdrawal. Though perhaps embellished by eager reporters, his quote became legendary in the Marines: "Retreat, hell, we're simply advancing in another direction."

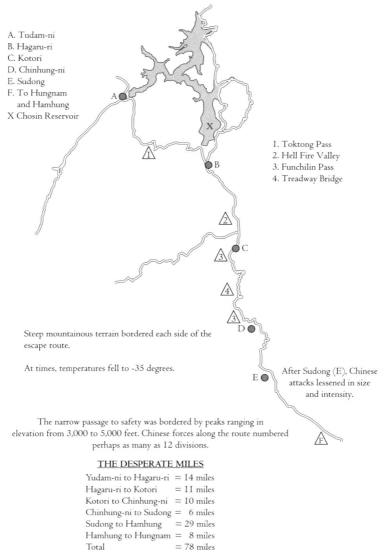

A. Tudam-ni
B. Hagaru-ri
C. Kotori
D. Chinhung-ni
E. Sudong
F. To Hungnam
   and Hamhung
X Chosin Reservoir

1. Toktong Pass
2. Hell Fire Valley
3. Funchilin Pass
4. Treadway Bridge

Steep mountainous terrain bordered each side of the escape route.

At times, temperatures fell to -35 degrees.

After Sudong (E), Chinese attacks lessened in size and intensity.

The narrow passage to safety was bordered by peaks ranging in elevation from 3,000 to 5,000 feet. Chinese forces along the route numbered perhaps as many as 12 divisions.

THE DESPERATE MILES

Yudam-ni to Hagaru-ri	= 14 miles
Hagaru-ri to Kotori	= 11 miles
Kotori to Chinhung-ni	= 10 miles
Chinhung-ni to Sudong	= 6 miles
Sudong to Hamhung	= 29 miles
Hamhung to Hungnam	= 8 miles
Total	= 78 miles

The Retreat from Chosin Reservoir

As some scholars have noted, great generalship is determined by what leaders did *not* do as much as for what they did. Had Smith aggressively followed the order that came from MacArthur and Almond to attack and "barrel through" to the north, the entire X Corps would have almost certainly been destroyed. He rejected that directive—which had been given him by perhaps the nation's most legendary general.

As the first step in the breakout, Smith ordered the forces posted north around Yudam-ni to consolidate and fight their way south to Hagaru. Those units packed their supplies and equipment and, during the daylight hours of November 30, began the move away from Yudam-ni. The 5th Marines walked the road to protect the vehicle train while the 7th Marines worked the hillsides to break up roadblocks and disrupt ambushes. Two artillery battalions hopscotched to provide continuous support and counter the almost constant resistance.

On the way south they would have to clear a major obstacle, Toklong Pass, which dominated the landscape and controlled access to Hagaru. On December 2, the Marines secured the pass, opening the road. Though fighting persisted all through the journey, they reached Hagaru on December 3. Cold and bedraggled, they had struggled through 14 bitter miles under almost constant attack. As they entered the American lines outside Hagaru, they formed up and marched in singing "The Marine Hymn" as they passed a British unit and other Marines holding the perimeter.

It is thought that as many as three Chinese divisions may have been rendered ineffective during the move. Those were in addition to the four that had been shot to pieces at Hagaru and other actions around Yudam-ni.

The presence of the units from Yudam-ni assured that the airfield at Hagaru could be held. Marine, Navy, and Air Force aircraft flew in ammunition and supplies to provision the force as it fought its way to the south. Casualties were also flown out in preparation for the move.

The additional forces also gave Smith sufficient manpower to clear the Chinese from East Hill. Driving the enemy from the heights along the northern perimeter removed a looming threat that would have disrupted withdrawal actions from the Hagaru area.

The breakout began at 4:30 in the morning of December 6, with the 1st Marines having first swept East Hill clear of opposition. The first to leave were the 7th Marines and soldiers from the 31st Infantry, leading Smith's "advance in another direction" toward Kotori.

What followed in the next few days—consistent, repeated examples of heroism, professionalism, and courage—made Smith and his men legendary. Altogether, about 14,000 Marines and soldiers came together in the Hagaru area and began the move toward safety. They took with them 1,000 vehicles—tanks, trucks, jeeps, wheeled artillery—in a column miles long. In the words of David Halberstam: "The [Marines'] breakout from the Chosin Reservoir is one of the classic moments in their own exceptional history, a masterpiece of leadership on the part of their officers and of single, relentless, abiding courage on the part of ordinary fighting men— fighting a vastly larger force in the worst kind of conditions."

Led by the 7th Marines, who cleared the ground on either side of the road, the column inched its way along the narrow, winding road toward Kotori. Before leaving Hagaru, they burned or destroyed everything of military value. The airfield, which had enabled the evacuation of 4,500 casualties and the replenishment of desperately needed food, supplies, and ammunition, was torn up and rendered inoperable.

The wounded that could not be sent out by air were loaded on trucks. The frozen bodies of those killed in action were also loaded on "six bys," strapped to hoods of jeeps, or in some cases fastened to the long barrels of the force's artillery pieces. Smith would remain at Hagaru that day and most of the next (December 7) before relocating his headquarters to Kotori.

As the move progressed, Marines fought for, and cleared, the high ground on each side of the road. The move was not anticipated by the Chinese, who apparently expected the column to be "anchored" to the roadbed. As had been the case with the move from Yudam-ni, American artillery was the great equalizer, with pieces being shifted to ensure continuous support all along the column, which eventually stretched for miles. The formation moved primarily by day and "buttoned up" at night, supported against Chinese attacks by cannon fire and night fighters from the Marine air wing.

In the immediate environs of Hagaru, six Chinese divisions (60,000 men) were arrayed against them. Between there and Kotori stood elements of five more, and major roadblocks had been set up in at least nine places. At Hell Fire Valley, the narrow defile where Task Force Drysdale had been decimated only a few days before, the column fought its way through, past the shattered hulks of Drysdale's vehicles and armor. Here, as at other locations along the tortuous road to Kotori, tracked vehicles with winches sometimes had to pull trucks, jeeps, and wheeled artillery out of ruts, up slippery embankments, and through damaged passages on the fractured roadway. In the face of unremitting cold, slowed by blown bridges, subjected to fire from Chinese units positioned on heights and in ambush positions near the road, the column pushed forward. Major elements passed through the Kotori defensive perimeter near sundown on December 7. The first phase of the breakout was complete.

The next section would be equally as daunting. The goal was Chinhung-ni, seven miles to the south. Units were briefly rested, replenished, and configured into a line of march. Meanwhile, Chesty Puller sent a force north from Chinhung-ni. Units from Kotori pushed south, squeezing the Chinese in between and forcing them off the heights and away from the roadbed. As the troops left Kotori, 600 casualties sustained during the passage from Hagaru were air evac'd to safety. That act was the last use of the Kotori airstrip, which was then destroyed. With forces now on the road headed south, Smith moved his headquarters to Hungnam to oversee the next push to Chinhung-ni and then to the sea and safety.

Before Chinhung-ni, however, lay Funchilin Pass. As Smith anticipated, the Chinese had now destroyed the long bridge, trapping the Americans north along the slender passageway on terrain later described by General Matthew Ridgway as "a narrow, frightening shelf with an impassable cliff on one side and a chasm on the other."

Smith and his staff, though, had prepared for the absence of the bridge. While his Marines battled Chinese infantry on the surrounding heights, Air Force "Flying Boxcars" under the overall command of Major General William H. Tunner air dropped Treadway Bridge components on areas near the site. In an amazing feat of combat engineering, on December 9, Marines and Army engineers constructed a trestle that spanned the gorge. By December 11, the entire column had cleared the pass.

Though the withdrawal rarely proceeded without opposition of some kind, the intensity slackened somewhat after Kotori. The last significant battle occurred at Sudong when 3rd Infantry Division troops—tasked with providing flank and rearguard cover for the withdrawing units as X Corps decamped from North Korea—beat back an ambush by large numbers of Chinese. Soon after, when units reached Hungnam, the 3rd and 7th Infantry Divisions and the ROK I Corps provided perimeter defense, supported by naval gunfire from ships standing offshore.

Lead elements of X Corps reached Hungnam after fighting almost continuously for 15 days. There, men and equipment were organized for departure. Marines left in mid-December, followed by the 7th Infantry Division, the ROK I Corps, and 3rd Infantry Division. In less than two weeks the entire force with equipment, along with thousands of Korean refugees, had been taken aboard ships and put safely to sea. The last combat elements from the 3rd Infantry left Hungnam on the afternoon of December 24. The port was then systematically destroyed.

In the two plus weeks during which the Marine and Army units had fought their way to the sea, Smith believed they had been opposed along the way by as many as seven full divisions and parts of at least three others.

From November 27 to December 11, the Marines lost 561 killed, 182 missing, 2,894 wounded, and other 3,600 who suffered mainly frostbite injuries. Total X Corps casualties for the same general time frame numbered about 10,500 battle and 7,500 non-battle casualties, a figure that included Marine, U.S. Army, ROK, and British forces.

Chinese losses are more difficult to ascertain. It is clear that they were enormous and their forces suffered horribly from lack of preparation and from winter weather as well as from American artillery and air power. Many estimates place the total at about 60,000. Figures later officially released by the Chinese regime assert 19,202 combat and 28,954 noncombat casualties. Based on reports indicating the number of replacements requested by Chinese units during the fighting, some Western analysts were inclined to think the figure of 60,000 is probably more realistic. Whatever the number, the effect on the Chinese was significant. In actions around the reservoir and during Smith's "advance in another direction" four Chinese divisions were rendered ineffective and put out of action.

Military historian Brigadier General S. L. A. Marshall described the 1st Division's actions and Smith's leadership in these words: "This campaign is perhaps the most brilliant divisional feat of arms in the nation's history. Smith made it so, through his dauntless calm, his tender regard for his regiments, and his unshakeable belief that rest when needed, rather than precipitate haste, was the only thing which could bring his men through the greatest of combat trials. In battle, the great Marine had more the manner of a college professor than a plunging fighter. But our services have known few leaders who could look so deeply into the human heart."

Before and After

Oliver Prince Smith was born in Menard, Texas, on October 26, 1893, but spent most of his youth in Northern California. After graduating from the University of California in 1916, he entered the Marine Corps as a second lieutenant in the spring of the following year. The next 24 years, until the United States' entry into World War II, saw an eclectic series of moves, training schools, and duty assignments, a dozen or so billet changes altogether, a pattern not unusual for Marine Corps officers at the time. The moves took him overseas to Guam, Haiti, France, and Iceland, to headquarters jobs in Washington, DC, and to embassy duty in Paris. Notable assignments included command of the Marine detachment aboard the USS *Texas* and attendance at the École Supérieure de Guerre in France, where he became the first Marine Corps officer to graduate from that famed institution. That assignment, and a subsequent series of instructor billets, led to the nickname that followed him for the remainder of his career: "The Professor." Along the way, Smith also developed a reputation as an expert in amphibious assaults, an area in which, during the years ahead, the Marines would become renowned for their proficiency.

Smith was in a headquarters job in Washington when in May 1942 he was assigned to duty with the 1st Marines in the Pacific. He commanded the 5th Marine Regiment on New Britain and Cape Gloucester and later became assistant division commander during the assault on Peleliu. In November 1944 he became deputy chief of staff of the Tenth Army and served in that position during the Battle of Okinawa.

In July 1945, Smith rotated back to the United States for duty as commandant of the Marine Corps School at Quantico, Virginia. While still in that billet, in January 1948, he was "dual-hatted" as commanding general, Marine Barracks, Quantico. In May of that year he was posted to Washington, DC, to become assistant commandant of the Marine Corps and chief of staff, Headquarters Marine Corps.

In June 1950 he was assigned as commanding general of the 1st Marine Division and led the unit through the landing at Inchon, the capture of Seoul, the landing at Wonsan, and the actions around the Chosin Reservoir.

After the X Corps was evacuated from Hungnam, the unit was transported south, where Smith quickly readied them for renewed action. On Christmas Day, 1950, he hosted a memorable open house for unit commanders and division staff members at the corps bivouac location near Musan.

After their attacks against the Eighth Army and X Corps, the Chinese offensive carried south across the 38th parallel. Their drive was not stopped until Seoul was again in their possession. Smith remained as commander of the 1st Marines through the United Nations' last major campaign, Operation Dauntless, which began in August 1951. The 1st Division, along with a ROK division, pushed north against initially light opposition to reclaim territory in Central Korea. As the Marines and ROK soldiers moved forward, the formation was suddenly attacked by hidden Chinese units. In desperate fighting, the Marines held on, averting a momentary crisis that developed when the ROK unit collapsed during the onslaught, leaving a portion of the Marines' line "uncovered." In the fighting that followed, the Marines inflicted severe casualties on the Chinese, stabilized the front, and eventually enabled the advance to continue.

Though scheduled for reassignment to the United States, Smith remained in command of the 1st Marines through Operation Dauntless. By this time, X Corps had been folded into the Eighth Army and General Matthew Ridgway had replaced General Walton Walker, who had been killed in a jeep accident in December. As the officers met for the first time, Smith asked Ridgway for only one thing: that Marines would never again be placed under Ned Almond's command. Ridgway readily agreed.

In May Smith returned to the United States with duty as commander of Camp Pendleton. There, over the next two years, he played a decisive role in developing the Twenty-Nine Palms training area, the Marines' largest installation. In July 1953, concurrent with his promotion to lieutenant general, Smith moved to the U.S. Naval Base at Norfolk, Virginia, to take command of Fleet Marine Force Atlantic, a position he held until his retirement effective September 1, 1955. Smith was promoted to general on the retired list the same day.

Smith spent his retirement years quietly in California, devoting much time to gardening and corresponding with Marines who had served with him. He died on Christmas night, 1977, at age 84. He was buried at Los Altos, at Golden Gate National Cemetery.

Smith was, as David Halberstam recorded, "one of the special, quiet heroes of the Korean War." Then, as now, few people outside of the United States Marine Corps know his name.

Chapter Three

Vietnam

The Path to War

The building pictured in the scene with a helicopter on the roof and an impossibly long line of people climbing toward it is often mislabeled as the American Embassy. In reality it is a nearby facility that housed U.S. Agency for International Development offices and served as top-floor space for the CIA deputy chief of mission. In the bigger scheme of things, the designation matters little. It is the photo itself that speaks to the ages. It is one of the saddest images in American history.

To some, the picture evokes memories of a war frustratingly fought, ineptly led, and subsequently "lost." To others, it connotes a last bitter episode in a long downward spiral of divisive fury that for nearly a decade tore at the soul of a nation. Whatever the view, the poignancy of the scene cannot be dismissed. A commitment that began with bright intentions and high expectations is captured as it ended; with a hopeless queue of desperate people clambering to board a military helicopter—all that remained of America's presence in Vietnam.

Vietnam remains the nation's most enigmatic conflict. Decades after direct U.S. involvement ended (April 19, 1973), the debate endures. Every aspect at every level evokes controversy.

Was the war *legal*?

If so, *should* the United States have become involved militarily?

If so, *how* should the war have been fought?

The arguments persist. They will likely continue to provide fodder for PhD theses for generations to come.

Tracing the path to war can be equally perplexing. As many scholars have noted, the narrative depends on where one enters the discussion. For the North Vietnamese and National Liberation Front (Viet Cong), the conflict was at different times and varying intensities a colonial war, a civil war, and a war of liberation. For the Republic of South Vietnam, it was a civil war and a defensive war against communism. For the United States, Vietnam began as a rather modest application of the nation's "containment policy." Giving credence to the "domino theory," which postulated the spread of global communism if the movement was left unchecked, American involvement grew exponentially over the years in terms of men, money, and materiel. It began in 1950 with a small $15 million dollar package of military and economic aid intended to assist France in combating communist insurgents waging guerrilla war in French colonies in Indochina. By 1959 there were 1,000 American advisors in South Vietnam. By 1963, 15,000. The employment of combat troops began in March 1965 with the introduction of 3,500 Marines in what was ostensibly intended to be an air base protection mission. A peak strength of 543,000 was reached in April 1969. Eventually, 2,707,918 American men and women—about 10 percent of their generation—would serve there.

The seminal events that triggered major U.S. involvement occurred in the Gulf of Tonkin in early August 1964. As with many aspects of the Vietnam War, the circumstances are murky. On two consecutive days North Vietnamese torpedo boats were thought to have attacked U.S. Navy ships. Of the first encounter, the facts have not been much in dispute. Three torpedo boats struck at the destroyer USS *Maddox* and were engaged by that vessel as well as by naval aircraft from the carrier USS *Ticonderoga*. Two North Vietnamese craft were thought to have been damaged, and one was reported dead in the water.

It is the second incident that has generated the most enduring controversy. Commander (later Admiral) James Stockdale was the lead pilot on the air strikes that took place on both occasions. On the second night, he did not see any enemy combatants. Later, the skipper of the *Maddox* acknowledged that the apparent attack may not have happened: weather phenomena and an inexperienced radar operator might have resulted in a misreading of events by his ship and the accompanying destroyer USS *C. Turner Joy*.

The reason for the U.S. Navy's presence in the Gulf adds another layer of controversy regarding the causes of the conflict. To some, the circumstances are clear: the ships were there to demonstrate "presence" and to affirm the right of passage along the coast of Vietnam—and, at any rate, the event most assuredly occurred in international waters. Those in opposition assert that the vessels were engaged in direct or indirect support for South Vietnamese military operations on nearby islands. Thus, attacks on the ships—if they did in fact occur—were not entirely unprovoked.

Though senior officials in the American government, including President Lyndon B. Johnson and Secretary of Defense Robert S. McNamara, were aware of the ambiguities associated with reports of the engagements, they chose to use the incidents as justification for escalating American involvement in the conflict.

Thus, the war's most direct causal event is itself shrouded in controversy. Perhaps more than any other of the country's conflicts, Vietnam was, both politically and militarily, an extraordinarily complex and divisive war.

More than 2.5 million Americans served in Vietnam; 58,220 lost their lives. Estimates of Vietnamese casualties vary widely. The Democratic Republic of Vietnam eventually approximated the combat losses of North Vietnamese and Viet Cong forces at 1.1 million (a figure that, interestingly, exceeded the U.S. estimate). A quarter of a million South Vietnamese soldiers are thought to have died in the fighting. As with so many other statistics associated with the war, there are wide disparities in the estimates of civilian losses. Some reputable sources place them as high as two million.

The timeline shown below provides a more detailed perspective of the war's major events.

March 1945: Japanese troops occupying Indochina carry out a coup against French authorities and announce an end to the colonial era, declaring Vietnam, Laos, and Cambodia independent.

August 1945: Japan is defeated by the Allies, leaving a power vacuum in Indochina. France seeks to reassert its authority over Vietnam.

September 1945: Communist leader Ho Chi Minh declares an independent North Vietnam and models his announcement on the

American Declaration of Independence in an attempt to win support from the United States.

July 1946: Ho Chi Minh rejects a French proposal granting Vietnam limited self-government. The Viet Minh begins a guerilla war against French authorities.

January 1950: The People's Republic of China and the Soviet Union formally recognize the communist Democratic Republic of Vietnam, and both begin to supply economic and military aid to communist cadres.

June 1950: The United States identifies the Viet Minh as a communist threat and increases military assistance—initially providing $15 million—to combat the insurgency.

March–May 1954: French forces are decisively defeated in a major battle at Dien Bien Phu. The defeat signifies the end of French rule in Indochina.

April 1954: President Dwight D. Eisenhower states that the fall of Indochina to the communists would create a "domino" effect in Southeast Asia.

June 1954: The Geneva Accords establish North and South Vietnam as separate, independent nations with the 17th parallel as the dividing line between them. The agreement stipulates that elections will be held within two years to unify the Vietnams under a democratic government. The elections never take place.

1955: Ngo Dinh Diem, a Catholic nationalist, emerges as the leader of South Vietnam. In the years ahead, Diem's government displays favoritism toward South Vietnam's Catholic minority, alienating his administration from much of the nation's population. Ho Chi Minh assumes control of North Vietnam, installing a communist regime.

May 1959: North Vietnam begins to build a supply route through Laos and Cambodia into South Vietnam. The route, later known as the Ho Chi Minh Trail, supplies Viet Cong forces in their growing war against Diem's forces in the South.

July 1959: The first American soldiers are killed in South Vietnam when guerrillas attack their living facilities in Saigon.

December 1960: The National Liberation Front (NLF) is formed with North Vietnamese backing as the political wing of the insurgency in South Vietnam. The U.S. regards the NLF as an army of the North Vietnamese regime and labels the military wing of the NLF as the Viet Cong—short for Vietnam Cong-san (Vietnamese communists).

May 1961: President John F. Kennedy sends helicopters and 400 Green Berets to South Vietnam and authorizes secret operations against the Viet Cong.

January 1962: U.S. aircraft begin spraying Agent Orange and other herbicides over rural areas of South Vietnam. Called Operation Ranch Hand, the purpose was to destroy vegetation that would offer cover and food for guerrilla cadres.

May 1963: Widespread protests occur in the South. During the "Buddhist Crisis" Diem's government opens fire on a crowd of Buddhist protestors in the city of Hue. Eight people, children among them, are killed.

June 1963: In a newspaper photo shown around the world, a Buddhist monk immolates himself as a protest against Diem's government. In the coming weeks others follow suit, further straining the U.S. government's relationship with Diem's regime.

November 1963: Diem and his powerful brother, Ngo Dinh Diem, are brutally killed in a South Vietnamese Army coup. In the two years that follow, 12 different coups install one military government after another.

August 1964: In an ambiguous encounter, the destroyer USS *Maddox* is believed to have been attacked by North Vietnamese torpedo boats in the Gulf of Tonkin. U.S. President Lyndon B. Johnson responds by ordering air strikes on nearby North Vietnamese installations. On August 5 U.S. Navy Lieutenant JG Everett Alvarez Jr. is shot down and becomes the first U.S. airman to be taken prisoner. Alvarez would remain a POW for eight years and seven months before being released on February 12, 1973.

August 1964: Congress responds to the incidents in the Tonkin Gulf by passing the Gulf of Tonkin Resolution, authorizing the president to "take all necessary measures, including the use of armed force" to retaliate against attacks.

November 1964: The Soviet Politburo increases its support for North Vietnam, sending aircraft, artillery, ammunition, small arms, radar, air defense systems, food, and medical supplies. The People's Republic of China sends military engineers to assist in building defense infrastructure.

February 1965: President Johnson orders the bombing of targets in North Vietnam in retaliation for Viet Cong attacks on U.S. installations at Pleiku and Camp Holloway.

March 1965: Operation Rolling Thunder, a bombing campaign targeting military facilities in North Vietnam and the Ho Chi Minh Trail, begins. The initial campaign lasts for three years. That same month, U.S. Marines—the first combat troops to enter Vietnam—land near Da Nang. The Marines' initial mission, force protection for an American base, soon morphs into offensive combat operations.

August 1965: A force of 5,000 U.S. Marines strikes a Viet Cong regiment in the first ground offensive by U.S. forces.

November 1965: The first large-scale battle of the war occurs at Ia Drang Valley in South Vietnam's Central Highlands. In what would become standard practice in the war, U.S. troops are inserted and withdrawn by helicopter. Heavy casualties are sustained by both sides, and each claims victory.

1966: U.S. troop strength reaches 400,000.

June 1966: U.S. aircraft attack targets in and around Hanoi and Haiphong, the first attacks on cities in the North.

1967: U.S. troop strength reaches 500,000.

February 1967: U.S. aircraft bomb Haiphong Harbor and airfields in North Vietnam.

April 1967: Large antiwar protests occur in Washington, DC, New York City, and San Francisco.

September 1967: Nguyen Van Thieu wins the presidential election in South Vietnam under a newly enacted constitution.

November 1967: At Dak To in the Central Highlands, U.S. and South Vietnamese forces defeat a major offensive by communist forces.

January–April 1968: At Khe Sanh, in a siege that lasts 77 days, U.S. Marines and South Vietnamese units hold out against heavy attacks by North Vietnamese main force units.

January 1968: The Tet Offensive begins. Attacks are launched against more than 100 cities and military sites across South Vietnam. Hue and Saigon are heavily attacked, as is the U.S. Embassy. Though the attacks are ultimately defeated, their size and scope shock U.S. officials and mark a turning point in the war.

February 11–17, 1968: The bloodiest week of the war: 543 American soldiers are killed.

February–March 1968: In large engagements at Hue and Saigon, U.S. and South Vietnamese soldiers clear Viet Cong guerillas from both cities.

March 1968: At My Lai, more than 500 civilians are killed by U.S. forces in a "search and destroy" mission intended to find and destroy terrorist units. The event becomes known internationally as the My Lai Massacre.

March 1968: President Johnson institutes a bombing halt north of the 20th parallel and announces that he will not seek reelection.

May 1969: In brutal combat at Ap Bia Mountain—a location later labeled as "Hamburger Hill"—American paratroopers defeat entrenched North Vietnamese units, temporarily shutting off infiltration from Laos into South Vietnam.

December 1969: The U.S. government introduces the first draft lottery since World War II.

1969–1972: As part of President Richard M. Nixon's "Vietnamization" strategy, U.S. troop strength is gradually reduced from a peak of 549,000 in 1969 to 69,000 in 1972. As American troop numbers are drawn down, South Vietnamese military forces take on larger portions of the combat burden.

February 1970: National Security Advisor Henry Kissinger begins secret peace negotiations in Paris with North Vietnamese representative Le Duc Tho.

March 1969–May 1970: In a secret bombing campaign, U.S. bombers strike communist base camps and supply routes in Cambodia.

April–June 1970: U.S. and South Vietnamese forces cross into Cambodia to attack communist bases.

June 1970: In an attempt to reassert congressional authority over the prosecution of the war, Congress repeals the Gulf of Tonkin Resolution.

January–March 1971: South Vietnamese troops with U.S. support invade Laos in an ultimately failed attempt to cut off the Ho Chi Minh Trail.

June 1971: In a series of articles, *The New York Times* publishes "The Pentagon Papers," encapsulating leaked Department of Defense papers revealing aspects of the government's long and secret involvement in the war.

March–October 1972: North Vietnam forces launch a large three-pronged attack against South Vietnamese and U.S. forces. Known as the Easter Offensive, the attack gains control of additional territory in South Vietnam but fails to deliver the decisive blow intended by North Vietnamese leaders.

December 1972: In concentrated attacks against Hanoi and Haiphong, President Nixon launches Operation Linebacker, the most intense aerial offensive of the war. The attacks are believed by air power advocates to have shattered the political will of the North Vietnamese leadership.

January 27, 1973: The Selective Service announces the end of its draft. The United States institutes an all-voluntary military establishment.

January 27, 1973: President Nixon signs the Paris Peace Accords, ending direct American involvement in the war. The North Vietnamese accept a ceasefire agreement, the provisions of which are almost immediately violated.

February–April 1973: North Vietnam returns 591 American prisoners of war.

January 1975: President Gerald R. Ford rules out any further U.S. military involvement in the conflict.

April 1975: Saigon falls to North Vietnamese forces; the government of South Vietnam surrenders. In a final 18-hour rescue effort, American helicopters evacuate more than 1,000 Americans and 7,000 Vietnamese refugees from the city.

Forgotten Leader: Robin Olds

The Leader, and the Mustache, That Became Legend

One of the most charismatic American leaders of the Vietnam War, Olds revitalized a key fighter wing and devised Operation Bolo, a trap that destroyed a third of North Vietnam's first-line fighter force. Olds argued that unduly narrow rules of engagement restricted the advantages of U.S. air power and unnecessarily placed American airmen in harm's way. U.S. AIR FORCE—8TH TACTICAL FIGHTER WING

The name Robin Olds is not extensively known outside the United States Air Force. But, to the "blue suiters" of the World War II–Vietnam generations particularly—and most especially to the fighter pilot community—the name evokes images often associated with that breed of aviator: hard charging, hard partying, daring, flamboyant. Colonel Robin Olds was all of those things, a swashbuckling, charismatic leader with consummate flying skills whose luster shown in an era when individualism and unique personalities were characteristics not always valued or welcomed by the military establishment.

Olds's service in Vietnam was best known for his leadership of the 8th Tactical Fighter Wing and for the planning and execution of Operation Bolo, a trap he devised for an air battle that destroyed a third of North Vietnam's first-line fighter force. For the Air Force in Vietnam, Operation Bolo provided a rare moment of outside-the-box, improvised brilliance.

Hamstrung by rules of engagement, which in their view restricted the inherent capability of air power, and by limitations on target sets imposed by Washington planners, air warfare proponents chafed at limitations placed on their mode of combat. To the aviation community, Operation Bolo was a ray of sunshine, an example of what might be achieved if the tethers were loosened and the capabilities of aerial weapons were more fully exploited.

Olds took command of the 8th Tactical Fighter Wing based at Royal Thai Air Base Ubon, Thailand, in September 1966. The wing's reputation was less than stellar at the time. During the three months prior to Olds's arrival, the wing had lost a squadron's worth of airplanes and 20 pilots. Aggressiveness was lacking, and there seemed to be no guiding force to the unit's operations. That "low energy" ambiance changed quickly under Olds's leadership. He began flying missions immediately, injecting intensity and spirit into the wing's operations, training, and support functions. Soon after taking command, he brought Daniel "Chappie" James into the unit as deputy commander for operations. James, a friend and colleague, would eventually become vice commander of the wing. (Later still, Chappie would become the Air Force's first African American four-star general.) The Olds-James leadership team eventually drew the sobriquet "Blackman and Robin" from Air Force audiences. The move strengthened the wing's command structure, making the leadership cadre one of the strongest of any flying unit at any time during the war.

The threat to Air Force F-105 Thunderchief strike forces from North Vietnamese MiG-21s sparked the idea for Operation Bolo. F-105s were equipped with radar-jamming pods that greatly reduced their vulnerability to surface-to-air missile (SAM) attacks. However, the Air Force initially lacked sufficient numbers of pods to equip the F-4 Phantoms that flew cover for the F-105s and escorted them in and out of their target areas. The absence of the protective pods on the Phantoms caused their flight pattern to be restricted to the boundary of SAM coverage. In the chess match that followed, that circumstance freed up MiG-21s to attack the bomb-laden F-105s as those formations approached their targets. Absent the Phantoms' presence, the MiG-21s posed grave threats to Thunderchief missions.

In concert with J. B. Stone, an 8th TFW officer, Olds devised a plan that would lure MiG-21s into attacking a formation of Phantoms "disguised" as F-105s. F-4s would be equipped with jamming pods and use call signs, code words, and flight profiles routinely associated with F-105 missions. The MiGs, it was hoped, would mistake the Phantoms—ready and fully equipped for aerial combat—for a strike force of F-105s. Flights of Phantoms arriving from different quadrants would cap the four North Vietnamese airfields at which the MiGs would recover, preventing them from landing or, if all else failed, running them out of fuel. Separate flights of F-4s would block escape routes of any MiGs that might seek refuge in China. Olds discussed the MiG-21 situation with Major General William Momyer, Seventh Air Force Commander, and received Momyer's approval to proceed with the Bolo mission.

After an intensive period of planning, maintenance preparations, and crew briefings, Bolo was initially scheduled for New Year's Day, 1967. Altogether, the strike force, supported by tankers that would refuel the F-4s along entrance and egress routes, would comprise 16 to 18 flights of Phantoms. After a weather delay, the operation was launched the following day under marginally better conditions. Solid overcast conditions persisted over North Vietnam air bases, home to the MiG-21 force, as Olds led the first flight of F-4s into the skies above some of the most heavily defended territory in North Vietnam.

Olds's first pass over the main MiG base drew no response. On his second run, though, MiGs began popping up through the cloud layer apparently intending to box in the supposed F-105s with strong attacks from the front and rear. The MiG-21s, however, were themselves ambushed, caught in a cauldron by Bolo's Phantoms. Seven were shot down, almost half of North Vietnam's inventory at the time. Olds was credited with one of the kills. There were no losses to USAF Phantoms.

In the next few days, after MiGs attempted to interfere with RF-4 reconnaissance aircraft, a similar Bolo-type mission was launched on January 6. Two more MiGs were shot down, effectively rendering North Vietnamese fighter activity nonexistent for several weeks afterward. The major purpose of Operation Bolo, to destroy or materially reduce the threat of MiG-21s to missions over the North, was achieved in a convincing manner.

Olds flew his last mission as commander of the 8th TFW on September 23, 1967. Though officially recorded as his 100th mission, it was actually the 152nd that he had flown. During the course of his tour he added a second MiG kill on May 4 and two more on a May 20 mission. Olds later acknowledged that he had passed up chances for additional kills because of his concern that if he became an ace (five kills), he would be sent home to engage in public relations tours. Some accounts have him shooting down as many as three more MiGs but awarding those kills to other pilots.

The official combined total of four kills in Vietnam and the 12 he achieved in World War II made him a triple ace. (Reports also persist of a 13th kill in World War II, but official verification from the Air Force Historical Research Agency credits him with 12.) The F-4C Phantom that he flew in Vietnam was placed on permanent display at the National Museum of the United States Air Force at Wright-Patterson AFB, Ohio.

Olds's Southeast Asia tour did not end with his exploits in Operation Bolo and his MiG kills. On March 30, he earned a Silver Star (his fourth) for leading a low-level, three-ship strike on blast furnaces at Thai Nguyen in northeastern North Vietnam. The raid was noted for its extremely low-level—25 feet or less at times—approach to the target through narrow defiles in terrain that featured some of North Vietnam's tallest peaks.

Dozens of batteries protected the furnaces, firing salvos at the three Phantoms as they made their runs toward the target. Olds's approach was so low that his aircraft was actually struck from *above* by flak from gunners posted on rooftops firing down at his aircraft as he raced toward the furnace complex. All three aircraft struck the targets, making solid hits across the compound.

Olds's plane was hit several times during his run to the target. With flames streaming out of a wing that momentarily caught fire, he coaxed the damaged craft to a rendezvous with a tanker that stayed with him all the way home to Ubon.

On August 11 Olds led a covering force that attacked the Paul Doumer Bridge that spanned the Red River near Hanoi. The mile-long bridge was vital to the North; it supported vehicle and rail traffic from China and a major industrial area nearby. Only recently removed from the list of restricted targets, the bridge was one of the most heavily defended sites in North Vietnam. The attack dropped two spans of the bridge, the opening round of a continuous damage-repair-damage cycle fought throughout much of the remainder of the war.

Olds's experience in Vietnam and those of the 8th TFW and other fighter wings vindicated his long-standing conviction regarding aerial combat and pilot training. During an era when the Air Force's senior leadership was significantly influenced by officers with bomber backgrounds, Olds argued that pilots were ill-prepared for warfare of the type waged in Vietnam. "We weren't allowed to dogfight. Very little attention was paid to strafing, dive-bombing rocketry . . . it was thought to be unnecessary . . . [the Vietnam War] proved the need to teach tactical warfare and train fighter pilots. It caught us unprepared because we weren't allowed to learn it or practice it in training."

Despite the seeming lethargy of senior officials, lessons learned in combat and the impetus of Olds and other commanders gradually drove changes in tactics that improved operational effectiveness and enhanced aircrew survivability. In 1965 one aircraft was lost for every 17 SAMs launched by the North Vietnamese. With better tactics and improved electronic countermeasures, that figure was rather quickly reduced to one for every 35 and eventually, by 1972, one for every 60 SAMs expended. As Olds and other commanders noted, these improvement did not come without costs, or nearly as quickly as many of them believed possible.

The impact of U.S. bombing efforts on the North Vietnamese military establishment and its civilian labor force is an aspect of the war not often elaborated on by Western media or recognized by many observers. At the height of the aerial campaign, the North Vietnamese employed about 600,000 laborers, mostly women, to repair bomb damage. During the course of the war, it is believed that 145,000 personnel were allocated to air defense duties.

No works about Robin Olds would be complete without reference to the famous (infamous?) mustache and the story behind it. In Vietnam Olds became known for the sporty, far-outside-regulation mustache that became an integral part of his swashbuckling persona. The mustache was a dashing World War II–type model that burnished his reputation as a maverick. In his own words, the mustache became "the middle finger I couldn't raise in

PR photographs . . . my short last words in the verbal battles I was losing with higher headquarters on routes, targets, and fighting the war."

Olds's gesture of defiance quickly caught on with the wing's pilots and support personnel and soon became the source of morale for others, spreading to units throughout the theater. Over time, "Mustache March" became a ritual in which units and individuals throughout the Air Force grew mustaches as well. When Olds entered Mitchell Hall at the Air Force Academy for the first time as commandant of cadets, the rows of cadets stood at attention—all wearing fake mustaches.

Before and After

If ever a person was predestined to be a pilot, surely that individual was Robin Olds. Born in Hawaii on July 14, 1922, Olds was the son of Robin Olds, a military pilot who achieved major general rank in the Army Air Corps. The younger Olds grew up in military quarters frequently visited by airpower pioneers such as Carl "Tooey" Spatz, Eddie Rickenbacker, Ira Eaker, Hap Arnold, and many others. His father was aide-de-camp to Billy Mitchell and testified for Mitchell at his famous trial. Young Robin attended a session of the tribunal—in uniform—as a three-year-old.

Olds's charisma and leadership skills were evident early on. He was president of his high school class for three consecutive years and starred on a football team that won the Virginia state championship. Encouraged by his father, Olds aspired from an early age to attend the United States Military Academy at West Point. It was a goal he achieved when he was accepted for admission in June 1940 (class of 1944).

Olds's time at the academy was notable for several reasons, but foremost among them was his prowess on the football field. Olds was a rugged 200 pounder, six feet, two inches tall. In 1941 and 1942 he played both offensive and defensive tackle on varsity teams coached by the legendary Earl "Red" Blaik. Olds was an outstanding player, achieving All-America status in 1942. That same year he was selected as *Collier's* "Lineman of the Year." Famed sportswriter Grantland Rice chose him as "Player of the Year in College Football." (In 1985 he would be enshrined in the College Football Hall of Fame.)

In October 1942, with the United States ten months into World War II, the academy adopted a three-year curriculum and modified the course for cadets identified for flight training. Along with academic work, Olds completed a primary flight training program at Tulsa, Oklahoma, and advanced training at Stewart Field, New York. On May 30, 1943, Hap Arnold personally presented pilot wings to Olds. Graduation from West Point took place the following day.

Olds left "The Point" with somewhat mixed feelings toward the institution and an acquired reputation—which would remain with him throughout his career—for mischief and for pushing the envelope. Though dedicated to "Duty, Honor, Country," he came to oppose the way the Academy applied the Honor Code. Punishment for an alcohol-related incident (he was "busted" from cadet captain to cadet private and walked tours until graduation), solidified his belief that the code was misused as a tool for enforcement of petty disciplinary infractions. In his view, the code process would be better employed to teach and enhance integrity at the personal level and throughout the corps.

After training phases in California and Arizona and gunnery practice in Texas, Olds was assigned to Muroc Army Airfield, California, in August 1943 for training in the P-38, a twin-engine fighter.

The stay at Muroc was of short duration. Early in 1944 he was transferred to Lomita, California, as part of a cadre to activate a new fighter squadron—the 434th. After extensive flying time the unit embarked for Europe aboard the USS *Argentina*. Along with two sister squadrons in the 479th Fighter Group, the 434th arrived in Scotland on May 14, 1944, then entrained for RAF Wattisham in East Anglia, where Olds would be posted for the entirety of his two combat tours.

Much to his dislike, Olds's initial flights from Wattisham mainly involved patrols and bomber escort duty. More to his satisfaction, on June 6 his squadron flew top cover for the Allied landings that assaulted beaches along the coast of Normandy. After two weeks of providing beachhead cover, the squadron's mission was switched to interdiction strikes against bridges, rail yards, supply depots, and troop concentrations.

In July, Olds became a flight commander. Promotion to captain followed, effective August 1. On August 14, while on a mission to attack a bridge at Chalon-su-Saone, Olds got his first and second kills, downing a pair of Focke-Wulf 190s. As the unit gained experience, fighter sweeps became an increasing part of their combat repertoire. Flying ahead of bomber strikes, clearing the sky of enemy fighters, brought frequent encounters with the Luftwaffe. During the course of his two tours, 10 more kills, FWs and ME-109s, would follow. (He was also credited with 11.5 destroyed on the ground.)

In September, the squadron transitioned from P-38s to P-51s. Olds's final seven kills were achieved flying the P-51 Mustang. Though not yet 23 years old in March 1945, he assumed duties as squadron commander and was promoted to major. He was twice awarded the Silver Star for his World War II service.

The end of World War II took Olds away from the milieu that most animated him. Much to his frustration and despite repeated requests for reassignment, he would miss the next conflict (Korea), often being posted instead to staff positions for which he had scarce enthusiasm and derived little satisfaction. His first postwar assignment, though, was unusual and fascinating.

For the 1945 session, at the personal request of Coach Red Blaik, Olds was assigned as an assistant football coach at West Point. When the season ended, with the backdoor assistance of friends at the Pentagon, Olds wangled an assignment to March Field, near Riverside, California, to fly the Air Force's first jet fighter, the P-80 "Shooting Star." Olds was clearly in his element as the soon-to-be-independent Air Force put the new aircraft through its paces.

For Olds, 1946 would be an eventful year, marked by involvement in several unique events. A multicity mass formation flight of P-80s was quickly followed by a notable "first"—a four-ship, one-day coast to coast transcontinental flight. Later on, he finished second in the jet division of the Thompson Trophy Race.

Soon after arriving at March, Olds and another officer, Lieutenant Colonel John C. "Pappy" Herbst, formed what may have been the Air Force's first jet aerobatic demonstration team. Their prowess in demonstrations—unique, highly acclaimed, and well-attended—ended in tragedy when Herbst was killed in a Fourth of July crash.

Olds's time at March was notable in another area as well. While there, he met movie star Ella Raines. The two were married in 1947, a union that would last 29 years.

While attending a three-month tactical school at Tyndall Field in Florida in October 1948, Olds was assigned as an exchange officer with No. 1 Squadron of the Royal Air Force at RAF Tangmere, flying Gloster Meteor jet fighters. In addition to flight duties, the assignment brought a significant professional achievement. From October 1948 until September 1949 he served as squadron commander, the first foreigner to command an RAF unit in peacetime.

Completion of the exchange tour brought a return to the base at Riverside, California (no longer March Field but now officially March AFB, the Air Force having become a separate service in 1947). At March, Olds signed in as operations officer of the 94th Fighter Squadron, 1st Fighter Group. The unit flew an aircraft still new to the Air Force inventory—the F-86A Sabre jet. Later he was assigned to command the 71st Fighter Squadron, which was eventually split off from the 1st Fighter Group and, after brief intermediate stops at George AFB, California, and Griffiss AFB, New York, based at Greater Pittsburgh Airport.

Olds would come to regard that assignment as one of the low points in his career. In June 1950, North Korea had attacked South Korea. He was bitterly disappointed that his numerous requests for reassignment to Korea were turned aside. He chafed at the circumstance of training pilots for combat but not being allowed to partake himself. Those feelings were hardened by the fact that he saw little purpose for an air defense unit (his squadron's primary mission) at a place like Greater Pittsburgh Airport. Not only was the location incongruous, but, in fact, Olds regarded air defense as a less-than-key component in the Air Force's menu of capabilities. To Olds, air power was at its core an offensive weapon. He desperately wanted to return to action and employ it as such. Though he was bumped up to base commander, his dissatisfaction led him to submit his resignation ostensibly so he could seek a test pilot position with a major aircraft company. His boss talked him out of what may have been a half-hearted attempt. Olds was soon reassigned as a staff officer at Eastern Air Defense Force, Stewart AFB, New York.

Olds had found few redeeming features in his time at Greater Pittsburgh. His duties at Stewart AFB also left him ambivalent and dissatisfied. Air Defense consumed a sizable portion of the Air Force budget. Olds believed those resources were misallocated, and the emphasis on nuclear warfare ignored the more likely possibility that the U.S. would at some point surely find itself engaged in conventional conflicts.

In May 1954 Olds was returned to Greater Pittsburgh for a brief stay as director of operations and training. At age 33, he was promoted to full colonel. After a year, he received orders for Landstuhl, Germany, as commander of the 86th Interceptor Group, a unit whose primary mission was air defense of Western Europe. The group's secondary mission—delivery of tactical and strategic nuclear weapons—was reflective of the alignment of forces in that part of the world and day-to-day tensions of the Cold War era.

August 1956 brought a new posting to Wheelus Air Base in Libya. Olds's position as chief, Weapons Proficiency Center placed him in charge of fighter weapons training for all Air Force units in Europe. The base's location, a few miles from Tripoli, with miles of open space and year-around favorable weather, made it ideal as a gunnery range and training facility. Activity levels at Wheelus steadily increased—Olds's time there coincided with ongoing weapons construction and modernization initiatives. Olds's efforts transformed the range from a camp into a true weapons training center with dummy airfields, bridges, supply dumps, and convoys replicating those Olds was sure the Air Force would be called upon to strike in future conflicts. By the time he left, two years later, facilities at the main base, including runways, maintenance structures, housing, and clinic, were also in place or nearing completion.

In July 1958 Olds's follow-on assignment took him to the Pentagon as deputy chief of the Air Defense Division. As with other staff postings during his career, the job was not to his liking. As per usual, he requested the assignment be changed or canceled. Also as usual, his requests were denied. He later characterized the job as "mindless, soul-searing, thankless, and mostly unproductive drudgery."

As his Pentagon tour wore on, his duties increasingly butted up against two of his mostly strongly held convictions: (1) the Air Force lacked sufficient capability to conduct conventional warfare, and (2) conventional conflicts were the most likely type of combat the nation would face in the future.

After slightly more than a year, his duties were changed by a transfer to the Operations Directorate on the Joint Staff. Rather quickly, he clashed with officers senior in the hierarchy who disputed, and tired of, his advocacy for conventional warfare preparations and his misgivings regarding the military's current lack of capability in that area. The only conflict the U.S. had recently been engaged in (Korea) had been waged with conventional weapons—a type of combat he believed the Air Force was no longer ready to fight.

After two years on the Joint Staff, Olds attended the National War College at Fort McNair in Washington, DC. Graduation in mid-1963 brought on assignment to the 81st Tactical Fighter Wing at RAF Bentwaters in the United Kingdom. There, he connected with Chappie James, who served as his deputy commander for operations. Olds's duties as commander of the unit flying F-101 Voodoos were generally satisfying and pleasant. Eventually, though, in trouble with a superior for conducting an unauthorized air show, he was shuttled off to Shaw AFB, South Carolina. (Olds's version of the story is that he deliberately ran afoul of his boss in a manner that ensured that his name would be removed from the list of officers identified for promotion to general. Generals did not fly in combat, and Olds was determined to get to Vietnam in a job that allowed him to engage in combat operations.) Olds spent a year at Shaw as assistant director for operations at 9th Air Force Headquarters. The 9th had control of the fighter squadrons in the eastern United States and responsibility for the combat training preparations that readied fighter pilots for assignments to Vietnam.

Finally, at long last, and much to his delight, it was his turn. After a hurried five days getting checked out in the F-4 Phantom at Davis-Monthan, Arizona, Olds was on his way to Vietnam.

Olds's first post-Vietnam public encounter—like many noncombat episodes throughout his career—won him no accolades from senior officials. After a Pentagon meeting with the Air Force chief of staff who told him to shave his mustache, he was told that the president wanted to see him. He quickly shaved and went to the White House for a meeting with Lyndon Johnson. During the discussion, Olds went against the party line by strongly advocating a bombing campaign that would close North Vietnamese ports, destroy bridges and rail lines, and eliminate supply dumps, telling the president, "With all due respect, the way to end the war is just to win the damn thing."

Olds shared the view of many Air Force strategists who had argued from the earliest days of the war that North Vietnam's industrial base resided in China and the Soviet Union. Thus, airpower as it was employed in Vietnam could not be decisive. Instead, Air Force planners urged the destruction of facilities around Hanoi and, most particularly, the bombing or mining of Haiphong harbor. Those actions, Olds and others believed, would materially reduce the supplies flowing into North Vietnam, and the effects would favorably influence the combat situation in the South. A more properly conceived air offensive would abet an aggressive ground campaign in several ways. Closing the harbor at Haiphong would severely restrict the North's war supplies at the major point of entry. Those that remained would be further reduced during their transit south where a full scope of interdiction and close air support actions would shield and support allied units engaged on the ground.

To Olds's surprise, Johnson asked that he talk with National Security Advisor Walt Rostow the following morning. Before that, however, Olds, just back from the war zone, exhausted, and barely having had a chance to see his family, endured a contentious meeting with the Pentagon press corps. To a question regarding how the U.S. should end the war, Olds replied again by saying—or shouting—"Win it." He was chastised by a senior Air Force public relations officer for responding in that manner and for using that term.

After his meeting with Rostow—at which he reiterated his requests for stronger action against North Vietnam—Olds was finally free to leave and prepare for his next assignment as commandant of cadets at the United States Air Force Academy.

The position, accompanied by promotion to brigadier general, was a nonflying billet. As per his usual reaction, Olds was initially less than excited about stepping into it. Numerous colleagues encouraged him to do so, believing that his drive and warrior ethos would help jump-start an organization in need of reinvigoration. Eventually, his doubts subsided, and he came to enjoy the job and the location.

Along with occasional clashes with the academy hierarchy and judge advocate staff, Olds, during his three-year tour, promoted harmony with the academic branch, worked to restore morale as the academy emerged from a cheating scandal, and labored with mixed success to adjust the honor code as it was applied for punishment and discipline. Most of all, he enjoyed his interactions with the cadets and savored the increased camaraderie and esprit de corps visibly evident throughout the cadet structure.

Olds continued to speak out about the conduct of the Vietnam War, arguing as always that it be waged in a manner that would achieve victory. Public backlash for his pronouncements mandated "damage control" statements from the academy hierarchy. Eventually, a clash with the academy superintendent regarding the handling of a cadet disciplinary matter caused Olds to request reassignment.

Olds's next, and final, job in the Air Force was as director of aerospace safety at Norton Air Force Base, near San Bernardino, California. Olds came to regard it as "challenging and interesting" but also "frustrating and ultimately disappointing." He enjoyed the people but opposed the policies that seemed to him to influence the way they approached their jobs.

Deeply disgruntled by the way the war was being fought and by what he perceived as bureaucratic politics, Olds retired from the Air Force effective June 6, 1973. He made his retirement home in Steamboat Springs, Colorado—a home he would never leave. Olds filled his retirement years with dining-ins, fighter pilot reunions, golf, and fishing.

Until his health failed, he participated in speaking tours—34 in total during the years immediately prior to this death. His topics often turned to Vietnam and to his view that Washington policymakers had micromanaged the air campaign. Indeed, President Johnson was quoted as saying, "They can't even bomb an outhouse without my approval." High-value targets were placed off limits. Operation Rolling Thunder was intended to support the U.S. commitment to South Vietnam and, through an ever-increasing reign of destruction, break the political will of the North Vietnamese. Olds believed that limitations placed on targets and operational methods precluded prospects for success. In his view, administrative officials ignorant of local conditions and wary of widening the war detracted from the skill and valor of Air Force, Navy, and Marine pilots and diminished opportunities for victory that were otherwise present. Only in the final days of the war—12 days of intensive operations that may have broken the impasse at the Paris Peace Talks—was American air power employed as Olds would have liked—in dimensions that more nearly demonstrated its full, unfettered capabilities. When it was, according to some participants, the effects were notable. Ambassador George H. Aldrich, a member of the American negotiating team in Paris, said, "Prior to Linebacker II [the bombing campaign], the North Vietnamese were intransigent, buying time, refusing even to discuss a formal meeting schedule. After Linebacker II, they were shaken, demoralized, anxious to talk about anything."

Olds died at Steamboat Springs on June 14, 2007, aged 84. He was buried at the United States Air Force Academy Cemetery.

Special Mention:
The Tet Offensive—the Turning Point

The Tet Offensive—a countrywide, months-long campaign conducted by North Vietnamese and Viet Cong units—has come to be equated in significance by some military historians alongside battles such as Saratoga in the War of Independence and Midway in World War II. Tet, like the outcomes of each of those events, shaped the future course of the conflict. Like them also, the effects were not immediately understood at the time.

By any criteria, Tet was a watershed event in the long history of the conflict. Indeed, the phrases "Tet Offensive" and "Vietnam War" are often paired in tandem. As historians have noted, there is considerable irony attached to the battle and its outcome. Tet is most often popularized as a military victory for America's adversaries. In fact, the Tet Offensive resulted in catastrophic losses for North Vietnam and Viet Cong formations. None of the objectives anticipated by Hanoi's planners before the battle were achieved. Tet, though, had a consequence unforeseen by either side. The sheer scale of the offensive, the countrywide devastation it wrought, and the headlines it generated, had the unanticipated effect of abetting the shift of public sentiment in the West to a more pronounced and pervasive antiwar sentiment.

Beginning in 1966 and continuing on an ever-increasing scale, the massive destruction visited on North Vietnam and Viet Cong forces prompted the leadership in Hanoi to conduct a lengthy reappraisal of the military strategy being employed against South Vietnam and allied forces. Unlike the French-Indochina War, communist cadres were being fought to a standstill and the North's economy was being wrecked by American airpower. There was an increasing concern among senior leaders that unless the pattern was broken, the results would eventually degrade, perhaps fatally, the ability to influence the military situation in South Vietnam.

The reassessment process took place over a prolonged period. Discussions were divisive and prompted major rifts within the leadership. Factions developed between disputing parties. Some favored negotiations, others advocated protracted guerilla-type warfare, and still others urged conventional war on the Soviet model. Before the disputes were resolved, changes in the leadership occurred and, over an extended period, several high-ranking officials were jailed—an outcome that at the time was little known in the West.

Hardliners favoring large-scale conventional war eventually won out. Subsequently, an operational plan for what officially was titled "The General Offensive/General Uprising" emerged from the tortuous process. The plan had several key objectives:

- Annihilate the South Vietnamese Army and cause it to disintegrate
- Overthrow the South Vietnamese government
- Destroy American troop strength and equipment to levels that would deny U.S. forces the ability to achieve their mission
- Force the U.S. to accept defeat and end hostile actions against North Vietnam

The central focus of the plan was to create "a spontaneous uprising in order to win a decisive victory in the shortest time possible." That overriding goal was premised on Hanoi's belief that the pronounced lack of popularity of the South Vietnamese government and its American allies would enable massive, countrywide attacks to prompt uprisings and result in a quick, overwhelming victory. That objective, they believed, was eminently attainable. The South Vietnamese Army was, in their assessment, no longer an effective combat force and the South's national government so bitterly disliked that it was ripe for overthrow.

In October 1966 the North Vietnamese Politburo decided to launch the attack concurrent with the Tet holiday, a decision that was reaffirmed by a plenary session of the North Vietnamese Communist Party Central Committee in January 1968. First though, there would be strikes along South Vietnam's borders intended to draw American and South Vietnamese forces away from the major areas that would be the primary targets of the assaults that would follow.

The final plan for the offensive—nationwide attacks on cities conducted primarily by Viet Cong units—was slated to begin January 30, 1968. Accompanying propaganda would encourage South Vietnamese soldiers to desert. Leaflets and broadcasts would incite insurrections among the South's citizenry. Meanwhile, diplomatic initiatives, more peaceable in tone, would disguise Hanoi's intentions. If necessary, follow-on phases of "General Offensive/General Uprising" would be launched in May and August.

The logistical buildup to support the offensive took months to assemble. Viet Cong cadres were equipped with new weapons. Supplies were stockpiled, and thousands of North Vietnamese regulars moved south along the Ho Chi Minh Trail. By the beginning of Tet in late January it is thought that North Vietnamese and Viet Cong forces in the South numbered about 325,000, of which possibly 130,000 were North Vietnamese soldiers. Service and support formations were bulked up in proportion. Combat units were complemented by artillery, antiaircraft, and sapper/engineer units.

Although allied intelligence officials had received some scattered inklings that strikes might be forthcoming, none correctly assessed the size and intensity of the attacks, or their timing. Earlier, Hanoi had announced a seven-day truce (January 27–February 3) to further put the allies at ease. They mostly succeeded: on January 30, senior Military Assistance Command, Vietnam (MACV) officials attended a pool party in Saigon.

The initial attacks, targeting several provincial capitals, began shortly after midnight on January 30. These first assaults generally followed similar patterns. Rocket and mortar bombardments, often heavy, preceded massed infantry strikes mostly conducted by Viet Cong formations in battalion strength. The units were often led to key targets by local Viet Cong cadres.

Despite achieving surprise at almost every location, these first assaults produced only mixed results. Most were defeated by sunrise or shortly after. Those actions, though, belied the fact that at higher echelons initial reactions to the numerous battles were generally lethargic.

In the early morning hours of January 31, attacks began on major cities, including Saigon and Hue, and on U.S. air and Army bases throughout the country. These assaults continued until February 10. By the end of the campaign every major U.S. airfield and Army base had been struck by mortar and rocket fire. In addition to the devastation wrought upon the South's major cities, 64 district capitals and dozens upon dozens of smaller towns had been assaulted.

From the start, the capture and destruction of several key targets in Saigon was intended as the centerpiece of the "General Offensive/General Uprising" plan. One portion of it, the attack on the American Embassy, although rather quickly overcome, captured headlines around the world. Fighting raged in parts of the city for days; the initial surge of the offensive did not recede until the second week of February.

At Hue, the historic imperial capital was minimally defended when communist units first moved against the city. When the size of the attack became apparent, U.S. and Army of the Republic of Vietnam (ARVN) forces—primarily the 1st Marine Division and the 1st ARVN Division—were hurried into the fray. The resulting battle, one of the longest of the war, lasted 25 days and left much of the city in ruins.

The final phase of the campaign began in August. Though many attacks were aimed at cities and specific objectives within cities, military targets were also a major focus. As in the first portion of the campaign, targets along the border were attacked first in the attempt to draw defending forces away from cities. Saigon was struck again, though with less intensity and surprise than the initial January–February attacks. For a time, the widespread attacks brought pacification efforts to a near standstill; in places Viet Cong cadres temporarily ruled the countrywide. Eventually, though, South Vietnamese and American forces pushed back, inflicting heavy casualties and regaining ground lost at the outset.

Operations associated with "General Offensive/General Uprising" continued into the fall before finally being terminated by Hanoi. Militarily, the results were catastrophic for the communist forces. Hanoi officials acknowledge the loss of more than 45,000 North Vietnamese and Viet Cong soldiers killed. Other estimates range as high as 200,000 casualties. None of the planned objectives were achieved. There was no public uprising. The South Vietnamese government had survived intact, and the prowess of the allied military forces had not been diminished. In fact, as the year progressed, 20,000 communist troops defected to the Saigon regime.

Losses on all sides were extreme. Often overlooked in discussions of Tet is the extent of the devastation visited upon the population of South Vietnam. Civilian casualties were approximated at 14,000 dead and possibly 25,000 injured. An additional 630,000 refugees were created, joining the more than three-quarters of a million already displaced by the war. One estimate suggested that as many as 75,000–100,000 homes were destroyed or heavily damaged. By the end of 1968, one out of every 12 citizens of South Vietnam would be living in a refugee facility. For the South Vietnamese Army, the fight to repel the Tet Offensive made 1968 the costliest year of the war to that point. More than 27,000 ARVN soldiers were killed that year. The same was true for American forces; more than 16,000 were killed in action. During one week in February, amid the height of the initial Tet assaults, 543 Americans were killed, the highest figure for any week during the war.

The Tet Offensive wrecked a considerable portion of the Viet Cong force. Entire units were decimated, and their effectiveness as fighting formations was destroyed or greatly diminished. After Tet, filler replacements from North Vietnamese regular army units fleshed out an ever-increasing portion of Viet Cong units.

The horrific losses and the failure of the campaign to achieve any major objective caused a crisis of leadership in Hanoi and a lengthy "after action" reappraisal. The eventual assessment concluded that the North had not understood the resiliency of the allied forces, particularly their mobility and firepower. The South's population was not as ripe for insurrection as anticipated, and their own plan was too intricate—the countrywide attacks spread forces too thin and made coordination difficult. Bitter divisions developed and changes took place in Hanoi's leadership element.

Though Tet was a significant tactical setback for the North Vietnamese and Viet Cong, in the weeks ahead the results would come to be seen in a different light. The pervasive countrywide attacks, the enormous size of the forces that participated in them, and the depth of the planning that obviously went into them took the world unaware. Though in most cases the allies responded well and recovered quickly, the *impact* of the surprise and the fact that it had been almost total stunned knowledgeable observers and ordinary citizens alike. Coming as it did soon after several senior political and military leaders reassured American audiences that things were going well and that the corner had been turned added to the shock and discouragement.

For some media pundits in the U.S., the tipping point may have taken place on February 27. On an evening news broadcast, Walter Cronkite, America's most respected newscaster, stated, "We have too often been disappointed by the optimism of American leaders, both in Vietnam and Washington, to have faith any longer in the silver linings they find in the darkest clouds . . . we are mired in a stalemate that could only be ended by negotiation, not victory."

President Johnson was later shown a tape of the Cronkite broadcast. His comment to a White House staff member has been variously quoted as something akin to "If I've lost Cronkite, I've lost the average citizen."

Johnson's instincts were largely correct. Although initial polls taken after Tet showed support for the war generally holding firm, as attacks persisted and details and damage reports flowed in, the favorable numbers eroded. Johnson's public reaction was relatively muted—a position that did little to dissuade skeptics or assure supporters. Thus, to the considerable surprise of the leadership in Hanoi, a campaign that was in many ways a military disaster for the North Vietnamese and Viet Cong was transposed over time into a strategic triumph.

British historian Max Hastings assessed the consequences as follows: "Tet became a stunning manifestation of an important truth about modern wars: success or failure cannot be judged solely, or even peripherally, by military criteria. Perception is critical, and events of February 1968 became a perceptual disaster to American arms. The communists were deemed to have secured a triumph merely by displaying the power to engulf South Vietnam in destruction and death even though most of the latter fell upon their own fighters and hapless bystanders."

Two of America's most forgotten leaders from the Vietnam conflict led forces with exceptional foresight during the turbulence of the Tet Offensive. One of the officers, then-Major General Frederick C. Weyand, has been credited with making "one of the most critical tactical decisions of the war."

Forgotten Leader: Frederick C. Weyand

A Command Decision of Historic Importance

Weyand was one of the few senior officers who emerged from the Vietnam War with an enhanced reputation. Unlike most of his contemporaries, he anticipated the Tet Offensive and pre-positioned his forces to meet it. His determination to adjust his units and draw them closer to Saigon is regarded as one of the most astute leadership decisions made in any of America's recent conflicts. U.S. ARMY—U.S. ARMY HISTORY AND EDUCATION CENTER

Amid the chaos and confusion of the attacks that initiated the Tet Offensive, Major General Fred Weyand was perhaps the only senior American commander to emerge with a burnished reputation. Indeed, renowned military historian Max Hastings remarked that Weyand is "often hailed as the only senior officer who prepared for trouble, moving units into Saigon and cancelling his own operations. It was certainly thanks to Weyand, a former intelligence officer, that 27 maneuver battalions were deployed within reach of Saigon when the enemy struck."

In the fall of 1967, North Vietnam and Viet Cong units began a series of heavy attacks along South Vietnam's northern and western boundaries. These "border battles," as they became known, were large-scale operations that caused confusion within MACV headquarters. Aided unquestionably by his background as an intelligence officer, Weyand, unlike most of his contemporaries, correctly interpreted the massive attacks as diversionary actions intended to fix U.S. units near the border in place and lure others away from Saigon and other key locations in the interior. Weyand, and John Paul Vann, his astute advisor, were wary of the patterns that seemed to be emerging. They noted that enemy radio traffic in areas close to Saigon was increasing. Then, after the series of large-scale engagements along the nation's periphery, the number of contacts with opposing forces inexplicably began to diminish—a sign, as Weyand saw it, that the enemy was on the move.

Anticipating the attack, Weyand withdrew units from outlying posts and placed them in and around Saigon. As events would reveal, Weyand's prescient moves positioned American and South Vietnamese forces to withstand the tidal wave that was about to roll toward them.

Weyand's determination to reposition his exterior forces has been hailed as one of history's greatest operational decisions, commensurate with Admiral Raymond Spruance's actions at Midway and others of similar magnitude and consequence. His accomplishment is perhaps made even more notable by virtue of the fact that it was made in the face of opposition from his commander, General William C. Westmoreland.

Westmoreland's initial perceptions of the border clashes differed from Weyand's; he was inclined to view them as they outwardly appeared to be—large-scale attacks whose objectives, while murky, were best addressed decisively. Early in 1967, when North Vietnamese forces perhaps numbering as many as 20,000–40,000 attacked the isolated U.S. Marine post at Khe Sanh, Westmoreland responded with overwhelming force. Thinking perhaps that the assault might be a precursor to an attempt to overrun South Vietnam's northern provinces, he dispatched nearly a quarter of a million men, half of MACV's maneuver battalions, to address the threat.

Weyand, charged with defense of the Capital Military District, correctly interpreted the attack as a feint, and eventually received Westmoreland's permission to redeploy maneuver battalions from areas along the Cambodia border to the vicinity of Saigon. After denying earlier requests, on January 10, 1968, Westmoreland approved Weyand's plan to reposition forces inside the "Saigon Circle," a fortified protective zone that surrounded South Vietnam's capital city. Weyand's move bulked up the number of combat battalions to 27, almost double the total that had previously been in place there. When the Tet Offensive began less than three weeks later, Weyand's generalship cost North Vietnamese and Viet Cong formations horrific numbers of casualties and repelled the massive attack that formed the centerpiece of what was envisioned by leaders in Hanoi as being a war-winning offensive.

Weyand's preparations for the coming battle included establishing a resilient communication system that enabled him to rapidly identify positions under duress and shift units to quickly address existing and emerging threats. At a time when much of MACV was thrown off balance by the size and intensity of the attacks, his preparations anchored the defense that saved the battle.

With the rousing message "Crack the Sky, Shake the Earth," North Vietnamese and Viet Cong cadres attacked Saigon and numerous other cities in the Capital Military District in the predawn hours of January 31. Major objectives included the National Radio Station, South Vietnam's Army and Navy Headquarters, the American Embassy, Independence Palace, and Tan Son Nhut Air Base. Peripheral attacks were conducted on the central police station and other military establishments. Simultaneously, targeted assassinations were launched against officials and civil servants throughout the city.

The initial attacks on major targets such as the radio station aimed at seizing the objectives and holding them long enough—48 hours was thought to be sufficient—for reinforcements to fight through to their relief. In the aftermath, thanks to unexpectedly stiff resistance from ARVN and American units, and Weyand's foresight, none of the attacks had the necessary staying power. The radio station was retaken within six hours, the U.S. Embassy was cleared of snipers in six hours, and most of the other targets were also reclaimed before or soon after sunrise.

At Hue, the ancient imperial city, the story was different. The city was struck in the early-morning fog of January 31. Hue was not, initially, strongly defended. Though heavily outnumbered, some ARVN forces and a scattering of 200 or so Americans managed to cling to a few positions; most of the city, including much of the Citadel—an ancient bastion—was overrun by an attacking force that probably numbered close to 8,000. Both sides rushed reinforcements and supplies to the city. Eventually, in a struggle that lasted 25 days—one of the longest battles of the war—the 1st Marine Division and the 1st ARVN Division cleared the city in house-to-house fighting. Thanks in part to Weyand's resilient communications system, U.S. forces were shifted quickly—often over considerable distances and in large numbers—to address threats and relieve embattled defenders.

In the end, Tet was a battle militarily won—rather decisively—by U.S. and South Vietnamese forces, but politically and strategically lost—equally as decisively—in American and international public opinion.

Weyand's strained interactions with Westmoreland were not confined to the problem of getting approval for his plan to realign his forces to better protect Saigon. Weyand disagreed rather fundamentally with Westmoreland's conventional war strategy. In his judgment, over the long haul, search-and-destroy missions and reliance on massive firepower did not promise success in the type of conflict being waged in Vietnam. Years after the war ended, an editorial in *The New York Times* revealed—with Weyand's consent—that he had been the source of a 1967 story written by *Times* reporter R. W. Apple Jr. titled "Vietnam: The Sign of a Stalemate." Weyand was quoted in the article as saying, "I've destroyed a single division three times. . . . I've chased main-force units all over the country and the impact was zilch. It meant nothing to the people. Unless a more positive and more stirring theme than simple anti-communism can be found, the war appears likely to go on until someone gets tired and quits, which could take generations."

Weyand was known to speak often of the anguish and futility of dispatching troops to an area, clearing it at the cost of some number of American lives, only to later have to repeat the process, perhaps multiple times. "One of the agonies you'd go through," he said, "is that you'd send out a sweep operation . . . maybe take 15 dead. Then, after the operation, we'd have to pull out of there . . . and then when we'd go back a month later, we had the same problem all over again."

He was convinced that success was possible only if, after the enemy was cleared, the ground was held and made secure for the local population. He disagreed with Westmoreland's assessment that U.S. firepower and maneuver battalions could defeat the enemy through attrition. That strategy, he believed, ignored the fact that, in the absence of infantry, it was virtually impossible for the Americans to secure much of anything beyond the range of its heavy artillery. In his view, "the key to success in Vietnam was in securing and pacifying the towns and villages of South Vietnam."

Perhaps for that reason, unlike some commanders of ground forces, Weyand was an advocate of air power. At the outset of the Vietnamization project, he was quoted as saying that if the program had any hope of success, "our air is going to be the glue that holds all this together . . . if it weren't for the air, which is driving [the enemy] up the wall, we'd be in very bad shape . . . and yet those people back in Washington keep wanting to whack at that, too." He was convinced that as American troops came home, air power would become the principal weapon at the disposal of President Nixon and Secretary of State Kissinger.

In his later years, Weyand often spoke of the young American soldiers he had been privileged to lead in Vietnam. He believed their reputations had been unfairly tarnished. An unfortunate legacy of the war, he thought, was the belief that American soldiers had sometimes failed on the battlefield. Nothing, in his judgment, could be more divorced from reality. Drawing on his experience in Vietnam, Weyand observed that "the American Army is really a people's army in the sense that it belongs to the American people, who take a proprietary interest in its involvement. When the army is committed, the American people are committed. When the American people lose their commitment it is futile to try to keep the army committed."

U.S. Army forces "in country" were assigned to posts in one of the four corps regions shown on the accompanying map. At various times each was the scene of heavy combat. During the 1968 Tet Offensive, fighting raged throughout the nation's length and breadth.

During the course of the war, 2.71 million American men and women (about 9.7% of their generation) served in Vietnam.

U.S. Army Corps Areas During Vietnam War

A. Da Nang

B. Pleiku

C. Phu Cat

D. Tuy Hoa

E. Nha Trang

F. Cam Ranh Bay

G. Phan Rang

H. Bien Hoa

I. Tan Son Nhut

J. Binh Thuy

The scope of the war is illustrated by the number of U.S. Air Force bases in South Vietnam and by their dispersal throughout the countryside. Missions were also flown from bases in Thailand (Don Muang, Korat, Nakhon Phanom, Nam Phong, Takhli, Ubon, Udorn, and U-Tapao), Guam (Andersen AFB), and the Philippines (Clark AFB). Kadena Air Base, Okinawa, served as a key transportation hub and staging point for forces transiting to Vietnam.

American Air Bases in Vietnam

Before and After

Frederick C. Weyand was born at Arbuckle, California, about 45 miles southeast of Sacramento, on September 15, 1916. "The slow-spoken Californian" saw action in World War II, Korea, and Vietnam. Commissioned in 1938 through the Reserve Officer Training Program at the University of California at Berkeley, Weyand entered active duty at the Presidio of San Francisco in December 1940. Stateside assignments and professional schooling culminated in a 1943 posting as an intelligence officer in the U.S. War Department. The Washington, DC, billet was followed in March 1945 by service in the China-Burma-India Theater at Chungking, China, as assistant chief of staff for intelligence on the staff of General Joseph Stillwell.

The end of the war brought duty in senior intelligence positions in Washington, DC, and elsewhere. After the Pentagon tour as a branch chief, in 1946 Weyand was sent to Hawaii, where he served as assistant chief of staff, G-1, at Headquarters, U.S. Army, Pacific. While in that billet, he was "dual-hatted" as a Joint Task Force 7 member, a group responsible for conducting the 1948 nuclear tests at Eniwetok.

In 1950, having transferred to the infantry, Weyand graduated from the Advanced Infantry School at Fort Benning, Georgia. During the Korean War, Weyand saw combat as commander of the 1st Battalion, 7th Infantry Regiment, before serving as the 3rd Division's assistant chief of staff for operations.

An eclectic series of moves followed his wartime duty:

- Infantry School faculty at Fort Benning
- Armed Forces Staff College
- military assistant, Office of the Assistant Secretary of the Army for Force Management
- military assistant and executive officer to the secretary of the Army
- Army War College

European assignments followed graduation from the War College:

- commander, 3rd Battalion, 6th Infantry Regiment
- Office of the United States Commander, Berlin
- chief of staff, Communications Zone, United States Army, Europe

Weyand returned from Europe in 1961 as deputy chief and, later, chief of legislative liaison for the Department of the Army.

In 1964 Weyand took command of the 25th Infantry Division, with headquarters at Schofield Barracks, Hawaii. The following year, he moved with the unit to Vietnam, leading its operations for two more years through major campaigns, including Operation Cedar Falls and Operation Junction City. Weyand was well known for his frequent presence on battlefields, and was noted for having personally directed the rescue of a trapped company and the safe recovery of a reconnaissance patrol caught behind enemy lines.

In March 1967 he became deputy commander, and not long after, commander of II Field Force, responsible for the III Corps area, encompassing 11 provinces around Saigon. Weyand was in that position—commander of II Field Force—when the North Vietnamese and Viet Cong launched the Tet Offensive.

Weyand's service during Tet did not culminate his involvement in Vietnam. In 1969 he was called to Paris to serve as military advisor during the Paris Peace Talks. After a brief Washington, DC, assignment as assistant chief of staff for force development, he returned to Vietnam in 1970 as deputy to General Creighton Abrams, MACV commander.

When Abrams was named Army chief of staff, Weyand took over as commander, MACV, effective June 30, 1972, a role that made him the last American commander in Vietnam. Over the next six months he supervised the withdrawal of all American combat units from the embattled country.

Weyand's post-Vietnam duties took him to the highest positions in the United States Army. After serving first as commander in chief, United States Army, Pacific, he returned to Washington, DC, as vice chief of staff, United States Army (1973–74) before being appointed chief of staff, a position he held from October 3, 1974, until September 3, 1976.

In 1975, following North Vietnam's full-scale invasion of South Vietnam, President Gerald Ford sent Weyand to Vietnam to assess the situation and meet with South Vietnamese President Nguyen Van Thieu. At the administration's directive, Weyand advised Thieu that though the U.S. would provide moral support as well as some financial assistance, American forces would not be sent into combat. Weyand returned to Washington to report that in his judgment the North Vietnamese invasion could not be repelled and South Vietnam could not be saved without decisive American intervention. For Thieu's government and for South Vietnam, the clock had struck midnight.

Weyand's final days as chief of staff were immersed in rebuilding the Army after the trauma of Vietnam. Weyand's efforts, and Abrams's before him, were the beginning steps in a process that came to fruition with the service's performance during Operation Desert Storm.

Weyand died in Hawaii on February 16, 2010. He was 93 years old. He was buried at the National Cemetery of the Pacific—the "Punch Bowl"—on Oahu.

A HistoryNet obituary said this about Weyand: "He was arguably the best American general of the Vietnam War."

Forgotten Leader: Olinto Mark Barsanti

"The 101st Airborne Division Is Present for Duty"

Barsanti planned and led Operation Eagle Thrust, the transfer of the 101st Airborne Division from the United States to Vietnam. The operation was the largest transfer of men and equipment directly into a war zone. Like Frederick Weyand, Barsanti was prepared for the Tet Offensive and had his forces ready to respond. U.S. ARMY—U.S. ARMY HISTORY AND EDUCATION CENTER

Major General Olinto Mark Barsanti commanded the 101st Airborne Division, the "Screaming Eagles," for one year. It was, in every significant aspect, an eventful 12 months. His time as commander would be recalled principally for two major achievements. The first, Operation Eagle Thrust, was at the time the largest transfer of men and equipment directly into a combat zone ever conducted. The second was his division's performance in defeating Viet Cong and North Vietnamese attacks during the Tet Offensive.

After taking command of the 101st at Fort Campbell, Kentucky, in July 1967, Barsanti immediately began preparing his soldiers for combat. Planning was accelerated and training was intensified to levels not previously experienced by the division's veterans. By mid-November, the 101st was ready to move. The bulk of the forces were in place by mid-December. By year's end, more than 10,000 troops and 14,000 pounds of basic combat gear had been flown 9,700 miles straight into a war zone. The significance of the lightning move was readily apparent. Eagle Thrust had quickly and considerably increased the combat punch of the allied forces in Vietnam.

On December 13, General Barsanti and his soldiers were greeted by MACV Commander General William C. Westmoreland and other dignitaries in ceremonies held at Bien Hoa Air Base, South Vietnam. Barsanti saluted Westmoreland and reported that the "101st Airborne Division is present for duty." The operation was a remarkable demonstration, to friends and foes alike, of the nation's capability to project power on a global scale. Barsanti immediately established an extensive civic action program to assist the South Vietnamese populace.

The timing of the 101st's arrival would prove to be fortuitous. A month and a half after the division's soldiers stepped onto the tarmac at Bien Hoa, communist forces launched the series of nationwide attacks that became known to the world as the Tet Offensive. The assaults, massive in scale, struck more than 100 cities and towns and dozens of U.S. bases and facilities. Combined units of Viet Cong and North Vietnamese regulars numbering in the tens of thousands were unleashed in actions that leaders in Hanoi believed would defeat the Americans and destroy the South Vietnamese government.

For the allied cause, Barsanti's presence during this critical time was of considerable consequence. Other than Major General Frederick Weyand, Barsanti was one of the few senior officers who anticipated and prepared for the violence that would blanket the South Vietnamese nation. On January 21, 1968, ten days before the massive assault began, Barsanti told his troops, "During the [Tet] holiday period, we need to be especially watchful and security conscious. The enemy will take advantage of any opportunity to conduct subversive activities among the people and raid our base camps. The Viet Cong have broken truces before. We must therefore maintain the maximum degree of vigilance in our security posture."

Barsanti's rapid repositioning of troops nearer Saigon and other high-value cities and military installations complemented Fred Weyand's preparations for meeting the strike that he and Barsanti, but few others, believed was coming. From locations in the capital region where they had been posted since arriving "in country," Barsanti dispatched units of the 101st into Saigon to help clear attackers from key sites in the city. Other formations fanned out to threatened areas across the countryside, including the ancient city of Hue. There, the communist attack initially captured all but a small portion of the lightly defended city. After a prolonged period of desperate fighting inside the city and along the Perfume River, allied units combined to clear Hue of enemy cadres.

During the bloody, difficult days of the communist offensive, Quang Tri, Bien Hoa, Song Be, and other cities were restored to South Vietnamese control as Barsanti adroitly positioned units to address the multiple attacks, first stopping them and then throwing them back.

After major Tet-related actions subsided, Barsanti focused the 101st's actions along the coastal plains of South Vietnam. In a series of major operations, including Jeb Stuart, Nevada Eagle, and others, he used frequent night operations and multiple axes of attack to take the initiative from the enemy and destroy the cohesiveness of Viet Cong and North Vietnamese formations. Barsanti became known for his rapid concentration of forces in mass strikes against enemy strongpoints as well as for exploiting the use of specialized equipment in airlift and night operations. These actions, and others, sought to deny access to rice crops and the use of the A Shau Valley as an infiltration route and base camp refuge to enemy formations.

Barsanti's tour of duty with the 101st ended in July 1968. Before departing he had begun preparations for reorganizing the 101st, restructuring it from an airborne division into a combat force labeled as an airmobile division. The new title reflected the transition from airplanes to helicopters as the primary method for inserting the 101st's troops into combat. (In 1974, the unit would be further redesignated as an air assault division.)

Barsanti's time in Vietnam is recalled by those who served with him as having consisted of a whirlwind of activity. A colleague from the Korean War said, "The man has an almost inconceivable amount of energy." On two occasions, he personally led the rescue actions that saved squads trapped behind enemy lines. Two of his *seven* Purple Heart medals were earned in frontline combat in Vietnam.

When Barsanti first arrived in Vietnam, he told his soldiers that "the mission of the 101st Airborne is to find the enemy and destroy him. Inherent in this mission is an incumbent responsibility to respect the proud people we are here to assist." During the long, bitter agony of the Vietnam War, few commanders fulfilled these duties as well as Barsanti.

Before and After

One of the most decorated soldiers in U.S. Army history, Barsanti earned more than 60 awards, including five Silver Stars and seven Purple Hearts.

Born in Nevada on November 11, 1917, to Italian immigrant parents, Barsanti became one of the Army's youngest battalion commanders during World War II, its youngest regimental commander during the Korean War, and one of its youngest general officers and perhaps its finest division commander during Vietnam.

Commissioned in June 1940, Barsanti was initially assigned to the 38th Infantry at Fort Sam Houston, Texas. The year 1942 brought a notable posting with the 2nd Infantry Division as the director of Ranger battle training at Fort McCoy, Wisconsin. The training regimen he installed— night patrols, radio proficiency, camouflage techniques, hand-to-hand combat, ordnance and demolition, and map reading—would serve him and his soldiers well during the course of three major conflicts.

When the 2nd Division was transferred to Northern Ireland in October 1943, Barsanti accompanied it as the newly minted commander of the 1st Battalion, 38th Infantry. On June 7, 1944 (D-Day + 1), Barsanti, now the commander of the 3rd Battalion, and his unit crossed Omaha Beach and moved through St. Laurent sur Mer, France. Over the next several months, from the hedgerows of Normandy to the Ardennes Forest in Belgium, his unit was engaged in some of the European Theater's heaviest combat. Barsanti was wounded five times. He received one Silver Star for stopping a German counterattack and a second for assailing a key fortification. During the Battle of the Bulge, he led his battalion during a four-day battle that repelled a German advance near the town of Kinkelt. He was one of only two battalion commanders in the 2nd Infantry Division who survived the war.

After the war ended, brief stops in Oklahoma and Texas preceded attendance at the Army's Command and General Staff College at Fort Leavenworth, Kansas, where Barsanti reported in February 1946. After graduating with high marks, he was sent to Camp Carson, Colorado, only to be almost immediately called back to Fort Leavenworth to join the Command and Staff College faculty. He taught at the school until July 1949. A second brief stay at Camp Carson, this time as executive officer of the 38th Infantry Regiment, was soon followed by reassignment to General Headquarters, Far Eastern Command, with duty in Tokyo.

Barsanti had barely settled in when, on June 25, 1950, North Korea invaded South Korea. He was one of a handful of officers immediately sent by General Douglas MacArthur to lay the groundwork for the thousands of American personnel who would soon flow onto the Korean Peninsula. Barsanti set foot on Korean soil two days after the shooting started. The command post he and his colleagues established at Suwon covered the full menu of preparations essential for absorbing the incoming forces. Barsanti, along with 10 others, was charged with "preparing all necessary systems and facilities for administration, receipt of replacements, care of prisoners of war, billeting and transportation, as well as strength and casualty reporting."

Barsanti's actions in Korea soon became the stuff of legend. He was one of the first to arrive at Inchon, scene of the amphibious landing on September 15, 1950. Four weeks later, he drove 150 miles, alone, behind enemy lines on a two-day trek to deliver vital correspondence to the commander of two embattled South Korean divisions. Frequently under fire, he somehow wove his way through the treacherous mountains of North Korea over roads that were at the time almost impassable.

Several weeks later he was assigned as executive officer of the 2nd Infantry Division, and not long after, commander of the 9th Infantry Regiment. At the time, he was a 33-year-old lieutenant colonel, the youngest regimental commander in Korea. The 9th Infantry saw heavy action during Barsanti's time as commander. To accompany the Distinguished Service Cross he earned for his behind-the-lines odyssey, he was awarded the Bronze Star and another Silver Star for actions near Inje, where he personally led the assault against a key North Korean fortification. Injured during the campaign, he was sent back to Japan in August 1951 after more than a year "in country."

Early 1952 brought an assignment as assistant chief of staff, VI Corps, with duty at Camp Atterbury, Indiana. Like many of Barsanti's postings, the tour was relatively brief. Summer of 1953 brought attendance at the Armed Forces Staff College at Norfolk, Virginia. Duty in Heidelberg, Germany, with Headquarters U.S. Army, Europe, followed in 1954. The next summer brought relocation to Berlin as Chief of Staff, Berlin Command. He completed a much-lauded tour in the divided city in January 1957. Barsanti then returned to the United States to attend National War College. Two significant Pentagon postings followed graduation in 1958. The first, a three-year assignment, was as Chief, Requirements Division, Office of the Deputy Chief of Staff for Personnel, Department of the Army. The second took him to the Joint Staff as Chief of the Manpower Division, where he remained until mid-1963.

After his extended time in Washington, tours in the Pacific and in Europe followed. In the Pacific, he was Assistant Division Commander for Combat Operations with the 7th Infantry Division based at Camp Casey, South Korea. He pinned on his first star on September 1, 1963. Exactly one year later, he was in Europe as Comptroller, Headquarters United States European Command. He held those duties until May 1966, when he became Chief of Staff V Corps. After only four and a half months in that billet, he was reassigned to Washington DC, as Comptroller and Director of Programs with the U.S. Army Materiel Command. He was in that position when he was promoted to major general on May 1, 1967.

In July, General Barsanti took command of the 101st Airborne Division. His tenure lasted only one year, but his accomplishments and those of his fabled division during that time were among the most significant in the fabled history of the unit.

Following his service in Vietnam, Barsanti was appointed Chief of Staff, Fifth U.S. Army. He assumed those duties on August 15, 1968, at Fort Sheridan, Illinois. His career cut short by cancer, Barsanti retired from active duty on August 31, 1971, after 33 years of service.

Though desperately ill, he worked for a few months as executive assistant to the president of the American Automobile Manufacturers Association. Eventually, when the illness became debilitating, he relocated to Chicago. He died there on May 2, 1973. He was buried at Arlington National Cemetery.

THE DISSENTERS

Even today, decades after the last shots were fired by an American soldier on a Vietnam battlefield, the war will not "go away." Discussions—often divisive in nature—persist regarding many aspects of the conflict. Books and articles whose titles reflect the divergence of views continue to be published: *Autopsy of an Unwinnable War: Vietnam* (William C. Haponski, Jerry J. Burcham et al., Casemate, 2019) and *Vietnam: The History of an Unwinnable War, 1945–1975* (John Prados, University of Kansas Press, 2009) share bookstore shelf space with "The War We Could Have Won" (Stephen J. Morris, *New York Times*, May 1, 2005).

Among the most controversial issues, even among those who supported America's participation in the conflict, is the lasting debate regarding the manner in which U.S. political and military leaders chose to fight the war. Aided often by the benefit of hindsight, over the years many analysts have called into question General William C. Westmoreland's overriding emphasis on massive firepower in an attempt to hammer Viet Cong and North Vietnamese forces into submission.

There were, however, an intrepid few who, during the course of the conflict, called that strategy into question despite risks to their own reputations and careers. Foremost among them were John Paul Vann, Edward Lansdale, and Victor Krulak.

Vann, Lansdale, and Krulak held substantial positions during the war. While their time "in country" sometimes overlapped, their duties did not often bring them together professionally in any direct, meaningful way. Vann and Lansdale were friends and mutual admirers. All were acquaintances. Their views on the war and how best to wage it differed to some extent in nature and the emphasis each gave to certain aspects, but collectively their notions were supportive and had elements in common.

Dissenter: John Paul Vann

"The Closest America Comes in Vietnam
to Having a Lawrence of Arabia"

One of the most legendary figures of the Vietnam conflict, Vann spent years in Vietnam as an Army officer and later as one of the few civilians ever to command troops in combat. He ingratiated himself with the civilian populace and believed the keys to success were to provide security to the countryside, pacify it mainly through small unit actions, adequately train the South Vietnamese forces, and reform the Saigon regime. U.S. ARMY—U.S. ARMY HISTORY AND EDUCATION COMMAND

Along the continuum of America's extended involvement in Vietnam, John Paul Vann was the second of the major dissenters to arrive in country. (Edward Lansdale was the first, serving an initial 1954–56 tour.) Almost from the time in March 1962 that Vann first set foot on the soil of Vietnam, he became a larger-than-life figure—"the closest the U.S. came in Vietnam to having a Lawrence of Arabia." He carried with him an ebullient conviction that the United States would ultimately prevail if the war was fought with sound strategy and tactics.

Vann's reputation, established immediately, was that he was "outspoken professionally and fearless in battle." He became an early critic of American strategy, judging it to be ineffective and needlessly brutal. A better approach, he believed, would be to deploy small units on aggressive patrols rather than commit large formations backed by massive firepower, which he thought was too often wielded indiscriminately. In his judgment, understanding of, and interaction with, Vietnamese society was essential to success, as was a much more profound commitment to effectively training South Vietnamese forces. Unlike many of his colleagues, he accepted the fact that the war would be a long one, but believed that if it was conducted effectively it could be successfully waged at a lower level of intensity.

Vann's first tour in Vietnam ended in April 1963. Subsequently assigned to the Pentagon, he retired from the Army as a 39-year-old lieutenant colonel on July 31 of that year. Vann spent his final three months in Washington, DC, cautioning senior officials and military decision-makers that the war was being mishandled and advocating a revised political approach and a revamped military strategy.

Vann returned to Vietnam in 1965 as a U.S. government civilian employee, working ostensibly in pacification programs. Until his death seven years later he seldom left the country. When he did so, the trips were often Christmas visits or, in later years, occasions that allowed him to brief senior personages such as President Richard Nixon, Secretary of State Henry Kissinger, or Secretary of Defense Melvin Laird. He rose eventually to major general equivalency and in an unparalleled circumstance became the first American civilian to command major forces in battle.

A battle fought during his first tour played a seminal role in shaping Vann's views and establishing his persona among colleagues and members of the media. Vann, "a wire-thin stick of ferocious energy and aggression," was serving as an advisor to the ARVN 7th Division in the Mekong Delta. On January 2, 1963, the division fought Viet Cong formations at Ap Bac, a small hamlet 14 miles northwest of the larger town of My Tho. The battle was a debacle. Intelligence misstated enemy strength; ARVN command-ers lacked aggressiveness; there were grave shortcomings in fire support, communications, and medical evacuation. A myriad of other areas were exposed as seriously deficient. It was as if the South Vietnamese Army had been introduced to the principles of war and had consciously chosen to violate all of them.

Vann was outraged. His accusation of incompetence on the part of Vietnamese commanders was not a burning ember that most American officials dared to touch. Equally bothersome in his view was that the American chain of command reaching to the very top had a "tendency to play down the real picture." He went so far as to caution high-ranking officials that General Paul D. Harkins, commander, MACV, was allowing himself to be duped by misleading reports that sugarcoated failures and ascribed positive outcomes to encounters that were at best drawn battles if not outright defeats.

Early on, Vann became convinced that prospects for success in the war were hindered greatly by the character of South Vietnam President Ngo Dinh Diem's regime and urged that it be overhauled. He was highly critical of the incompetence, vice, and venality he observed in the senior officer corps of the ARVN forces but was equally as incensed with the American military system as it operated in Vietnam, judging it to be arrogant and rife with corruption. He would later also object strongly to the tour rotation policies employed by American military services. His assessment of the effects of the rapid turnover of personnel has been famously quoted: "The United States has not been in Vietnam for nine years, but for one year nine times."

His concerns about Ap Bac and conditions in general, voiced openly to senior civilian and military officials, were ignored. Reports from the ambassador and ranking generals to counterparts in Washington, DC, continued to paint a picture of almost universal success. Vann, almost constantly in the field, saw the situation as deteriorating. He responded to the lack of attention given to his assessments by cultivating relation-ships with influential members of the media and leaking meticulously documented material to them.

Ap Bac, or more precisely Vann's actions following it, made him a favorite, a trusted source, for journalists such as David Halberstam, *The New York Times*; Malcolm Brown, the Associated Press; and Neil Shee-han, United Press International. To them, Vann's "irreverent candor was a refreshing antidote to the overweening optimism of prominent American officials both in Saigon and Washington." Vann had openly asserted that "Ap Bac had been a miserable damn performance" and commented on the enemy's skill and the ARVN's seeming reluctance to fight. From the days following Ap Bac until he left Vietnam for the first time, he advised media, and his superiors, of instances of malfeasance, bungling, and deceit.

These media leaks and Vann's freewheeling relationship with the press infuriated his superiors. He was frequently threatened with firing. Undeterred, he continued to supply information that contradicted the "official version" of the war flowing to the media from the embassy and MACV channels.

General Harkins likely concluded that firing Vann would outrage the media, whose correspondents regarded him as being one of the few officials whose word was trustworthy. Perhaps also because of his energy, battlefield exploits, and obvious competence, Vann's presence was tolerated until his tour ended.

In 1965, two years after he retired from the military, Vann returned to Vietnam as a senior U.S. government civilian employee. Foreign Service officer Douglas Ramsey described him at the time as "smart, determined, [with] reverse-slanting eyes, somewhat reminiscent of movie star Lloyd Bridges, which transfixed you like blue-gray laser beams. His voice was slightly harsh, with a southern Virginia accent. He was fairly short, with blond hair thinning at the front and at forty-one, he was beginning to develop a slight paunch." Another source depicted him as a "small man with an outsize command presence." Colleagues almost unanimously cited his extreme physical vitality and a level of energy that with four hours of sleep routinely carried him through 16-hour workdays.

Vann was eventually assigned to rural pacification operations in 11 provinces in the central highlands area, holding a civilian-grade equivalent to that of a two-star general. As usual, he was a dynamo of action, flying missions and driving an International Scout—a four-wheeled utility vehicle—over roads that few others dared to travel.

His management style was intense, all-consuming, aggressive. As described by his colleague Doug Ramsey, "He wanted to know everything about everything. With his prodigious memory, and eye for detail, he could have been an immensely successful administrator . . . save that he cherished a passion for action. He described himself as a Virginia redneck at heart, and maybe he was. His loyalty to friends and loathing for foes was absolute. He was a fabulous networker, cultivating ruthlessly and usually successfully the acquaintances of anyone who might fit his purpose." Those who worked with him thought that he may have been personally acquainted with more Vietnamese than any other American. He ingratiated himself with the civilian population by often staying in hamlets with ARVN soldiers.

Along the way, he accumulated critics as well as admirers. He was seen by some as acting the part of a local warlord. Most others saw him in a more positive light. General Frederick Weyand said, "He was one guy I would have trusted with my life." Another acquaintance spoke of Vann's grasp of the realities in Vietnam and of the war in general, and his unwillingness to "play games" to please American officials and audiences.

While Vann never hesitated to use whatever force the circumstances demanded, he remained a critic of rampant bombing and shelling, labeling the (in his view) indiscriminate use of firepower as cruel and self-defeating. In 1967, he told General William C. Westmoreland, Harkins's successor as MACV Commander, that his (Westmoreland's) strategy was not working in the countryside; indeed, security was worsening. A short time later, these comments were vindicated when, in January 1968, North Vietnamese and Viet Cong forces launched the massive, nationwide Tet Offensive.

Vann's views on how to fight the war contrasted significantly with Westmoreland's in another area as well. Vann believed the South Vietnamese Army should be shown how to fight and then, with American assistance, prodded into waging it with conviction. In contrast, Westmoreland believed that massive American firepower should be employed to destroy Viet Cong and North Vietnamese formations, after which the war could be turned over to South Vietnamese units.

Political and social actions programs—key aspects of Vann's approach—did not hold much interest for Westmoreland. Vann thought that as long as South Vietnam had a government relatively unconcerned with the welfare of its citizens, one that institutionalized injustice and depredation on the rural citizenry, military actions alone would not suffice. Too many government leaders, he thought, were morally bankrupt or incompetent.

Almost to the last, Vann believed that if the South Vietnamese government was reformed, and the army and the civilian population were given an alternative to turn to, the social revolution could be "stolen" from communist cadres. In much of the countryside controlled by Viet Cong cadres, Vann assessed their hold as being shallow. The population, in his judgment, had not bonded with the occupiers.

Vann's early and persisting impression of the South Vietnamese Army was that large segments of it had a sense of inferiority due to incompetent leadership, low morale, and poor discipline. Army units seemed intimidated by their adversaries. Then, too, ARVN soldiers too often mistreated prisoners and abused civilians. By contrast, the Viet Cong's treatment of civilians, if not always pristine, was markedly better than that of ARVN units and government functionaries. If properly handled, Vann believed all those problems could be fixed.

In Vann's paradigm, good things would happen by providing security to the rural areas: better intelligence would be forthcoming, and stable conditions would allow the establishment of schools and medical facilities. Clean water systems and unthreatened crop cycles would be more readily attainable. In Vann's idealized view of the military profession, the soldier was the champion of the weak.

The change of administrations in Washington, DC, brought Richard Nixon to power and, with it, a plan for eventual "Vietnamization" of the war. Though Nixon later admitted that he had no "secret plan" for ending the war (contrary to his assertion during his campaign for the presidency), he did have the firm conviction that periodic troop withdrawals would buy time from the American public while the combat role could increasingly be turned over to a better trained and equipped South Vietnamese Army.

Nixon's notion was in general conformity with Vann's view that substantial U.S. forces could be withdrawn if the South Vietnamese were shown how to fight and then prodded into doing so. U.S. forces would assume an advisory role and provide technical support and aviation assets.

In retrospect, it seems that Vann's idealized notion would have called for U.S. troops to secure Saigon and the posts, airfields, and inland cities that could not, as a matter of prestige, be lost. American soldiers would serve as a garrison and emergency reserve force. They would be deployed offensively only in those rare occasions when a large enemy force had been well located, circumstances favored the Americans, and there was little danger of civilian casualties. The primary (unspoken) mission of U.S. troops would be political—to provide the muscle to stop the roulette wheel of coups and countercoups and bring Saigon generals to heel. Behind this shield, the U.S. would in essence take over the regime and gradually interpose leaders who were not fundamentally corrupt. South Vietnamese forces, not American troops, would do most of the fighting in the countryside. ARVN formations would be reorganized to carry the burden of fighting and pacification in the hamlets. This could be accomplished by creating a "joint command" in which Americans would issue the orders in a combined leadership arrangement.

Late in the war, Vann was provided with an opportunity to test his theories. He was allowed to install an experimental program in the 11 provinces under his jurisdiction. A single official (Vann, ostensibly, in concert with a cooperative South Vietnamese general) would control all military units—U.S. as well as South Vietnamese. Operating through a separate chain of command with higher headquarters, the official would also guide all aid and pacification programs. The leader would also possess the responsibility for the hiring and firing of military officials—American advisors included—and civilian provincial administrators. Under Vann's tutelage, the quality of the latter group was quickly and decidedly improved. In a short time, Vann stopped the forced relocation of civilians in the countryside and halted unobserved artillery and mortar fire in most areas.

In a mutually agreed-upon arrangement, Vann shared command of 158,000 ARVN troops. Though somewhat covert in nature, the structure was made possible (and successful) because of Vann's strong personal relationship with his Vietnamese counterparts. In his interactions with the Vietnamese, he sought to spotlight their presence, thus making their units and commanders more visible. Concurrently, he mentored the leadership cadre and, where useful, integrated unique American capabilities into local unit operations. At the tactical level, a product of his networking and contacts was his ability to quickly call upon B-52 strikes in dire circumstances. It was an aspect of his leadership much lauded and highly appreciated by his ARVN counterparts.

On March 30, 1972, the North Vietnamese launched a massive thrust—the so-called Easter Offensive—against the South. Intended as a war-winning strike, the incursion was, like Tet, immense in size and scope. Vann, in his two-star equivalent capacity, shifted his forces and met the assault with a crescendo of air strikes that obliterated some attacking units, inflicting perhaps as many as 40,000 casualties. Max Boot, among other historians, concluded that Vann had "rendered invaluable assistance in stopping the offensive."

B-52 strikes and similar heavy firepower interventions gradually assumed a more prominent role in Vann's warfighting repertoire as overall conditions across the country became more tenuous. Along the spectrum of war, combat was shifting from a guerilla insurgency focus toward more conventional warfare between main force units of North and South Vietnam. Vann noted the change and altered his approach accordingly, although he seemed never to have abandoned his basic beliefs regarding the utility of small unit actions, the need to reform the government, and the essential requirement to "win" at the local level. Toward the end, out of necessity in the face of changing conditions, Vann's views morphed in the direction of the combat-heavy approach that he had criticized early in the war.

Frustrated or perhaps made incredulous by the way the war was playing out—a war he thought the U.S. could win—he developed an obsession for victory that transformed him. In the last months of his life Vann waged war with prodigious energy, flying combat, reconnaissance, and resupply missions; personally directing air support, calling in air strikes, and goading commanders to be more aggressive.

During the course of the campaign Vann flew into countless battles, seemingly indifferent to incoming rounds, taking risks that far surpassed the bounds of reasoned prudence. The encounter that took his life on June 8, 1972, was representative of dozens of other death-challenging missions he had flown in recent months. On a Kiowa helicopter flight from Pleiku to Kontum, he directed his substitute pilot to intervene in an ongoing firefight. Flying in conditions of low visibility, rain squalls, and fog, the helicopter crashed. All on board—the pilot, who, it is conjectured, may have experienced vertigo; a passenger; and John Paul Vann—were killed.

Vann's funeral at Arlington National Cemetery a week later was attended by, among others, the secretaries of state and defense, and his fellow dissenter, Edward Lansdale. Among the eight official pallbearers were General William C. Westmoreland, now chief of staff, U.S. Army; General Bruce Palmer Jr., Army vice chief of staff; Lieutenant General Richard Stilwell; deputy chief of staff for military operations; William Colby, director of the Central Intelligence Agency; and a South Vietnamese Army colonel.

Following his funeral, the Vann family went to the White House where President Nixon, prohibited from awarding the Congressional Medal of Honor because of Vann's official status as a civilian employee, posthumously presented him with the Presidential Medal of Freedom.

Vann's death was seen by some as the end of an era. In the words of one scholar, "Vann treated Vietnam as if the struggle was his personal property, so that observers found it impossible to imagine Vann without war and war without Vann. His courage was that of a near madman, yet one who was intelligent enough maybe to know, in his heart, that he was striving to defy destiny."

While Vann's views shifted over the years, it seems apparent that his central convictions—a need to reform the South Vietnamese government and the essential role of South Vietnamese military forces—remained firm. His words to U.S. Ambassador Henry Cabot Lodge years before were prophetic: "If the war is to be won, it must be done by the Vietnamese—nothing would be more foolhardy than the employment of U.S. (or any other foreign) troops in quantity. We could pour our entire army into Vietnam and accomplish nothing workable."

Dissenter: Edward Lansdale

"One of the Most Unconventional Generals"

Lansdale's initial notoriety came from assisting the Philippines in defeating a communist insurgency. When the Geneva Accords divided Vietnam, Lansdale facilitated the transfer of nearly a million North Vietnamese to the South. He was a constant advocate of social programs for the people and urged the South Vietnamese political leaders to meet and interact with the civilian population. He maintained those views throughout the conflict, despite a combination of circumstances that reduced his influence in the later stages of the war.
U.S. AIR FORCE—U.S. AIR FORCE HISTORY OFFICE

Edward Lansdale was a most unusual warrior who, if allowed, would have waged counterinsurgency warfare by very uncharacteristic means. Like John Paul Vann, Edward Lansdale was sometimes referred to in Lawrence of Arabia terms. Like Vann also, Lansdale was an advocate of "soft power." The key to successful counterinsurgency, he believed, was to create legitimate, democratic government institutions that were accountable to the people and could command their loyalty and support.

While Lansdale recognized the need for violent measures against armed insurgents, he thought that properly designed political and social actions programs could relieve or eliminate the roots of rebellion. Large formations of foreign troops were counterproductive to that goal. Lansdale advocated what would come to be known as "population-centric" counterinsurgency doctrine. Terrorists would be identified and hunted down while effective government programs administered by trained, dedicated military and civilian officials would attract the support of the civilian population.

Many who later assessed his career—critics and admirers alike—attributed his effectiveness to an almost otherworldly gift for establishing rapport with foreign nationals. Lansdale first worked that magic in the Philippines, helping Secretary for National Defense, and later President, Ramon Magsaysay put down the Huk (Hukbalahap) rebellion and establishing a functioning, democratic government that had undisputed popular support. Later, he assisted South Vietnamese President Ngo Dinh Diem with the birth of the South Vietnamese republic. Walt Rostow, one of President Lyndon B. Johnson's key advisors, said of Lansdale, "I've met a handful of people in my life who have this particular genius for dealing with people in ways that make them feel dignified. Ed Lansdale was one such man."

Another colleague said, "What I respected [about Lansdale] was that with both American and Vietnamese, he was a good listener and a smooth calculator. He displayed a very good understanding of what was possible and what was not."

Lansdale's exploits in the Philippines paved his road to Vietnam. His work in helping Magsaysay defeat the communist insurgency earned him the reputation as one of the United States' most knowledgeable experts on guerilla warfare. Lansdale and Magsaysay made a formidable team. Lansdale became Magsaysay's closest companion, traveling with him, advising him, providing him with ideas and material for speeches. Under the guidance of Lansdale, a former public relations man, Magsaysay became a folk hero to Filipinos. Lansdale made him visible, moved him among the rural population, had him speak of unity and the future, and urged him successfully to implement programs with widespread popular appeal: water purification, road building, education, and many others. Land reform legislation was also introduced, and lawyers were provided to defend tenants against landlords. Election laws were fairly and fully enforced. Army training emphasized treating the population with civility. Inept officers were removed. With Lansdale's encouragement and guidance, Magsaysay's reforms won over the Filipino populace. The ever-increasing swell of popular support enabled the two men to create an excellent intelligence service. Their success in this area was further abetted by reforms that turned the Philippine Army and paramilitary constabulary into disciplined organizations with high morale. Huk cadres began surrendering in large numbers and were given amnesty. With popular support declining, the rebellion withered on the vine. Lansdale and Magsaysay had waged a brilliant, successful counterinsurgency campaign.

The war in the Philippines was a transformational experience for Lansdale. His deep and prolonged immersion in counterinsurgency warfare shaped his convictions on how to wage that unique type of combat—and, in the words of one noted historian, made him "one of the most unconventional generals in U.S. history."

After the French defeat at Dien Bien Phu in 1954, the Geneva Peace Conference carved Indochina into a communist North, a democratic South, and a neutral Laos. In the muddled situation that followed, many analysts in the United States became alarmed by actions taken by the North, which seemed to evince a clear ultimate intention of gaining control of the South. Low-intensity strife began almost immediately, and large-scale assassinations of village and provincial leaders soon followed.

To many observers, including Secretary of State John Foster Dulles, the flow of events seemed to reprise the early days of the struggle in the Philippines. Dulles called on Lansdale, instructing him to go to South Vietnam and "do what you did in the Philippines."

Lansdale arrived in Vietnam on June 1, 1954. He was 49 years old. Slim and slender at five feet, ten inches tall and 160 pounds, he maintained a youthful appearance throughout his life. Later, he added a clipped mustache that complemented his closely trimmed hair. There was no mistaking his military background.

Lansdale's mission was to assemble a team "to undertake paramilitary operations against the enemy and to wage political-psychological warfare." As a first step he established an organization called the Saigon Military Mission, a mostly covert group of soldiers and intelligence agents. The mission cadre included "dirty tricks" specialists whose purposes, among others, included sowing dissention between Hanoi and China and fostering anti-communism in the North. Later, after the signing of the Geneva Accords, several agents were embedded in the North. None of these first initiatives achieved anything more than minimal results.

More successful—markedly so—was Lansdale's role in the massive movement of refugees from North Vietnam to the South after the Accords were signed. In many ways, the enormous exodus—nearly a million people total—was a precursor to the flight of the boat people that would take place 21 years later. Lansdale abetted the move, plying on religious themes, rumors of atrocities perpetrated by Hanoi, superstitions, and bribes to astrologers that predicted coming catastrophes. Perhaps 600,000 of those who fled to the South were of the Roman Catholic faith—a bloc that would provide Ngo Dinh Diem and his government with an ardent anti-communist constituency.

Constantly in motion, Lansdale propelled Operation Exodus, as the evacuation was labeled, to unanticipated levels of success. Rather quickly, entire villages were emptied as residents fled south. In some areas, as much as 65 percent of the North's rural population joined in the flight. Orchestrated with his assistance, the U.S. Seventh Fleet and a CIA-run Civil Air Transport organization (operated by Claire Chennault of Flying Tiger fame) transported evacuees to the south. Many analysts believe that without Lansdale's efforts, the U.S. venture in Vietnam would have failed from the outset.

To skeptics who attributed the overwhelming response to his manipulations, Lansdale replied, "People don't just pull up their roots and transplant themselves because of slogans. They honestly knew what might happen to them, and the emotion was strong enough to overcome their attachment to their land and their ancestors' graves. So the initiative was very much theirs—and we merely made the transportation available."

It seems unlikely that Ngo Dien Diem's presidency would have survived without him. The former ad man with the persuasive charm established a personal relationship with Diem that seemed to hold considerable long-term promise. In the months that followed, Lansdale, through finesse, bribery, cajoling, and coercion, thwarted a coup attempt by senior military officers, defeated Cao Dai and Hoa Hoa sects (both with private armies) that sought to exert control, and eventually marginalized the Binh Xuyen, a powerful organized crime society that wielded considerable influence in Saigon.

Lansdale spent portions of almost every day with Diem, helping him plan and encouraging him to "win the hearts and minds" of the Vietnamese people. As in the Philippines, he pressed Diem to launch land reform programs that would undercut the communists' appeal and to take action to stop the injustices perpetrated by provincial landlords. Lansdale cautioned Diem that the establishment of a South Vietnamese nation must become a visible, heartfelt cause to which the populace would attach themselves. He urged Diem to hold public forums throughout the country, form a coalition of democratic parties, and adopt a democratic constitution.

In October 1956 South Vietnam held a nationwide referendum to determine the fledgling nation's head of state. Opposing Ngo Dinh Diem was Emperor Bao Dai. Lansdale's efforts contributed to Diem's overwhelming victory. Among other actions, Lansdale had Diem's ballot printed in red—a lucky color in the Vietnamese culture. Bao Dai's ballot was printed in green, a color connoting misfortune. By some accounts, his actions may have denied the communists the level of instability that would have fueled their attempt to gain control.

Critics inside and outside the American administration were concerned by Diem's tendency toward authoritarianism. Lansdale defended Diem in the face of an attempt by U.S. envoy J. Lawton Collins to remove him. In a briefing to President Dwight D. Eisenhower, Lansdale convinced the administration to stay with Diem, arguing that Diem could govern successfully and that South Vietnam could be built into a viable nation and a reliable ally of the United States.

Lansdale's first tour in Vietnam ended in 1956. Though for a considerable time in the early years the Diem regime fought the insurgent forces to a standstill, the majority of the reforms urged by Lansdale never took hold or were indifferently pursued. Several factors contributed to those outcomes. First and foremost was Lansdale's absence. Without his presence, there was no countervailing pressure to urge Diem toward reforms. Under Lansdale's tutelage, Diem's visits to the countryside were mostly well, if modestly, received, but Diem was always an uncomfortable, reluctant campaigner. When Lansdale left, positive momentum dissipated. Diem became increasingly influenced by his brother Nhu and his sister-in-law Madame Nhu (eventually labeled the "Dragon Lady" by the Western press). Both were dominant and autocratic personalities. Another brother, Ngo Dinh Thuc was the Catholic archbishop of Hue. A third, Ngo Dinh Can was the political boss of the central region of South Vietnam. Collectively, the family exerted considerable influence over the political life of the new nation. Priorities, in both the military and civil sector, were heavily influenced by cronyism. Incompetent officials were seldom removed. Graft in monumental proportions became pervasive. There were very few successful or concerted attempts to restrain the malefactors or reform the structure.

Lansdale's follow-on assignment after South Vietnam was in Washington, DC, where he remained from 1957 to 1965. Except for a brief one-month sojourn in 1958, when President Eisenhower sent him back to

Vietnam to undertake an objective analysis of the military assistance program, Lansdale remained in various Pentagon positions for the next seven years. He returned from the Eisenhower-directed mission advising continued political support for Diem and continued military aid to his regime. On this and other occasions, Diem asked that Lansdale be allowed to return to Vietnam to assist him.

Soon after assuming the presidency in 1961, President John F. Kennedy requested an updated analysis of conditions in Vietnam. Lansdale was alarmed by the deteriorating situation and urged Kennedy to increase aid to Diem. In a warning that apparently stunned Kennedy, Lansdale told Kennedy that the U.S. must "show [Diem] by deeds not just words alone, that we are his friend."

Lansdale suggested that Diem be urged to broaden his government's base by establishing a Complaints and Action Commission (perhaps a forerunner of the Truth and Reconciliation Commission later instituted in South Africa). Accompanying that mission would be the forming of a coalition of opposing parties in a government of national reconciliation. An economic development commission would also be instituted, and land would be given to Viet Cong defectors. Concurrently, a psychological warfare operation would be launched against North Vietnam, and the number of American military advisors would be increased. U.S. troops would not engage in combat, but Lansdale thought their presence would be useful in bolstering the regime and providing fiber to ARVN units.

In February of that year, Lansdale was named assistant secretary of defense for special operations. Walt Rostow, now an advisor to Kennedy, urged that Lansdale be returned to Vietnam to assist newly appointed ambassador Frederick Nolting. Concurrently, Diem again officially requested Lansdale's presence.

In April, President Kennedy convened a formal Presidential Task Force on Vietnam. Lansdale was appointed Operations Officer, but his influence on the outcome was modest, despite Roswell Gilpatric, another Kennedy advisor, having said at the time that "General Lansdale is the most highly qualified officer on active duty serving in the area of counterinsurgency affairs."

Lansdale met fellow dissenter John Paul Vann at the Pentagon early in 1963. Not long after, he also became acquainted with dissenter Victor "Brute" Krulak, an influential U.S. Marine Corps officer. The outcome was not a happy one for Lansdale, who was serving at the time as Pentagon point man on Vietnam policy. As he was preparing to brief senior Department of Defense officials on his plan for Vietnam, Krulak had the briefing canceled apparently because of apprehension that it would run counter to, and divert resources from, his own proposals for conducting the war. Eventually, Krulak would usurp much of Lansdale's role and influence in this area. To those who knew Lansdale, that outcome was not a total surprise. Lansdale never acquired a facility for dealing successfully with the federal bureaucracy. Others, including Krulak, manipulated and worked through it in ways that secured more favorable outcomes.

By this time, Lansdale's views were already at loggerheads with those of many senior defense officials. Lansdale believed South Vietnam's internal problems could be successfully addressed. Many, he believed, would exist even in the absence of outside aggression. At a time when the U.S. had about 20,000 troops "in country," he did not support sending additional troops, nor did he advocate bombing North Vietnam. Instead, he favored increased emphasis on "psyops" and "black ops" and efforts to transform South Vietnam from a junta-type government to a truly broad-based democratic one more representative of the general population.

Late in the year, opponents in the bureaucracy torpedoed a proposal to return Lansdale to South Vietnam as U.S. ambassador to the increasingly troubled country. Chief among his opponents was Secretary of Defense Robert S. McNamara, a consummate bureaucratic infighter. McNamara, whose systems analysis approach placed overriding emphasis on quantifiable measures, had little patience for "hearts and minds" initiatives of the type advocated by Lansdale. Programs that were difficult or impossible to measure by putting numerical calipers around them were given short shrift, receiving low priority or none at all. McNamara shunted Lansdale into the shadows and eliminated his planning role in Vietnam matters.

Lansdale thought that the Kennedy administration should not have supported the overthrow of the Diem regime. He believed Diem to be unusually cosmopolitan and tolerant for his time and culture. With him, as with Magsaysay in the Philippines, good things could perhaps be achieved. Indeed, in the revolving door of coups that followed, the generals who succeeded Diem often seemed to have all of his shortcomings and none of his strengths. Of Diem's assassination, Lansdale said "it was morally wrong and strategically stupid to divide our political base in Vietnam when that base, small as it was, was facing an energetic and exploitive enemy."

Lansdale returned to Vietnam in 1965. By early 1966 it was clear that he would accomplish little. The old Washington, DC, cliché, to the effect that the longer the duty title, the smaller the influence, was apropos of

Lansdale's circumstance. Officially, he was "chairman of the U.S. Mission Liaison Group to the Secretary General of the Central Bureau Reconstruction Council." His duties, if they could be labeled as that, were vague and ill-defined. His role was strictly advisory; he had no power to implement or compel. And, even if he had those levers, he was given no resources to carry his proposals forward. General Westmoreland had resources to give. Ambassador Henry Cabot Lodge had the power to give them. But little if anything was forthcoming from either source. Lansdale was marginalized and ignored.

At any rate, by this point in the war, prospects for counterinsurgency programs were increasingly dim. President Johnson, with U.S. prestige and his own reputation at stake, wanted the war to be fought urgently and forcefully. Cooperative efforts with South Vietnamese and counterinsurgency programs would take too long. Support for hearts and minds initiatives, already limited, subsided further.

Eventually, Lansdale worked mainly in pacification matters, using his remaining reservoir of credibility to do what he could to influence opinions on issues of significance to him. As an advisor/liaison without any real power, he had ideas and proposals that were sometimes seen as meddling or as a challenge to the authority of the officials and bureaucrats who held positions of influence. Many were not reluctant to undercut him or indict him in leaks to the media. Lansdale completed his second tour in Vietnam in 1968, having accomplished little of substance.

Still, Lansdale's reputation was such that he was asked to brief the incoming Nixon administration on the situation in Vietnam. In a meeting with President-elect Nixon and his National Security Advisor Henry Kissinger, Lansdale noted that a politically viable South Vietnam nation did not yet exist. He believed that North Vietnam, with its combat capability steadily improving, had the momentum militarily, whereas, at the same time, the American public was growing tired of the war. Still, he cautioned against either withdrawal or further escalation, suggesting instead that additional aid to South Vietnam be contingent "upon their doing their utmost to live up to the ideas and principles of their own constitution."

Lansdale's meeting with Nixon and Kissinger was one of his last substantive activities. Soon after, he retired from government service.

After his service in World War II, Lansdale had been ahead of his contemporaries in his assessment that, in the future, the United States would be engaged far more often in guerilla-type conflicts than in large-scale conventional warfare. Along with his belief that the American military establishment was not adequately prepared to operate in the environment, it was a conviction he would maintain throughout the rest of his service.

Three proposals were representative of the many that would follow over the years. None of the three was enacted to the fullest extent. The first, had it taken root, would have been the most sweeping. The idea called for U.S. military personnel to be indoctrinated in counterinsurgency warfare. The second was to assign counterinsurgency specialists to the Military Assistance and Advisory Groups (MAAGs) stationed around the globe. Third, Lansdale called for U.S. troops to periodically attend counterinsurgency seminars.

It appears that despite the travails of his being shunted aside and his ideas ignored, Lansdale never lost his faith in counterinsurgency programs or his conviction that proper application of them would have made a difference. His belief in "soft power" seemingly never wavered. He advocated scaling back massive application of firepower while taking steps to make the Saigon regime more accountable, legitimate, and popular. He believed that the actions of individual soldiers could be very influential, and that it was important for the military establishment to identify with the people. Not only should native forces be trained in military matters, but they should also be prepared to assist in projects—roads, flood control, pacification, and others—that would tie them more clearly to the nation's citizenry.

Similarly, in Lansdale's paradigm, the example set by American advisors assumed enormous importance; they should provide a national ideal for indigenous troops to admire and emulate. To Lansdale, the best weapon in fighting a guerilla insurgency was a well-rounded soldier, diplomat, or agent who could deal sympathetically with the local population. It is, he said, "damn hard for guerillas to get the people to help them throw down a government that the people feel is their very own."

Lansdale's proposal met with mixed reactions, not only among his colleagues and superiors but also among members of the American media that, as the massive buildup of forces took place in the mid-1960s, swarmed into Vietnam in impressive numbers. Some of these relative latecomers saw him as naïve, a romantic loose cannon. To his harshest critics, statements such as "Communist guerillas hide among the people. If you win the people over to your side, the guerillas have no place to hide. With no place to hide, you can find them: Then, as soldiers, fix them . . . finish them" smacked of chamber of commerce slogans. Others assessed him as being a foreigner who did not understand the complexities of the local culture, and whose proposals, though well-intentioned, were of little consequence on those rare occasions when they were enacted.

Conversely, to some students and scholars, and to his legions of devoted supporters, Lansdale was a visionary who exemplified the best kind of American representative—a military expert adept not only in warfare but also in helping the people of the nation under duress.

In later years some observers commented that the most vocal critics were those latecomers who had known Lansdale and the situation in Vietnam only from a mid-1960s perspective. By that point, Lansdale was in an advisory position without real influence. Most had not seen him in action or known of his accomplishments—Operation Exodus, for example, or his role in establishing and holding together a new nation—in the early days.

To the very end, he advocated inserting Americans of exceptional talent in appropriate areas of the South Vietnamese government and military to instill the spark that was often missing and provide operational guidance. Even as the war increased in intensity, he believed that approach held more promise for success than large numbers of foreign troops tramping around the countryside and massive applications of firepower that too often resulted in unacceptable numbers of civilian casualties. He did not, however, advocate the complete withdrawal of American forces, and he accurately predicted the bloodshed and mass exodus that would follow when American troops departed. In Lansdale's ultimate assessment of the conflict, the basic U.S. approach was flawed: "We [the U.S. military] sought to destroy enemy forces. The enemy sought to gain control of the people."

Throughout their later lives, colleagues who sympathized with his views continued to believe that Lansdale's program of social actions could have saved South Vietnam. Others, not quite as certain that the outcome could have been altered, thought his approach would have made the war less costly and more politically successful.

When the war and Lansdale's life were over, it was the considered assessment of William Conrad Gibbons, a noted chronicler of the Vietnam War, that "one of the tragedies of the whole thing was that [Lansdale] was never put in charge . . . he had more of an ability to deal with people than almost any other American. . . . Of all the people, he had the best understanding of what we ought to do."

Edward Lansdale died February 23, 1987. He was buried at Arlington National Cemetery.

Dissenter: Victor H. "Brute" Krulak

A General Who Understood the Mind of His Enemy

"Brute" Krulak was one of the few officers in the military who had "the capacity for innovative genius." Krulak shared many of the views of Vann and Lansdale and advocated a Combined Action Program that merged military action, mainly through embedded small units, with civic action programs. He suggested integrating American and South Vietnamese units. Krulak directly confronted both General William C. Westmoreland, commander of U.S. forces in Vietnam, and President Lyndon B. Johnson, contradicting their views and arguing forcefully for a different approach to the war. U.S. MARINE CORPS—U.S. MARINE CORPS HISTORY DIVISION

The third of the major dissenters was a diminutive five-foot, four-inch, 138-pound lieutenant general in the United States Marine Corps. "Brute" was a sobriquet hung on him by his Naval Academy classmates. Intended to poke fun at his small size, the label stuck, to his great satisfaction. He would revel in it for the rest of his life—even his wife called him "Brute."

Krulak did not begin the war in Vietnam as a critic. Early in the conflict, not yet immersed in the dynamics of the war, he was inclined to tolerate, if not fully accept, the attrition-based strategy of General Paul Harkins, U.S. military commander in Vietnam. An aggressive, highly ambitious self-promoter, Krulak was not initially prepared to "rock the boat" on an issue that could hinder his goal of becoming commandant of the Marine

Corps. His views would change markedly over time, and he would come to share the frustrations felt by John Paul Vann and Edward Lansdale.

On February 16, 1962, with President Kennedy's approval, Krulak (then a major general) was appointed to the newly created position of special assistant for counterinsurgency and special activities with direct reporting to Secretary of Defense Robert S. McNamara. Krulak's appointment was seen by most observers as a logical progression in the career of an officer who, inside the Marine Corps, was already viewed as near-legendary in status. Since his junior officer days, he had been a trusted advisor and confidant of senior officers who relied on him implicitly for counsel, planning, and leadership roles in make-or-break activities.

Vietnam would be Krulak's fourth war.

He was in Shanghai in 1937 when the Japanese attacked and overran the Chinese garrison. From his post in the International Settlement section of the city, Krulak inserted himself directly into the conflict. Sometimes finding himself in the middle of the fighting, he took photos and made detailed notes, transforming them into a report that, probably for the first time in a comprehensive way, delineated how the Japanese Army made war.

More importantly for the Marine Corps and the United States, he recorded in great detail the design of the Japanese landing craft he saw in action at Shanghai. At a time when the United States Navy had only 18 landing barges—those left over from the Spanish-American War—Krulak knew immediately that vessels similar to those used by the Japanese would be ideally suited to the Marines' mission. The Japanese craft featured bows that opened and forward landing ramps. After dispersing troops and equipment, the vessels could be reversed, backed off the beach, pivoted in the water, and returned to the parent ship for repeated loads.

What emerged over the next few years had elements of a Hollywood script. The Navy bureaucracy ignored Krulak's design and recommendations. Krulak built a model and, as a junior officer, demonstrated it to the commandant of the Marine Corps, winning his immediate approval. Krulak then formed a symbiotic relationship with shipbuilder Andrew Jackson Higgins, who quickly built a prototype vessel. Still not convinced, the Navy proceeded with its own plans. Eventually, after a series of bureaucratic impediments, a competition was arranged that pitted the Navy Bureau of Ships model against the Krulak-Higgins prototype. The clear superiority of the latter convinced even the most callous Navy observers.

The landing craft was not all that emerged from the Krulak-Higgins interaction. Krulak was a key instigator in the creation of the amtrac vehicle that would prove so useful on the coral reefs and islands of the Pacific. In 62 hours, Higgins devised and built the first of the vessels that would transport the landing craft to beachheads around the world. Among many others, General Dwight D. Eisenhower, who commanded Allied forces in the European Theater, believed Higgins's boat "won the war for us."

Krulak's baptism under fire in World War II took place on October 27, 1942, when he commanded the 2nd Parachute Battalion in an attack on Choiseul in the Solomon Islands. The assault, a diversion intended to shield the forthcoming major landing on Bougainville, was superbly led, achieving its objectives while sustaining very few casualties.

Early in 1945, Krulak was tasked with planning the 6th Marine Division's role in the invasion of Okinawa. Still relatively junior at the time, Krulak exerted influence far out of proportion to the rank he held. That circumstance was not always well received by his contemporaries. Krulak "was so smart, so assertive, so *right*, that he provoked feelings of jealousy and bitterness among some of his colleagues."

The immediate postwar period saw Krulak's beginning engagement in a long-term stop-and-start series of projects aimed literally at securing the survival of the United States Marine Corps. Working initially with a small cadre at Quantico, Virginia, Krulak would over the years remain first among equals in a group that opposed plans to instill a Prussian-like general staff and ultimately unify the nation's armed forces.

Advocated by General George C. Marshall, Eisenhower, and other notables, the initial proposal called for a senior military official to be placed in charge of all military services and made solely responsible to the president. The absence of civilian control was anathema to Krulak and his colleagues, as was—crucially—what seemed to be a rather transparent attempt to greatly reduce, if not eliminate, the Marine Corps.

In various forms, the struggle would go on for years. In incremental steps the Marines' views eventually prevailed. First, the notion of a Prussian-like general staff was dispelled and the value of the Marine Corps to the nation was affirmed with the aid of a 23-minute documentary written primarily by Krulak and shown to the Armed Services Committees of both houses of Congress, individual congressmen and senators, and key administration officials. Though a considerable step forward, from the Marines' perspective the Corps was still vulnerable because the legislation did not delineate the roles of the services.

That issue was a matter of considerable consequence to the Marines because, among other opponents, the president himself had weighed in on the argument. In late 1950 President Truman replied to a letter from a congressman that lauded the Marines and praised the Corps's contribution to the nation. Truman responded with a note that said, "For your information the Marine Corps is the Navy's police force and as long as I am President that is what they will remain. They have a propaganda machine that is almost equal to Stalin's." The congressman released Truman's letter to the media and placed a copy in the Congressional Record. Truman later issued a public apology.

Eventually, with assistance from groups including the Veterans of Foreign Wars and with subsequent amendments, legislation was enacted in early 1952, which, from the Marines' viewpoint, corrected the omissions of the original National Security Act of 1947. The bill made the Corps an essentially separate service within the Department of the Navy, assured the commandant a seat on the Joint Chiefs of Staff (JCS) when Marine Corps matters were being discussed (eventually the Marines would receive a permanent seat on the JCS; in 2005 Marine General Peter Pace became the first Marine to serve as JCS chairman) and established a minimum Marine Corps structure of three divisions and three aircraft wings. The Marines were guaranteed a separate budget to carry out their mission. The bill was enacted as Public Law 416. Ushered through congress by Senator Mike Mansfield, a former Marine, the essential provisions had been written by Brute Krulak—yet another accomplishment to burnish a growing legacy.

It would not be the last.

As early as 1946, when the primitive helicopters of the day were fragile, slow, short-ranged, and limited to carrying two passengers, Krulak captured a view of the future. While most observers in all services saw the helicopter as a utility vehicle, generally limited to roles such as close-in reconnaissance and scouting, Krulak envisioned it as a potential major instrument of war. Emerging technology could, he believed, make it the pointed end of the spear in the Marines' warfighting repertoire.

Krulak, with the approval of the commandant, set out to make it happen. In a reprise of his interaction with Andrew Jackson Higgins, Krulak worked with helicopter pioneer Igor Sikorsky to begin the process of integrating helicopters into the Corps. By 1948, he had produced a 52-page manual on helicopter procedures. "Vertical envelopment" would quickly become a major facet of how the Marines went to war.

Two years later, in fighting around the Pusan Perimeter in Korea, Krulak and his Marines were already using helicopters for recon, intelligence gathering, flank security, courier service, laying communications wire, and evacuation of wounded. At the Chosin Reservoir, Krulak employed helicopters as the Marines' "eyes in the sky" during the Corps's legendary "attack in the opposite direction" move to Hungnam and safe evacuation by sea. On September 30 of the following year, 224 Marines landed on Hill 844, the first insertion of combat troops by helicopter directly into a battle. A decade later in Vietnam, helicopters would form a vital, essential component of America's ground combat striking power.

In 1955 Krulak became the first of his Naval Academy class to achieve flag rank. Another promotion and his posting as a key advisor to the president and secretary of defense seemed further evidence of a career with a virtually unlimited horizon.

Two months into his new job, Krulak's name surfaced in context with the war in Vietnam. In August, the Diem regime instituted a "strategic hamlet" initiative designed to separate the rural population from guerilla insurgents. The program was not overly demanding of U.S. resources and Krulak supported the concept, probably assessing it as being complementary to Harkins's efforts. A somewhat similar program had been employed by the British in Malaya and had met with general success. In Vietnam the program was, overall, a tactical success, but that result was achieved at considerable social and political cost.

In some areas, entire villages were uprooted and moved to locations where conditions of terrain and environment made them more suitable for defense. These moves often separated peasants from traditional tillage areas and displaced them from the family burial plots so venerated in their culture. The majority of the rural populations affected by the program did not wish to move. When analysts mentioned the negative impacts, Krulak was quoted as saying that "[the U.S.] would force the peasants to do what's necessary to make the program succeed." It was not one of his finer moments.

As the war ramped up in the months ahead, the strategic hamlet program received less emphasis. Eventually, overwhelmed by events and displaced in priority, the program withered away. Krulak supported the strategic hamlet initiative but had little connection with its application. He would soon emerge as an advocate for other programs that had population security and pacification as central themes.

On June 4, 1962, in a speech at the National War College titled "Tactics of Insurgency and Counterinsurgency," Krulak was almost dismissive of the utility of the United States' enormous military strength as a factor in the counterinsurgency battle. He told the war college students that the battle in Vietnam would be won or lost in "nameless villages and hamlets and the objective in general to be gained is not a hill or a city, but the hearts and minds of thousands of little people without whose support there can be no victory."

Soon after, he published a major paper titled "Joint Counterinsurgency Concept and Doctrinal Guidance" intended to help educate military and civilian decision-makers. With the possibility of major U.S. involvement in a different form of war increasingly apparent, Krulak saw the need for informed officials as being particularly important. Unfortunately, the document was little read by Washington elites.

While continuing at this stage to publicly support Harkins, Krulak pushed his own ideas about what for the armed forces of the day would be a new form of conflict. In a lecture to State Department officials, Krulak said that "protection is the most important thing you can bring. [Providing protection brings] health . . . land, property, education."

In September 1963 Krulak again drew the notice of senior leaders. With the war becoming an increasing concern, President Kennedy dispatched a fact-finding mission, sending Krulak and State Department representative Joseph Mendenhall to Vietnam. During a four-day tour, Mendenhall talked primarily with officials in Saigon, Hue, and Qui Nhon. Krulak hopscotched around the country, speaking with American and South Vietnamese military officers in the field.

They returned with different conclusions. Mendenhall was appalled by what he heard and saw. Krulak, by contrast, was optimistic, believing that things in general were on the right track. He told Kennedy that "the shooting war was going ahead at an impressive pace." After both men had completed their presentations, Kennedy famously asked, "You two did visit the same country, didn't you?"

It was not the first time, nor would it be the last, that decision-makers received contradictory opinions regarding the war or prospects for ultimate success.

In November 1963, subsequent to the assassination of President Ngo Dinh Diem, and with progress in the war stalemated if not deteriorating, administration officials held a major conference in Honolulu to assess proposals on how to proceed. The conferees recommended a proposal devised by Krulak. Later labeled Op Plan 34A, Krulak's idea was sponsored by Secretary of Defense McNamara at the Honolulu meeting. Following President Kennedy's death, President Johnson quickly accepted McNamara's counsel to proceed with Krulak's program.

Op Plan 34A called for large-scale clandestine warfare to be launched against the North. Believing the coastline of North Vietnam was vulnerable to hit-and-run operations, military leaders planned destructive raids that would cause substantial damage and result in economic hardship. The scope and intensity of the raids would increase incrementally as ever larger and more sweeping attacks would be forthcoming. The target set included rail lines, bridges, fishing boats, and other shipping. Eventually, strikes on larger targets such as radar sites would be conducted by parachute teams dropped farther inland. Over time, saboteurs would be dispensed throughout the North. Op Plan 34A was activated on February 1, 1964, with raids conducted by teams composed of Vietnamese, Chinese, and Filipino personnel.

The plan itself was a significantly bulked up version of an initiative originally proposed and activated a few years earlier by William Colby during his time as CIA station chief in Saigon (1959–62). Colby strongly advised against implementing the plan, citing the abject failure—"notoriously unsuccessful" in his words—of his earlier efforts. In the end, Krulak's version proved to be as devastating in cost and human lives as Colby's had been. It was later terminated, but not before bequeathing one significant footnote to history. In August 1964 U.S. Navy vessels shadowing raids by South Vietnamese commandos were attacked by North Vietnamese patrol boats. The "Gulf of Tonkin incident" sparked the eventual mass intervention of American forces and the major conflict that followed.

For a time after being appointed as special assistant for counterinsurgency, Krulak had been content to essentially accept the view of General Harkins and rely on his assessments to the president. He retained those perceptions for a considerable period, still holding them after the debacle at Ap Bac when the coterie surrounding Harkins had put a positive spin on the outcome.

A 29-page report, mostly authored by Krulak, concluded that "the essential ingredients for success have been assembled in Vietnam." The report dismissed Ap Bac as hyperbole generated by ill-informed newsmen.

As many later noted, Krulak was far too smart to continue to be taken in by reports that fictionalized events on the battlefield and constantly shaded outcomes in a favorable light. That shift in convictions was accompanied by a growing recognition that the attrition strategy, favored by some senior Army commanders, was deeply, and quite possibly fatally, flawed. Gradually, inexorably, Krulak lost confidence in the way the war was being handled and with the people who were handling it.

As Krulak became more steeped in issues associated with Vietnam, he grew rapidly as an expert on guerilla warfare. In the view of one scholar, he was a rarity in the U.S. military: "He had acquired the distinction of becoming an American military leader who understood the minds of the men in Hanoi." To those who knew him, that facility came as no surprise. Throughout a long and distinguished career, he had achieved a superb reputation—an officer whose capacity for innovative military thinking "could be described without exaggeration as genius."

For a time, like others before him, Krulak attempted to work through the system to generate the changes he believed necessary. His efforts never succeeded in changing the trajectory. In the end, like his fellow dissenters Vann and Lansdale, his attempts would close in frustration.

On March 1, 1964, Krulak was promoted to lieutenant general and assigned as commanding general, Fleet Marine Force Pacific. Headquartered near Honolulu at Camp H. M. Smith, Krulak's major official mission was to train and prepare Marines for assignment to Vietnam. Krulak construed his duties in much broader detail, extending advice to field commanders and interjecting his views on battlefield tactics and operational issues.

In the early months of 1965, Krulak selected the site of the future base at Chu Lai and drove the project to completion at a pace that shocked observers from other services. There was, at the time, no village named Chu Lai—in fact, the place chosen by Krulak was a generally flat, mostly unpopulated piece of real estate. Little known at the time was that "Chu Lai"—recalled from his days in Shanghai—was Krulak's name in Chinese.

On March 8 of that year Marines went ashore at Da Nang, the first use of U.S. ground troops in Vietnam. Ostensibly assigned to provide defense to the air base located there, these Marines were given a role that had no traction. Marines are not conditioned for defense.

Meanwhile, Krulak's difficult relationship with General William C. Westmoreland, Harkins's replacement as commander of U.S. forces in Vietnam, continued to deteriorate. Westmoreland wanted the Marines to be kept on a short leash; they were to fight the war in Vietnam the Army way. The Marines' approach was to spread security outward from populated areas. Eventually, that approach transformed into the Combined Action Program in which Marines joined with Vietnamese units. Based in hamlets, they interacted with the rural population and provided security for villages and the areas around them.

Westmoreland had little use for "hearts and minds" and believed that too many Marine resources that should have been allotted in support of his strategy were being assigned to pacification efforts. Westmoreland was irate at Krulak's speeches and proposals, which supported plans and ideas at variance with his own. During one shouted argument Westmoreland told Krulak, "Your way will take too long." Krulak replied, "Your way will take forever."

By late 1965 Krulak's disenchantment with the attrition strategy was complete. In December of that year he authored a comprehensive paper that consolidated the views that had formed after months of observation and research. Packaged in a format that he hoped would gather attention, the paper dissected the attrition strategy, pointing out its shortcomings in language that was almost clinical. The report called for action to be taken that would refocus the war and place it on a winning trajectory. There was still time to do that, he thought, but the necessary steps should begin soon.

Krulak assessed that across the spectrum of conflict, U.S. efforts were failing in both the North and the South. In the North, the gradual escalation of air raids was having little apparent effect. In the South, he warned that the ground war was nearing the point in which victory would be irretrievable.

In Krulak's judgment, attrition would continue to fail because it played directly into the enemy's hand. The North Vietnamese and Viet Cong welcomed close-in combat because it reduced the effectiveness of the U.S. advantages in artillery and air power. Further, the liberal use of massive firepower often resulted in civilian casualties. It seemed clear to Krulak that Hanoi believed that if they persisted in the war and continued to kill and maim U.S. soldiers in sufficient numbers, the American public's support for the war would eventually atrophy and the U.S. would withdraw. Krulak's attrition "arithmetic" lent further credence to his argument. In simple terms, attrition would fail because the North had more people to devote to the struggle. Krulak thought that the combined North Vietnamese and Viet Cong manpower pool numbered about two and a half million fighters. Even if the U.S. and its South Vietnamese ally achieved a 2.6 to 1 kill ratio (which he thought was optimistic), they would not "catch up" in attrition.

Despite the formidable obstacles, Krulak believed success could still be achieved. He devoted a considerable portion of his paper outlining a plan to do so. In many ways, his ideas paralleled those of John Paul Vann. Like Vann, Krulak placed emphasis on pacification, land reform, and the introduction of social and economic measures that would improve conditions, particularly among the local population.

To make that happen in the limited time that remained, Krulak called for what amounted to almost a takeover of the government of South Vietnam. In Krulak's view, the people of South Vietnam were the ultimate prize. Communist cadres derived shelter, sustenance, and intelligence information from them. The U.S. should respond by shielding the populated areas—denying them to the enemy—while concurrently pacifying the countryside and winning over the people.

Krulak thought the U.S. should focus its heaviest attacks against communist units located in sparsely populated regions where equipment capabilities and conditions of terrain were advantageous to the U.S. North Vietnamese and Viet Cong units could be hammered relentlessly from the air. Improved intelligence gathering was also a key. Much of that would come from the rural population as U.S. efforts increasingly assured their safety and reforms, which improved as their welfare took hold.

Krulak cautioned against reacting to communist initiatives by automatically seeking to bring their forces to battle. In his view, choice of strategies was a choice of outcomes. Pacification and social and economic reforms were a "design for victory." Attrition was "the route to defeat."

Krulak noted that the North was receiving increasing volumes of war materiel from the Soviet Union and China. Interdicting those supplies as they flowed South on roads and railways was ineffective, if not foolhardy, in Krulak's assessment. To be impactful, an air campaign was needed that would halt delivery to the North by bombing and mining Haiphong harbor and other ports and destroying the rail lines that entered the country from China.

Krulak devoted considerable time and effort to lobbying military and civilian decision-makers in an effort to "sell" his proposal. Like Vann's and Lansdale's, his efforts proved mostly futile. A 40-minute session with President Johnson ended abruptly when Johnson, frustrated and angry, escorted him from the Oval Office. He, and others, regarded the confrontation as foreclosing any possibility that he might someday be named commandant of the Marine Corps.

Still not willing to abandon his effort, Krulak then tried an entirely different approach. If he could not "sell" his plans to the nation's political and military leadership through presentations and briefing charts, he could convince them by demonstrating its advantages in a "live" test in the combat zone. Even General Westmoreland, he believed, would have to accept objective results on the battlefield.

Krulak established the I Corps area, South Vietnam's five northernmost provinces, as the place for his trial. If successful, the plan could then serve as a model for the rest of the country. Among other factors, Krulak chose the I Corps sector because Marines made up a significant portion of the U.S. forces assigned there, which would give him a bit more latitude.

Two other considerations—geography and population density—also made the region appealing for Krulak's demonstration. The five provinces housed a bit more than two and a half million people. Ninety-eight percent lived on one-fourth of the land area within 25 miles of the sea. Krulak's idea was to shield that population and make the area near the coastline as secure as possible. Pacification programs would then be extended outward from those base areas. As pacification progressed, those sectors would be linked together to enclose the arable land area. After that, it would not matter how many North Vietnamese and Viet Cong forces remained in the rain forests, jungles, and mountains that formed the rest of the landscape. Food, supplies, and recruits—most of which came from the local population—would no longer be accessible to them. Intelligence, the lifeblood of the enemy forces, would also be denied. Concurrently, enemy units in areas outside of Krulak's protected zone would be attacked remorselessly from the air.

In his quest to advance his proposal, Krulak had at least two friends in high places. Admiral Ulysses S. Grant Sharp, commander in chief, Pacific, and Marine General Wallace Greene Jr., Marine Corps commandant, both supported his conclusions regarding the war and his views on how best to fight it. On the ground in Vietnam, Marine Corps Major General Lewis Walt commanded U.S. forces in I Corps. Walt, a fellow Marine, shared Krulak's ideas, but his position would be difficult. In the warfighting chain of command he was directly subordinate to Westmoreland.

Westmoreland was the key—and his opposition and the actions he took would ultimately bring an end to Krulak's plans to reverse the course of the war.

Krulak had long been worried by Westmoreland's propensity to react to any and all enemy initiatives—essentially, in Krulak's opinion, too often ceding momentum to the opposing forces and allowing them to set the terms of combat.

Before Westmoreland's emphasis on the battle he had structured around Khe Sanh effectively brought an end to Krulak's experiment, Lewis Walt had worked tirelessly, and with considerable success, to cleanse hamlets of guerilla fighters and communist political cadres. He and Krulak had devised an innovative Combined Action scheme to merge Marine rifle squads with local South Vietnamese units. Marine NCOs led the combined units while a Vietnamese soldier served as deputy. Combined Action Platoons were then further merged into Combined Action Companies with the same shared leadership. Had time allowed, eventually Marines would be integrated in this fashion with every militia unit in the I Corps region. By April 1966 the units were launching 7,000 combined patrols and 5,000 night ambushes each month. At the same time, Marines were providing security for an encompassing civic action program which, under Walt's guidance, had for the first time been brought together under a single director.

Westmoreland objected that resources were being taken away from his attrition program and asserted that those that were assigned were not of the highest quality. Secretary of Defense McNamara supported Westmoreland, though Krulak had attempted to dissuade him with a long letter that encapsulated his views. In his correspondence Krulak noted that pacification efforts were achieving success. Roads throughout the five provinces in the I Corps region were increasingly safe for travel, for instance. Krulak wrote that body count—Westmoreland's primary measure of success—was an inappropriate index. Among other shortcomings, attrition wreaked havoc on the friendly inhabited areas and in the long run probably did more harm than good. To an Army officer's conjecture that the U.S. was "winning militarily," Krulak's rejoinder was that "the statement was meaningless. You cannot win militarily. You have to win totally or you are not winning at all."

As events played out, the Combined Action Program recessed in importance as thousands of American troops were fed into the struggle. It became clear that Krulak and Walt did not have sufficient forces to both support Westmoreland's strategy and do a full-scale implementation of their plans for I Corps. Westmoreland pressured Krulak and Walt, sometimes with McNamara's assistance, to get on board with his strategy. Their support was particularly important to him as he developed plans for the major set-piece battle at Khe Sanh.

As a response to communist incursions, Westmoreland determined to draw the enemy into a battle using Marines at an isolated outpost as bait. Believing that enemy leaders sought another Dien Bien Phu, Westmoreland planned to lure them into one that he would fight under favorable conditions. When the post had been invested by thousands of fighters, Westmoreland would then strike the attackers with a Niagara of aerial bombardment and artillery shells. To many, including Krulak, a reprise of

Dien Bien Phu was not a good idea. Krulak reminded Westmoreland of Mao's doctrine: "Uproar in the East, strike in the West." Krulak thought the incursions were aimed at disrupting an increasingly successful pacification program or were diversions intended to shield preparations for major attacks elsewhere. Indeed, the Tet Offensive followed soon after. Krulak accurately foresaw Khe Sanh as a failure in the making. He urged Westmoreland not to garrison the place. Eventually, 6,000 Marines would be thrown into the battle and tens of thousands of artillery shells, bombs, and mortar rounds expended on the attackers. Costly to both sides, the outcome of the battle proved to be of little consequence. Soon after the enemy forces withdrew from the fray, the post was abandoned.

Khe Sanh had another outcome as well. The butcher's bill paid for holding the post caused Krulak and Walt to abandon the pacification strategy. The aftermath was appalling. In Westmoreland's "big unit" warfare that followed, from 1967 to the end of U.S. involvement in combat operations, more than half of the American soldiers and Marines killed in action would fall in the I Corps region.

To Krulak, Khe Sanh was emblematic of the failed strategy that shrouded the entire war. When General Creighton Abrams replaced Westmoreland as commander of U.S. forces in Vietnam, he replaced Westmoreland's "search-and-destroy" strategy with a "seize-and-hold" approach and installed it in several areas across the country. There is some irony in that: the concept was in some features a modified version of Krulak's Combined Action Program.

It was all too little, too late.

Krulak retired from active duty on June 1, 1968, not having achieved his goal of becoming commandant of the Marine Corps. His postretirement years were spent in San Diego, California, where he remained active in civic affairs. He died on December 29, 2008, at age 95. He was buried at Fort Rosecrans National Cemetery.

Each of the three major dissenters, Vann, Lansdale, and Krulak, had the occasion to discuss their views with the presidents they served. Their interactions with senior officials varied considerably in their intensity and purpose as well in the length, scope, and nature of their communications. It was Krulak's fate to have the occasion—and the courage—to directly confront a president and openly contradict his views. Vann and Lansdale shared with Krulak a common virtue: the willingness to dissent. Their service, like his, was ennobled by their spirit.

In his masterful work *Brute: The Life of Victor Krulak, U.S. Marine*, Robert Coram includes the words that close this section. Not all may agree with the harshness of Coram's assessment, but to those who conjecture that war in some form will long be with us, the examples of Vann, Lansdale, and Krulak, and the words that follow, may be instructive.

> *In Vietnam, it was the job of active duty senior officers to present unvarnished advice to the president, but the generals, in every branch of the services, were silent and servile. At the end of the day, they were men of little integrity, and there is a school of thought that every one of them should have resigned in protest of LBJ's policies. Their actions, or lack thereof, did not reflect well on them or their respective branches of service, or on the fundamental character of American military leadership.*
>
> *Krulak, as far as can be determined, was the only senior general who confronted LBJ. Other generals may be quick to point out that Krulak was pushed aside and may ask what is the point of doing the right thing if you are no longer in a leadership role. But that is the response of a careerist. Krulak knew he would pay a price and he still did the right thing. At a time when he had everything to lose, he was the only general in the American military whose sense of duty and love of country were greater than his careerism.*

CHAPTER FOUR

Grenada

OPERATION URGENT FURY: THE INVASION OF GRENADA

Some pundits have suggested that an appropriate title for the Grenada chapter might be "Operation Urgent Fury: You Can Learn from a Bad Example." That title would not in any way be intended to demean the courage or the accomplishments of the military members of all branches of America's armed forces who participated in Operation Urgent Fury. Indeed, the performance of individual soldiers, sailors, airmen, and Marines was generally at a level commensurate with that associated with conflicts throughout the nation's history. Rather, the label would serve as an acknowledgment that the effort was hastily put together and revealed numerous problems in joint planning, deployment, communications, and equipment.

Though not extensively written about, Grenada was in retrospect a watershed event. The campaign revealed that the United States was inadequately prepared to conduct joint force operations in the modern era. It is to the nation's credit that the campaign was studied, lessons were learned, and, in a relatively short period of time, the problems were addressed and remedied.

THE PATH TO WAR

In late October 1983 Grenada, the smallest and most southerly of the Windward Islands in the Eastern Caribbean, became the scene of a Cold War–induced encounter that ultimately involved the deployment of more than 8,000 American troops. It was the first substantial employment of U.S. forces in combat following the end of the war in Vietnam.

Though ultimately successful, Urgent Fury, as the Grenada operation was labeled, revealed numerous major deficiencies in the planning and conduct of the battle. So pervasive were the flaws that a Senate Armed Services Committee staff report identified "serious problems in the ability of the Services to operate jointly."

The cumulative effect of the Committee's report and the similar conclusions drawn in the after-action assessments of the individual Services led to passage on October 1, 1986, of the Goldwater-Nichols Department of Defense Reorganization Act. The Goldwater-Nichols legislation instituted a massive revision in the way America's "war department" structured itself to wage combat in the modern age.

Since gaining its independence from Great Britain in 1974, the 10-mile-wide and 25-mile-long island of Grenada had been led by officials whose views were at variance from those of most contemporary nations. The first administration, led by Sir Eric Gairy, combined a bizarre foreign policy with corruption and political repression. After taking office in the middle of turbulence and a general strike, Gairy's beliefs in mysticism and psychic phenomena led to unusual and erratic manifestations of policy.

In an event welcomed by most Grenadians, Gairy's regime was overthrown on March 12, 1979, by a group whose leadership eventually devolved to Maurice Bishop. As circumstances would reveal, Bishop was an avowed Marxist who set about to establish Grenada as a mirror of the Soviet system. Citizens were instructed to call one another "comrade," a Young Pioneers Organization was established, and the names of the cabinet posts mirrored those of the Soviet Union. As Bishop made clear his intent to establish a People's Revolutionary Government, the nation's free press was shut down and other repressive measures were introduced. Peoples' Revolutionary Militia and Peoples' Revolutionary Armed Forces organizations were created, abetted by copious shipments of arms and munitions from Cuba. Three formal military agreements were signed with the Soviet Union as well. Eventually, the island became "one of the perhaps dozen most militarized states in the world in terms of population under arms."

Over the next three years, Bishop's regime invited increasing military, financial, and political support from Cuba, the Soviet Union, and other communist states. With the aid of 600–700 Cuban workers, the runway of the international airport at Port Salinas at the extreme southwestern end of the island was in the process of being expanded to 9,000 feet—a length that would provide both a staging base for the resupply of Cuban forces then engaged in Africa and a refueling stop for Soviet planes en route to Nicaragua.

From the American perspective, hostile control of the Antilles by Soviet proxies threatened U.S. strategic interests, most particularly the vital air and sea lanes through the Caribbean via which more oil flowed than transited the Straits of Hormuz.

Meanwhile, several factors led to growing unrest on the island. Heavy-handed actions of the large Cuban contingent fed increasing antagonisms on the part of the local population. A deteriorating economy led Bishop to propose closer ties with the West, a move bitterly opposed by a more radical Marxist faction led by Bernard Coard, the nation's deputy prime minister.

On October 13, 1983, with the backing of Grenada's military, Coard overthrew Bishop's regime. Coard, a clear favorite of the Soviet Union, was not widely popular among Grenada's citizenry, who continued to generally support Bishop and temporarily freed him from incarceration. Coard's cadre retaliated, again placing Bishop and members of his cabinet in police custody. Soon after, following more turbulence, Bishop, several cabinet members, and perhaps 100 other Grenadians were shot and killed.

The violence and widespread disorder that followed raised alarm among other Caribbean nations concerned for the safety of their citizens on the island and by the threats posed by a potentially aggressive Marxist regime in their midst. For the United States, the chaos following Coard's takeover brought special worries for the safety of the 600 American students attending medical school on the island as well as additional numbers of U.S. citizens residing there. Altogether, there were thought to be about 1,000 Americans on Grenada.

In the United States, Grenada-related planning began in a concerted way soon after Coard's takeover. At first, the focus was on rescue and evacuation operations; invasion options were not initially considered. That dynamic began to change as conditions on the island deteriorated amid increasing violence and unrest. A few days later the killing of

Bishop and dozens of others signaled the need to consider more aggressive planning options.

On October 21 leaders of six small Caribbean nations known collectively as the Organization of Eastern Caribbean States (OECS), met to consider collective action against Grenada. The leaders of Antigua and Barbuda, Dominica, St. Kitts and Nevis, St. Lucia, St. Vincent and the Grenadines, and Monserrat (still a British dominion) voted to intervene militarily. Recognizing that individually and collectively they lacked sufficient capability, the group appealed to Jamaica, Barbados, and the United States for additional help. The eventual request from the OECS was to assist in actions on Grenada that would restore law and order. Though the genesis of the note, its timing, and its method of delivery vary in the telling, a formal request was also received at some point from Sir Paul Scoon, the British-appointed governor general of Grenada, asking the coalition partners to intervene. Dominica, St. Lucia, St. Vincent, Antigua, Barbados, and Jamaica would eventually send troops to participate in operations on Grenada with Jamaica sending the largest contingent, 152 soldiers.

In the United States, the days following Coard's takeover and the assassinations of senior officials brought increasing concerns about the danger to American medical students. Planning for a military operation began in earnest on October 21. As eventually presented to President Ronald Reagan in the form of National Security Decision Directive (NSDD) 110A (October 23), the objectives of the operation would be threefold: assuring the safety of U.S. citizens, restoring a democratic government on Grenada, and eliminating present and future Cuban intervention on the island. Implicit in the objectives was, as needed, the evacuation of Americans and the disarming or destruction of hostile forces.

The Special Situation Group that met in Washington, DC, initially had very little information regarding Grenada. There was no CIA presence on the island, no aerial photographs had been taken for at least five months, and existing maps were inadequate. Each of those considerations was somewhat surprising given increasing concerns with events on the island. SR-71 and U-2 aircraft were in extensive use in other parts of the world. The Defense Mapping Agency was not alerted regarding prospective actions on Grenada. Hence, soldiers initially on the ground were relegated to using maps of the island prepared for British tourists. The lack of factual information and the hurried nature of the planning process were to plague the military's efforts throughout the campaign.

When work associated with Grenada began in a concerted way, General John Vessey, chairman of the Joint Chiefs of Staff, imposed special category (SPECAT) restrictions on message traffic. Vessey's directions were meant to preserve secrecy and assure favorable conditions for a coup de main operation that would involve simultaneous combat and rescue operations. The effect of Vessey's decision was to compartmentalize the planning process. Though well intended, the SPECAT restriction limited the flow of information to many members of the planning staff with expertise in key disciplines. The result was confusion. A series of late patchwork "fixes" was necessary to address deficiencies that became obvious as planning transitioned to live preparations. At any rate, news of the Grenada venture leaked very quickly and appeared in some news reports as early as October 21.

A second questionable decision by the Joint Chiefs was to task Atlantic Command rather than U.S. Forces Caribbean Command with responsibility for the operation. Atlantic Command was a "Navy heavy" organization with limited Army and Air Force representation. Lacking an adequate Joint Task Force operation, the 2nd Fleet was especially deficient in planning and conducting ground operations. Conversely, U.S. Forces Caribbean Command, though small, had a more robust joint flavor and tri-service experience. The latter consideration was important given that, in four days' time, Operation Urgent Fury would involve more than 20,000 troops from all uniformed services plus a sizable special operations contingent.

The initial version of the Urgent Fury plan called for the island to be seized by surprise attacks beginning at 0200 hours on October 25. A continuing series of changes—some related to operational necessities, others induced by equipment failures—pushed back the start time and contributed to the loss of surprise. Special operations actions began 36 hours ahead of the invasion when 12 SEALs and four Air Force Combat Control teams divided into two groups were air dropped into two Boston Whaler boats launched from the USS *Clifton Sprague*. Four divers went immediately missing after the jump. One whaler eventually headed for shore only to be plagued by engine trouble. Soon detected, the boat struggled back to the *Sprague* after an unsuccessful reconnaissance. A second attempt the following night also failed. Swept by rough seas, the whaler did not reach the beach and returned to the ship. In many ways, the special ops experience foreshadowed the dilemmas encountered by several units in the following days.

From the beginning, uncertainty plagued several aspects of the Grenada operation. U.S. planners were not sure of the strength of the opposing forces. The Peoples' Revolutionary Army was thought to number 1,200 to 1,500 soldiers. There were believed to be somewhere between 2,000 and 5,000 militia members and 300 to 400 armed police. The Grenada forces were known to have antiaircraft weapons and a contingent of armored personnel carriers. Additionally, there was thought to be a sizable representation of Cubans—perhaps 30–50 military advisers and 600 or more construction workers. The latter group, who were at work lengthening the runway at Port Salinas, were also armed. Many, if not most, were army reservists, and a sizable portion were veterans of Cuba's wars in Africa.

A second major intelligence shortcoming concerned the number and locations of the American medical students who were the focus of the rescue operation. At the outset, there were thought to be about 600 students, all at a single location—the True Blue campus in the city of St. George's. In reality, only a third were at that site. Two hundred more were at Grand Anse, about two and a half kilometers northwest. A final cluster, not located until several days later, was scattered across residences on the Lance aux Epines peninsula and elsewhere.

Final plans for Urgent Fury called for H hour attacks intended to seize St. George's and Port Salinas, which collectively comprised the island's capital, the residence of the governor general, and the international airport, as well as the presumed location of the American students. Those venues were situated at the southwestern tip of the island. Also on the H hour list was the Pearls airport on the opposite end of Grenada. Some scholars have questioned the choice of certain early targets, particularly the island's radio station and the prison at Richmond Hill, as not warranting the allocation of resources to objectives of low value that would have certainly fallen into American hands in the course of other operations.

Early attacks brought mixed results. The True Blue campus was seized without difficultly in 15 minutes. The Salinas airfield was in U.S. hands by 1000, although the path was anything but smooth. Scheduled to occur simultaneously with the Marines' heliborne assault on Pearls, the failure of the internal navigation system on the lead C-130 momentarily delayed the attack. En route confusion caused a shuffling and reshuffling of paratroop preparations on follow-up aircraft as decisions were reversed regarding aerial assault versus landing operations. Eventually, initial drops secured the airport and cleared the runway obstacles placed by the Cubans, allowing later-arriving C-130s to disembark their loads at the aerodrome.

Initial operations quickly revealed the severity of communications issues. Cross-service dialogue was made virtually impossible by incompatible equipment and the failure of CINCLANT to issue call signs and radio frequencies. Implausibly, the Navy command ship, the USS *Guam*, could not talk with the Army command posts ashore except occasionally by satellite—even though at times they were in sight of one another as the *Guam* cruised offshore.

Problems abounded: Air Force C-130 aircraft could not converse with Marine helicopters; Navy A-7s could not talk with Army Ranger and 82nd Airborne units, foreclosing the capability to respond to requests for fire support. Ranger and Marine units were equipped with incompatible radios, and some Marine units were assigned incorrect radio frequencies. On two occasions, A-7s attacked the wrong targets. The first killed 18 patients at a mental hospital located near a Grenadian Army command post. In a later friendly-fire incident, A-7s bombed an 82nd Airborne brigade headquarters, wounding 17 paratroopers, one of whom later died.

The first day's fighting brought mixed results. Perhaps considering the extent of the problems, U.S. forces were fortunate to have attained a modest level of success. By midnight on October 25, airfields at both Salinas and Pearls had been secured. The result of the battle at Port Salinas was, in comparison with events elsewhere, a notable outcome. A counterattack by Peoples' Revolutionary Army forces was defeated, and the vital facility was, with difficulty, secured and placed in American control. However, of the three counterattacks launched by Grenadian forces on the 25th, this was the only one that was successfully repulsed. A second, against the radio transmitter seized by Navy SEALs, drove the SEALs away from the station and forced them to retreat into the nearby jungle. The third was partially successful, pinning down a SEAL unit that had fought its way to Government House to rescue the governor general. The SEALs were trapped overnight, holding a tenuous perimeter until augmented by a Marine force the following day. At that point in the struggle only one of several Special Ops missions had been completed as planned. An American attack on Richmond Hill prison failed. By necessity, the campaign timetable was readjusted.

Over the next few days, as problems were ironed out and additional forces were brought to the island, the conflict turned in favor of American and coalition forces. Some Grenadian units began to surrender late on the first day. The Cuban contingent near Port Salinas followed soon after. Actions on the 26th freed the governor general. The first contingent of American medical students was evacuated, and prisoners held by the Grenadian government were released.

Army and Marine units then swept across the island, aided by Grenadian citizens who led them to arms caches, provided intelligence, lent them vehicles, and pointed out Peoples' Revolutionary Army officers who had donned civilian attire. Hostilities officially ceased on November 2.

On December 12, the U.S. command was disestablished, though 258 military police and a handful of civil affairs, communication specialists, and logisticians would remain for a time. Responsibility for military forces on the island was turned over to Caribbean coalition forces.

Aftermath

The official count of Americans evacuated from Grenada was 662, as well as 82 citizens of foreign countries. Most accounts show 19 Americans killed, though it should be noted that many of those were the results of accidents and helicopter crashes. There was one friendly-fire fatality. A high percentage of the more than 100 wounded or injured were also the result of accidents.

Twenty-five Cubans were listed as killed and 59 wounded. More than 600 were repatriated to Cuba. Grenadian forces were estimated to have suffered 67 killed and 358 wounded, though officials found it difficult to separate military from civilian casualties. More than 100 diplomatic personnel from Eastern bloc and Soviet-affiliated nations—USSR, East Germany, Bulgaria, North Korea, and Cuba—were evacuated as well. The Russian ambassador to Grenada was revealed as a military intelligence official.

Operations in Grenada were denounced by the United Nations and drew objections from the United Kingdom—President Reagan did not initially advise Prime Minister Margaret Thatcher of U.S. intentions. Though somewhat controversial at the time, Urgent Fury came to be seen in a more positive light in later days. Popular support in both the U.S. and Grenada was strongly in favor (85 percent) of the operation. Most citizens apparently saw U.S. actions not as an invasion but as a rescue mission. U.S. forces were, in fact, asked to remain longer. A democratically elected government was rather quickly restored. Grenada remains the "only Marxist regime in modern times to suffer invasion and military destruction by a western power."

Documents captured after the campaign revealed the extent of military aid projected for Grenada by the USSR, Czechoslovakia, Cuba, and North Korea. Five military agreements covering the next several years would have brought weapons, armored personnel carriers, antiaircraft batteries, seven aircraft, and six patrol boats to the island. Facilities were planned to accommodate Soviet submarines and surface warships.

The invasion undermined years of preparation by Grenadian, Soviet, and Cuban officials. Grenada under Bishop was being groomed as a militant Marxist state, a platform for the spread of subversive thought in the Caribbean. For Cuba in particular, Grenada was a humiliation and foreign policy misadventure. Castro, apparently foreseeing the possible negative implications, had ordered Cubans on the island not to initiate military actions and to return fire only if fired upon. When American forces assaulted the Port Salinas airport and moved into the surrounding area, shots were exchanged with Cubans who were garrisoned there. Cuban personnel—both official military and construction workers—became engaged in the fighting before surrendering late in the first day. Apparently dissatisfied with their performance, Castro reportedly sacked their commander after the contingent returned to Cuba, reduced him to private, and sent him to fight in Angola.

Throughout the campaign, U.S. officials were worried by the possibility that the large contingent of American medical school students might be taken hostage. It is not certain if that tactic was intended by Grenada authorities, dependent as the nation was on money from the students. Most students were initially unconcerned by the possibility. However, as tensions increased and fighting began, they felt increasingly threatened and welcomed the soldiers and Marines sent to rescue them. Several kissed the ground when they reached American soil. As one indication of the apprehension felt by many on the island, one British citizen, a schoolteacher on Grenada, was quoted as saying, "It [the invasion] was the first time ever I was glad to see an American."

REPERCUSSIONS (IN A POSITIVE WAY)

Urgent Fury revealed enormous flaws in U.S. capability to conduct joint military operations. Essential components, including communications, planning, and deployment, were glaringly deficient. Indeed, after-action reports described a litany of missteps, inadequate equipment, and shortsighted preparation in areas large and small. Problems abounded with radio codes, call signs, and frequencies. There were aircraft control problems, dangerous to an alarming degree as aircraft of different types and services flew over the same battle space with no capability to talk with one another. A major friendly-fire incident resulted in one death and double-digit numbers of injured. Last-minute reshuffling, the result of confusion and equipment problems, caused landings to occur on a piecemeal basis, destroying from the outset any possibility of a coup de main operation. Infantry troops were overburdened with personal gear to an extent that impacted their mobility.

There were also numerous shortcomings in tactical intelligence. Considerable uncertainty surrounded the size and capability of Cuban and Grenadian military units. The locations of more than half of the medical students the U.S. forces came to rescue were unknown. Perhaps as many as 21 were not located and left behind. The erroneous belief that helicopters could fly unmolested resulted in the loss of helicopters as well as casualties among the crews. Had the Peoples' Revolutionary Army possessed handheld SAMs, the results could have been devastating. Exacerbating all of the problems were the hurried, unrealistic timelines that formed the backdrop of the planning effort.

Urgent Fury highlighted the inherent weaknesses of the existing joint system and prodded Congress to undertake fundamental reforms. The problems, obvious in their scope and depth, were fully described in a Senate Armed Services Committee staff report. On October 1, 1986, a remarkably short period of time considering the sweeping nature of the changes, the Goldwater-Nichols Department of Defense Reorganization Act was enacted into law. One of the major changes was to assign areas of responsibility to designated commanders in chief with commensurate authority to plan and execute operations in that theater. The effects of Goldwater-Nichols would quickly become apparent in operations in Panama (December 1989) and Kuwait-Iraq the following year.

Forgotten Leader: George B. Crist

The Fix-It General

As liaison between the U.S. and allied Caribbean forces, Crist organized Caribbean units, coordinated their interactions with the U.S. military, CIA, and State Department officials, and established their major duties as a follow-on force and POW guards. Crist devised the operation's multinational command structure and advised officials on the evacuation of foreign nationals. His suggestion that media attention be given to the enormous cache of weapons captured by U.S. forces helped favorably influence popular opinion regarding the conflict. U.S. MARINE CORPS—U.S. MARINE CORPS HISTORY OFFICE

It may seem unusual for an officer not directly involved in commanding forces in combat to be singled out for special recognition during a military operation. That, though, is the well-deserved accolade accorded U.S. Marine Corps Major General George B. Crist. A review of the Urgent Fury campaign makes clear the caliber and importance of his contributions to the coalition's efforts. Crist was, in many ways, the glue that held important pieces of the process together.

It is indicative of the hurried nature of the Urgent Fury planning process that for a considerable time the senior leaders of the American and coalition forces did not know one another's names. Indeed, the commanders of the Caribbean contingent did not know the Urgent Fury designation. It was not until October 23, two days before the scheduled invasion began, that U.S. military officials learned that Caribbean forces would participate in the operation.

Crist, serving as vice director of the Joint Staff, was tasked by General John Vessey, chairman of the Joint Chiefs of Staff, to accompany American Ambassador Frances J. McNeil to a conference with representatives of the Caribbean nations, meet with counterparts, and advise the ambassador regarding the military capabilities of the coalition forces.

Crist quickly helped organize the Caribbean units into a more cohesive peacekeeping force and coordinated their activities with American military officials, the Central Intelligence Agency, and the State Department. Crist's orders from General Vessey posed a unique challenge: Vessey instructed Crist to set up a Caribbean force to perform "a visible but completely safe role." Indeed, the CINCLANT concept of operations completely excluded the force from any active participation. Crist remedied the situation by proposing that the Caribbean units be employed as a follow-on force to take custody of key government facilities captured by U.S. forces. Crist's initiative proved to be a valuable addition to the overall concept of operations. Beginning on the first day of the invasion and continuing through the course of Urgent Fury, Caribbean units relieved U.S. units holding Richmond Hill prison, Radio Free Grenada, police headquarters, Government House, and other key facilities.

The JCS executive order rather ambiguously directed "close coordination with the Caribbean community forces at the appropriate time." Vessey tasked Crist with improvising a multinational command arrangement once all forces were on the ground in Grenada. It was a duty accomplished quickly and well. As Vessey's liaison, Crist advised the senior naval officers

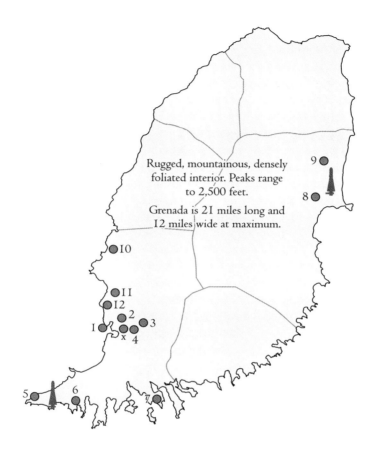

Rugged, mountainous, densely foliated interior. Peaks range to 2,500 feet.

Grenada is 21 miles long and 12 miles wide at maximum.

X St. George's (Capital City)
 1 Fort Rupert
 2 Government House
 3 Fort Frederick
 4 Richmond Hill Prison
 5 Grand Anse
 6 Port Salinas
 7 True Blue
 8 Calivigny
 9 Greenville
 10 Pearls
 11 Beausejour
 12 Grand Mal

SEAL team attacks, mostly unsuccessful, began hours ahead of H Hour at locations along the west coast.

H Hour targets included sites in the St. George's area, Port Salinas international airport, and Pearls airport. These attacks met with mixed results.

American medical students were eventually located at True Blue, Grand Anse, and other scattered locations around the island.

Invasion of Grenada—Operation Urgent Fury

in CINCLANT—Admiral Wesley L. MacDonald, commander CINCLANT, and Urgent Fury commander Vice Admiral Joseph Metcalf III—on the employment of Caribbean units and on politically sensitive issues such as internment and evacuation of foreign nationals, including citizens of Cuba, the USSR, and other communist bloc nations.

During the evening of October 26, U.S. soldiers and Marines began evacuating refugees and international residents. Crist coordinated both operations with the State Department, JCS, and Admiral MacDonald. That same day, he escorted Governor General Sir Paul Scoon and worked with him to assemble an interim government. Crist took psyops under his purview and found local announcers to broadcast on Radio Free Grenada. When commanders provided him with captured Cuban and Soviet documents, he requested CIA linguists to translate them. His suggestion to Admiral Metcalf that the documents and the impressive trove of captured weapons provided to the Grenadians by Castro and the USSR be publicly displayed was immediately approved. The immense stockpiles, with the evidence of more yet to come, aided considerably in quelling criticism of Urgent Fury in Canada and Western Europe.

In a campaign that was almost a textbook example of misadventures that can affect hurried, patchwork operations, Crist's contributions helped achieve a positive outcome despite difficult and persistent obstacles along the way.

Before and After

General Crist's career must surely rank as one of the most unusual and eclectic of any of America's senior military officers. Commissioned in 1952 from a Navy ROTC program, he served as a young officer in all three active Marine divisions, most notably with the 1st Marines in Korea. In 1955 he was detailed to the White House as an aide to President Dwight D. Eisenhower. That role would not be the last of its kind. Eleven years later he was named as aide-de-camp to the chairman of the Joint Chiefs of Staff, General Earle G. Wheeler.

Over the years, his diverse training and professional schooling assignments—Advanced Infantry Officer School, Airborne Training, Armed Forces

Staff College, and Air War College—complemented his broad range of duties and marked him as an officer of special promise.

Another unique special duty assignment occurred in 1959, when Crist was selected as a member of the U.S. Navy Mission to Haiti. In 1965 the first of Crist's two tours in Vietnam took him "in country" as a military advisor to the South Vietnamese General Staff—duties that involved him in combat operations across the country. Crist returned to Vietnam in 1972 as a battalion commander with the 3rd Marine Division and subsequently with the 9th Marine Amphibious Brigade, which assisted in repelling the North Vietnamese Easter Offensive.

Two consecutive three-year tours followed Crist's Vietnam service. The first, at Marine Corps headquarters in Washington, DC, was followed by duty with Fleet Marine Force Atlantic at Norfolk, Virginia, a posting that culminated in his promotion to brigadier general and duty as deputy commander.

In 1978 Crist was transferred to Europe where he served under Generals Alexander Haig and Bernard Rogers as deputy director of Operations, U.S. European Command. Promoted to major general in 1980, Crist returned to the United States as deputy chief of staff for reserve affairs, a position he held for two years. A fast-track Washington, DC, assignment followed as vice director of the Joint Staff, the position he held when called to assist with Urgent Fury.

In 1984, a few months after Grenada, Crist was promoted to lieutenant general. The advancement in grade led to a series of three-star billets at Marine Corps Headquarters, culminating in duties as chief of staff.

Crist was promoted to four-star general in November 1985, and in the same month he took command of the United States Central Command. He is renowned throughout the Marine Corps as the first active-duty Marine promoted to four-star general without previously having served as commandant or vice commandant of the Corps. He was also the first Marine officer to command a unified combatant command.

Crist retired, effective December 1, 1988, after 36 years of active duty. For a period of time after his retirement, he served as a military analyst for CBS News.

A Familiar Name in a Lesser-Known Role: H. Norman Schwarzkopf

The Essential Advisor

Several years prior to his notoriety in Desert Storm, Schwarzkopf served as a key advisor to the Urgent Fury commander, a U.S. Navy admiral. Placed in the role at the last minute by the chairman of the JCS, who recognized shortcomings in the staff, Schwarzkopf saw his role increase during the course of the conflict. He served as advisor, coordinated ground operations, adjusted boundaries, helped assign targets, and aided in the safe extraction of American medical students. In the final stages, he wrote the daily tasking orders for ground operations. U.S. ARMY—U.S. ARMY HISTORY AND EDUCATION CENTER

In America's pantheon of military leaders, General H. Norman Schwarzkopf is best known for his success as commander, United States Central Command, where he guided an international coalition of forces to victory in the Gulf War. Less remembered are his substantial contributions during Operation Urgent Fury.

Schwarzkopf's involvement in Urgent Fury came in the form of a last-minute appointment by General John Vessey, chairman of the Joint Chiefs of Staff. As the hurried preparations approached their conclusion, Vessey recognized that an adequate Joint Task Force organization did not exist. The 2nd Fleet Headquarters, in charge of the campaign, was primarily a naval staff with little or no experience in planning, coordinating, or conducting ground operations. On short notice, Vessey sent Schwarzkopf (a major general at the time) to advise Vice Admiral Joseph Metcalf and to coordinate ground operations. Vessey's choice was apparently based on Schwarzkopf's experience with airborne troops, Rangers, and Marines during a previous unified command assignment.

Schwarzkopf's initial status as an "advisor" was ambiguous and impeded his efforts to coordinate ground operations. Recognizing the hindrance, Admiral Metcalf designated him as deputy commander of the Joint Task Force. Schwarzkopf played a substantial role in several decisive events that followed. On October 26, the second day of Urgent Fury, Schwarzkopf shifted the assigned boundaries of the ground forces to enable the use of available Marine units to relieve besieged SEALs and secure Government House, allowing the safe extraction of Governor General Paul Scoon.

Evacuation of American students began that same day, aided by Schwarzkopf's commandeering of an available Marine helicopter unit to transport Army Rangers to the Grand Anse campus, where 224 students were airlifted to safety. Schwarzkopf's timely advice on matters such as attack times, boundaries, and bombing targets was well appreciated by Metcalf, who, as the campaign progressed, asked Schwarzkopf to handle daily planning and write task orders for Urgent Fury's ground operations.

Schwarzkopf's effective service during Urgent Fury foreshadowed the notoriety that would come seven years later during Operation Desert Storm.

CHAPTER FIVE

Panama

SETTING THE STAGE

Sandwiched between actions in Grenada (Operation Urgent Fury), the first significant deployment of American forces subsequent to Vietnam, and Kuwait (Operation Desert Storm), the massive encounter in the Middle East, the invasion of Panama (Operation Just Cause) in December 1989 may appear to some to be dimmed by the shadows cast by the two encounters that surrounded it. But by any standard—size, scope, significance—the conflict in Panama was of major political and military consequence to the United States.

Operation Just Cause was the first test of the Goldwater-Nichols Defense Reorganization Act of 1986. Enacted after operations in Grenada revealed "shortcomings in service cooperation and interoperability" and the bombing of the Marine barracks in Lebanon evidenced a cumbersome chain of command, the law, among many other changes, streamlined the military's command and control procedures and increased the power of the chairman of the Joint Chiefs of Staff, making that officer the principal military advisor to the president. In a major alteration, the legislation specified the operational chain of command as running directly from the president through the secretary of defense to the combatant commander who was also given authority over forces from all U.S. military services operating in the theater.

Ultimately, 22,000 soldiers, 3,400 airmen, 940 Marines, and 700 Navy personnel would be directly involved in Just Cause. It would be the largest military operation conducted by the United States since the Vietnam War. Forces committed to the struggle represented some of America's premier military units: elements of the 82nd Airborne, 5th and 7th Infantry Divisions, Rangers, Marines, Air Force and Army Special Ops units, Green Berets, Navy SEALs, Special Boat units, psyops specialists, and many others. The aerial assault conducted by the 82nd Airborne was the largest of its kind made by the United States military since World War II.

History recalls several "firsts" associated with military operations in Panama. Operation Just Cause saw the first use of the Air Force's Stealth aircraft (F-117) in combat. The Army's Humvee vehicles were also employed for the first time in a conflict environment. Notably, Captain Linda L. Bray, commander of a military police company, became by most accounts the first woman to lead U.S. forces in combat. During a three-hour firefight, Captain Bray commanded troops that captured a Panamanian weapons storage facility.

Operation Just Cause is the name now clearly associated with events in Panama. Interestingly, though, that title was late in arriving—it was not assigned until December 18, two days before D-Day. Throughout the planning and preparation stages, the operation was identified as Blue Spoon. By whatever title, it was a major operation and, not withstanding some notable glitches along the way, a major success.

To lead its forces in Panama, the United States selected an officer who looked more like an accountant than a warrior—"a small-framed man of average height with a large head and thick glasses." It turned out to be a wise choice.

THE PATH TO WAR

For the George H. W. Bush presidency and several preceding administrations, Panama was a long-festering sore. The overthrow in 1968 of the elected government of Arnulfo Arias by Colonel Omar Torrijos essentially marked the end of democratic government in Panama. Though pro forma "elections" were held, a series of dictatorships rife with killings, imprisonments, and disappearances followed in the years ahead. The militarization of Panama's Guardia Nacional—the National Police Force—and its integration into the nation's defense establishment placed coercive power directly in the hands of the dictator/president. With the passage of time, General Manuel Noriega murdered, bullied, and bribed his way to the top, eventually styling himself as "maximum leader for national liberation."

Noriega had a checkered past. Adept at playing both sides against the middle, he had a long association with the U.S. Army, working with U.S. intelligence agencies and taking U.S.-sponsored courses at Fort Bragg, North Carolina. For a time, he served as a CIA asset providing airfields and resources to support CIA Director William Casey's campaign to assist antigovernment Nicaraguan contras and thwart drug-related activities in other Central American countries. Noriega's conduct, though, became increasingly brutal, corrupt, and erratic, eventually exceeding the threshold the U.S. government was willing to tolerate.

June 1987 brought the first major confrontation. Massive public demonstrations opposing electoral fraud and Noriega's role in the murder of an opposition leader were savagely crushed. A series of moves and countermoves followed. The U.S. Senate passed a resolution requesting that Noriega step down. In response, a pro-Noriega mob attacked the American Embassy. In retaliation, the U.S. State Department cut off economic and military aid. At about the same time, Noriega, a known drug user and trafficker, was indicted by an American grand jury on several drug-related charges.

Noriega's response was a prolonged period of harassment against American servicemembers and families. Anti-gringo messages were broadcast by the national radio, and illegal detentions and beatings became more frequent. In 1988 more than 300 such incidents were recorded. Other forms of intimidation hindered the U.S.'s implementation of rights guaranteed by the 1977 Panama Canal Treaty.

Increasingly, Noriega turned to Cuba, Nicaragua, and Libya for economic and military assistance. A steady supply of communist bloc weapons and instructors flowed into the country. In early 1989 Libya provided $20 million in return for Noriega's permission to use Panama as a base to coordinate terrorist activities and insurgent actions throughout Central and South America. To further strengthen his hold on the country, Noriega organized "Dignity Battalions." The "Digbats" (in Pentagon parlance) were civilian defense committees, in essence quasi militias that were focused on intelligence collection and population control.

As Noriega's policies grew more openly belligerent, the American government became increasingly concerned that Panama could be used as a wartime base by the Soviet Union or other client states to interfere with U.S. naval operations and hinder or halt maritime commerce. In peacetime a communist foothold in Panama could support insurgencies throughout the region and facilitate drug-trafficking activities aimed at the United States.

In May 1989, amid a collapse in Panama's currency and nationwide unrest, elections were held. As validated by international observers, including former U.S. President Jimmy Carter, an anti-Noriega coalition led by Guillermo Endara overwhelmingly—by a three-to-one margin—defeated Noriega's hand-picked candidate. Three days after the vote, Noriega annulled the election results and sanctioned violence against the winning officials. Endara and his two vice-presidential running mates were publicly beaten by Noriega's thugs. Public demonstrations were quickly and brutally crushed.

Later that month, President George H. W. Bush ordered additional forces to Panama to protect U.S. citizens. On July 22, National Security Directive (NSD) 17 ordered military actions to assert treaty rights and keep Noriega off guard. The document provided a range of potential options. President Bush changed U.S. strategy from a massive buildup of forces intended to deter Noriega to a more forceful approach providing for military action as conditions warranted.

Late 1989 saw a further deterioration of relations between the United States and the Noriega government. On December 15 Panama's National Assembly passed a resolution asserting that a state of war existed between the United States and Panama. Concurrently, Noriega, while anointing himself as Maximum Leader, stated that "bodies of our enemies will float down the Panama Canal" and the people of Panama would win complete control over the waterway.

The following day, an off-post incident at a Panamanian checkpoint involving four American military officers resulted in Panamanian soldiers shooting at the Americans' vehicle, wounding three, one of whom later died. In a related incident, an American naval officer and his wife were apprehended. While in police custody they were both threatened at gunpoint, the officer was severely beaten, and his wife was subjected to sexual threats and intimidation.

On December 17 a final meeting was held at the White House between President Bush and his key advisors. Several major objectives were decided upon. The operation that would soon be labeled "Just Cause" would:

- safeguard the lives of 30,000 U.S. residents in Panama
- protect the integrity of the Canal and the American defense sites in the country
- help Panama establish genuine democracy
- neutralize the Panama Defense Force and bring Noriega to justice

The clear consensus of the participants was that the entire Panama Defense Force had to be dismantled. The whole structure was assessed as being so corrupt that if left intact, another Noriega variant would simply and surely assume power. The overall approach was agreed upon: surprise, swift, massive interdiction would decapitate the Noriega regime and prevent the Panama Defense Force from seizing American hostages. President Bush made the go-to-war decision that day. H Hour was set for 0100 on December 20.

OPERATION JUST CAUSE

"Our strategy in going after this army is very simple. First we are going to cut it off and then we are going to kill it." General Colin Powell's succinct comment describes the Just Cause operation rather well. Twenty-seven thousand American military personnel representing all branches of the armed forces—some already positioned "in country" and others flown in from bases in the United States—struck objectives in Panama on December 20 and the days immediately following. Major fighting, though relatively brief, was savage in places. The issue was mostly decided by the end of the first day.

American forces were confronted by a Panama Defense Force establishment of about 12,000 strong, consisting of soldiers, police, and national guardsmen. About 4,000 of that total were fully trained combat troops. Ground forces were structured in two infantry battalions, three light infantry companies, and one cavalry troop. The Panamanian air force numbered about 500 personnel who flew and maintained reconnaissance, training, and transport aircraft and some unarmed helicopters. The naval components had about 400 sailors who operated patrol boats, cutters, and launches. The defense establishment was augmented by the availability of an additional several thousand paramilitary Dignity Battalion personnel with varying degrees of competence and training. The "Digbats" were organized into 18 battalions.

H Hour on December 20 was initially set at 0100 hours. In a late evening broadcast on the 19th, CBS newsman Dan Rather reported U.S. aircraft in large numbers were departing Fort Bragg, North Carolina. The Panama Defense Force (PDF) reacted to the news in a mixed fashion: some units were activated and put on alert, others were required to check in every 30 minutes, some were not informed or did not respond. Uncertainty about how much the PDF knew and how its various components would react caused U.S. commanders to adjust H Hour. Ultimately, the loss of total surprise caused H Hour to be accelerated by 15 minutes.

In the late hours of December 19, just before D-Day, General Maxwell Thurman and John Bushnell, the U.S. deputy chief of mission in Panama, met with Panama's duly elected president, Guillermo Endara, and his two vice-presidents and briefed them on the Just Cause operation about to begin. The three officials were offered, and accepted, the opportunity to assume their elected offices and lead the effort to establish a new government. They were sworn in by a Panamanian judge shortly before midnight. Two days later, President Endara abolished the Panama Defense Force, which was reestablished as part of a new public law enforcement organization.

At H Hour on December 20, flowing from west to east across the country, massive paratroop drops isolated Panama City while pre-positioned forces struck PDF headquarters and other locations inside the city. At key points in Panama City and elsewhere, operations began with assaults on vital installations. The Pointe Paitilla Airport was struck immediately, as was an airfield at Rio Hato where Noriega was known to maintain a residence, a private jet, and a gunboat. La Comandancia, the central headquarters of the PDF located downtown in a heavily populated area, was an initial major objective. The opening series of attacks also included a special operations raid on Carcel Modelo prison to rescue a U.S. citizen,

Kurt Muse, convicted of espionage by Noriega. The successful operation lasted six minutes, faster than any of the several rehearsals.

Elsewhere, Fort Amador, a bastion that overlooked not only oil storage areas but also the Bridge of the Americas spanning the waterway and the entrance to the Canal, was an early target. The fort was especially significant, not only because of its position in proximity to vital assets but also because the installation housed command-and-control elements of the Panamanian military. Capture of the fort also secured a large U.S. housing area located on its confines, preventing the PDF from taking U.S. citizens as hostages. Forces were also dispatched to secure the U.S. Embassy.

Encounters between opposing forces varied in intensity as targets were attacked and taken during the day. Fighting was particularly heavy at Rio Hato where Navy SEALs were ambushed, losing four killed and nine wounded during an intense five-hour struggle. Likewise, the fighting at La Comandancia lasted three and a half bitter hours before opposition was eliminated. While the struggles for Rio Hato and La Comandancia were going on, Marines captured and held the approaches to the Bridge of the Americas.

Though freak ice storms in North Carolina delayed the arrival of some airborne units departing from Pope AFB, by the end of D-Day key objectives were in U.S. hands all along the waterway. Casualties from the day's fighting included 53 Panama Defense Force members killed in action, 55 wounded in action, and 1,236 taken prisoner. U.S. losses amounted to 19 killed and 99 wounded.

In the immediate aftermath, U.S. follow-on forces moved into western areas of the country and blanketed Panama City, eliminating pockets of resistance and occupying remaining key facilities. On December 21, D-Day plus one, the Canal was reopened, policing action in Panama City began, and the Marriott Hotel, where Americans were under threat and from which two American businessmen had been abducted, was secured. Eleven Smithsonian employees who were taken from an island near Colon were located on December 22 and safely evacuated.

Over the following days, operations expanded through the country. On Christmas Day (D-Day + 5), Rangers secured David, the last major city to be cleared of Panamanian forces. On January 2, 1990, Operation Just Cause was officially concluded.

Though events proceeded generally as planned and success was quickly and unquestionably achieved, there were occasional foibles on the path to victory. Before being halted, the rock music that was blared into Noriega's place of refuge met with general disfavor internationally and in the American press.

On December 29, U.S. troops entered a residence reported by an intelligence source to contain drugs and a cache of weapons. After some confusion with credentials and available documentation, the building was identified as being the residence of the Nicaraguan ambassador to Panama. Among other weapons, soldiers found Uzi machine guns, rocket-propelled grenade launchers, automatic weapons, and assault rifles. Subsequently, U.S. Embassy officials belatedly confirmed the diplomatic status of the residence. The weapons stores were returned to the Nicaraguans.

Nicaragua, and others, noted that the building was identified by a large seal on the front of the residence. U.S. troops asserted that the documentation for the residence was not immediately forthcoming, and that the presence of weapons violated diplomatic privilege. Nonetheless, the incursion drew unfavorable comments internationally and embarrassed the American government.

Total U.S. casualties for Just Cause were generally cited as 23 killed and 322 wounded. The distribution of the U.S. losses fell most heavily on Special Forces units—Rangers, SEALs, Green Berets, and Air Force Special Ops. The 4,150 members of special ops units sustained 50 percent of the total American casualties—11 killed, and 150 wounded. Casualties among other U.S. Army and Marine units numbered 12 killed and slightly more than 150 wounded out of the 23,000 engaged. Figures for Panamanian forces as stated in the Official Joint History of Operation Just Cause were 287 killed, 123 wounded, and 468 detained. Additionally, 36 armored vehicles, 7 boats, and 33 aircraft were captured. Entire buildings were discovered stacked floor to ceiling with Soviet bloc and Chinese weaponry. Eventually, the cache of weapons taken from Panamanian forces totaled 77,553 armaments of numerous types; 8,848 were recovered in a "weapons for dollars" initiative aimed at taking weapons off the streets and out of the hands of pillagers.

The number of civilians killed during Just Cause remains a source of controversy. In May 1990 the Panamanian government released an official total of 252, a figure that included both identified and unidentified fatalities.

A significant portion of the latter figure is attributed by various sources as resulting from the fires and destruction caused by Dignity Battalions and looters marauding through poorer areas of Panama City in the midst of the fighting or in its immediate aftermath. Noriega's earlier integration of the national police into Panama's defense force effectively meant that no one was available to stop the looting and burning, which continued unabated for about 30 hours. The United Nations and Americas Watch estimated civilian casualties at 500 and 600 respectively. Panama's Roman Catholic Church also reported a similar, low figure. Former U.S. Attorney General Ramsey Clark released a figure of 3,000 while CBS newsman Mike Wallace aired a number in the thousands. His broadcast caused that figure to gain prominence in the midst of highly disputed claims. The larger figures reported by Clark and Wallace are dismissed by many scholars who note that accounting mechanisms inside the country, including an internal ID/passport-like device, appear to support the much lower numbers cited in government reports. All adults in Panama are required to carry identity cards (the credula) that are renewed at regular intervals. When those cards were renewed the year after the invasion, there were no major discrepancies that would account for the absence of several thousand individuals.

As legal justification for the invasion, U.S. officials cited Article 31 of the United Nations Charter and Article 21 of the Charter of the Organization of American States, which assert the right of self-defense and allow appropriate measures to defend people and installations. Additionally, Article V of the Panama Canal Treaty provides for actions taken to protect and defend the waterway.

The Bush administration noted that Noriega's government had declared a state of war against the United States and had harassed and brutalized American citizens. Further, the legally elected Endara government, sworn in on December 19, had invited U.S. forces to enter the country.

The initial reaction to the removal of the Noriega government on the part of the Panamanian people was highly favorable. Indeed, a long-time critic of the United States, Roberto Eisenmann, the president of *La Prensa*, Panama's major newspaper, stated, "We are plainly convinced that the population of Panama considers the invasion of Panama a liberation."

In the United States, Operation Just Cause met with an 80 percent approval rating.

The war had the effect of showcasing the unmatched mobility of U.S. forces. Hundreds of sorties of C-141 and C-5 aircraft rapidly transported troops, equipment, and supplies over distances spanning a significant portion of the continent. High-tech features including C-130 gunships, guided munitions, and night-vision capabilities were exploited with impressive results and provided a learning platform for operations in Desert Storm, which would unfold less than a year in the future.

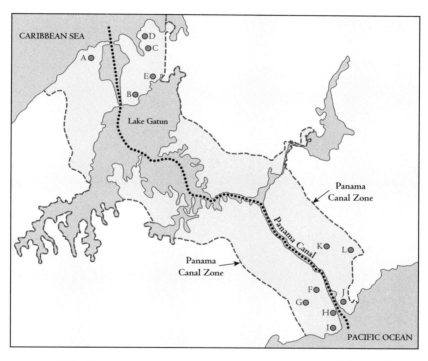

A. Fort Sherman
B. Fort Davis
C. France Field
D. Colo Solo Naval Station
E. Fort Espinar
F. U.S. Naval Ammunition Depot
G. Howard Air Force Base
H. Farfan Naval Base
 I. Fort Kobbe
 J. Fort Amador
K. Fort Clayton
 L. Albrook Air Force Base

Scale: 10 Miles

Operation Just Cause—Military Installations and Sites of Major Action

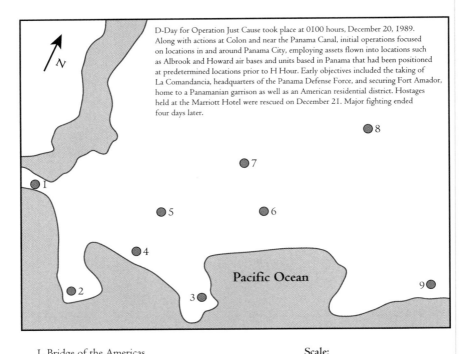

D-Day for Operation Just Cause took place at 0100 hours, December 20, 1989. Along with actions at Colon and near the Panama Canal, initial operations focused on locations in and around Panama City, employing assets flown into locations such as Albrook and Howard air bases and units based in Panama that had been positioned at predetermined locations prior to H Hour. Early objectives included the taking of La Comandancia, headquarters of the Panama Defense Force, and securing Fort Amador, home to a Panamanian garrison as well as an American residential district. Hostages held at the Marriott Hotel were rescued on December 21. Major fighting ended four days later.

Pacific Ocean

1. Bridge of the Americas
2. Fort Amador
3. Presidential Palace
4. La Comandancia
5. USSOUTHCOM
6. U.S. Embassy
7. Albrook AFB
8. Fort Cimarron
9. Marriott Hotel

Scale:
1 inch = 0.7 miles

Panama City Area

TRACKING THE DRUG LORD

Discussions of the events leading to the war in Panama and the larger story of the war itself cannot be separated from the saga of Manuel Noriega. Noriega's actions were so intertwined with the machinations of the Panamanian government that the two cannot be isolated in any meaningful history of the events of Operation Just Cause. From the American perspective, for all intents and purposes Noriega was *the* government of Panama, with all that entailed in terms of drug trafficking, harassment of American citizens, fomenting unrest in the region, and other nefarious activities.

The search for Noriega began almost from the time the first American paratrooper's boots hit the ground in the moments after H Hour on December 20. The dictator was known to maintain several residences in Panama City and throughout the country, making frequent moves from place to place as a security precaution. Initial searches of his known bolt-holes discovered an extensive cache of pornography, $83,000 in cash, witchcraft materials (two "witches" from Brazil periodically traveled to Panama to perform witchcraft rites with Noriega), and pictures of Hitler, whom Noriega greatly admired. Later, a stash of $8 million dollars was found, as was a valuable art collection. In the following days, lists of bank accounts in Switzerland and the Cayman Islands and three diplomatic passports were also discovered.

On December 24, after being relentlessly pursued and narrowly avoiding capture, Noriega sought refuge and was granted political asylum in the embassy of the papal nuncio in Panama City. A few days later a "sound barrier," consisting of loud rock music, was set up around the embassy. U.S. forces asserted that the action was intended to prevent reporters and others from eavesdropping via powerful microphones on sensitive negotiations between the papal nuncio and American officials. The music was also intended as a psychological ploy. The approach drew condemnation in part because it inflicted stress on the embassy staff. On December 29 the barrage of rock music was stopped and a less provocative noise jammer was put in place to safeguard the privacy of ongoing negotiations.

Noriega's days at the embassy were surrounded by a flurry of diplomatic activity. Several countries, including Spain, Mexico, and Peru, refused to grant asylum to him. An offer of asylum from Cuba was unacceptable to the United States. The U.S.'s request to the Vatican for Noriega's release was refused, as was an appeal from the Panamanian government. With events seemingly at an impasse, American authorities invited the senior Catholic prelate in Panama to tour Noriega's residences to develop a more informed picture of the dictator. Soon after, the ambassador wrote to Pope John Paul II advising the pontiff that Noriega had committed torture and murder, practiced devil worship and voodoo, and had stockpiled weapons and munitions in preparation for a guerilla war.

The indirect approach led to discussions between a Vatican representative and U.S. authorities. Against a backdrop of massive anti-Noriega demonstrations, a brokered settlement was reached in which, among other provisions, the death penalty was removed. On January 3, 1990, Noriega walked out of the embassy. He was immediately taken into custody by U.S. authorities and flown to Homestead AFB, Florida. Indicted by grand juries in Miami and Tampa on charges of racketeering, drug smuggling, and money laundering, he was convicted on several counts and confined in a U.S. prison. In 2010 he was extradited to France, where he was held for a year before being sent back to Panama. Noriega died in a Panamanian prison in May 2017.

Forgotten Leader: Maxwell Thurman

The Most Intense Man in the Military

Maxwell Thurman greatly compressed the time frame called for in existing plans for Panama. The revised design emphasized speed and surprise and employed overwhelming force. Thurman's objective was to end the conflict quickly, thus safeguarding the thousands of Americans in the country and preventing them from becoming hostages of the Panamanian regime. During the weeks before the invasion, his training regimen involving daily and nightly exercises accustomed Panamanian officials to American military operations and caused them to minimize the prospects for an attack.
U.S. ARMY—U.S. ARMY HISTORY AND EDUCATION CENTER

General Maxwell Thurman was a late addition to the Panama cast. In mid-summer 1989 President George H. W. Bush decided to replace General Frederick F. Woerner Jr., then commander of U.S. Southern Command (SOUTHCOM), with a more aggressive officer committed, if necessary, to forceful action.

General Woerner was a longtime advocate of seeking to dissuade conflict by incremental buildups in response to Noriega's programs of harassment and intimidation. Indeed, U.S. strategy under former administrations had amounted to "a sequence of subtleties and innuendos," intended to intimidate and create doubt about U.S. intentions. The idea was to demonstrate toughness without provoking an armed response from Noriega's regime. In the event hostilities did occur, plans at the time called for augmenting the 12,000 U.S. troops based in Panama with another 10,000 soldiers flown in over a three-week period from bases in the continental United States.

Noriega's increasing belligerence led the Bush administration to conclude that a prolonged buildup of forces might extend the period of conventional fighting, result in more casualties, and provide more opportunities for Noriega to take hostages or escape to the country's interior, from which he could transform the struggle into a guerilla war. Better, it was thought, to achieve surprise with a swift, overwhelming strike that would eliminate Noriega and the PDF.

Several recommendations by key officials led to the selection of Maxwell Thurman as Woerner's replacement. Admiral William J. Crowe Jr., chairman of the Joint Chiefs of Staff, described Thurman's "uncommon vigor, aggressiveness, and determination" as qualities that suited him for the SOUTHCOM duty. With the official change of command ceremony still several months away, Thurman, then serving as commanding general of the Army's Training and Doctrine Command, began familiarizing himself with the SOUTHCOM area of responsibility and exhaustively studying plans associated specifically with Panama.

If indeed aggressiveness was a trait that the Bush administration was looking for in an officer to take the reins at SOUTHCOM, Thurman was an understandable choice. Author Bob Woodward characterized Thurman thusly: "A bachelor workaholic, he thought nothing of working himself, and his staff, nights and weekends. He spoke with piercing directness, and did not accept excuses. There was perhaps no more intense man in the United States military."

Max Thurman was not an easy man to work for. His routine 14-hour workdays and actions such as conducting a staff meeting in the evening hours of Christmas Eve made him legendary throughout the Army—as did several acquired nicknames, including among them Mad Max, Maxatollah, and Emperor Maxmillian. There was no doubting his effectiveness, however. Thurman was primarily responsible for making the all-volunteer Army viable in the bleak aftermath of Vietnam.

One of the first steps Thurman took after studying and being briefed on Panama matters was to quickly compress the time projected for arriving forces to be inserted into the country from stateside bases. In Thurman's view, success would depend on surprise and speed. He intended to fight the war on U.S. terms, using overwhelming power that would paralyze the opposing army. His goal was to get it over with quickly, secure the safety of thousands of potential U.S. hostages, and win the support of the American people.

A second early step was to appoint Lieutenant General Carl W. Stiner, commander of the XVIII Airborne Corps, as his prospective operational commander in the event of hostilities. Thurman had not commanded forces in the field in more than a decade. He needed a battlefield commander to fight the war while he (Thurman) took care of the CINC duties.

Thurman's tenure as SOUTHCOM commander began with a flourish. In the late evening of October 1, the day following his change-of-command ceremony, a call from the local CIA station advised him of a potential plot against Noriega. In the first of many correct decisions Thurman made during his time in Panama, he decided the plot was fatally flawed, poorly planned, and poorly led—a failure in the making that the U.S. should stay away from. Indeed, the scheme quickly collapsed. Plotters intended to get control of La Comandancia while Noriega was not on the premises, block access roads, and direct Noriega to retire in the countryside with a full pension. After delaying for a full day, plotters attempted to launch a coup that by midafternoon was an acknowledged failure. The coup leader and his compatriots were beaten and killed by Noriega's henchmen.

Immediately after taking over, Thurman launched an intensive program of countrywide exercises. All major weapon systems, including tanks, aircraft, and amphibious vehicles, were employed. Helicopter exercises were conducted every night. These events were intended to appear random, but many involved actual targets that would be struck if conflict occurred. Large night exercises were held frequently to mask similar deployments that would take place in a real operation. These activities were further intensified after Thurman laid on additional measures following a credible bomb threat. The stratagem appeared to work. General Colin Powell, who succeeded Admiral Crowe as chairman of the Joint Chiefs of Staff, said the exercises "caused Noriega to believe the U.S. was trying to intimidate him. Consequently, he did not expect an attack." Thurman's insightful preparations proved fortuitous in many ways: revised guidance from the JCS instructed him to be prepared to mobilize forces within 48 hours for a large-scale attack.

Thurman was in Washington, DC, on December 16 when a U.S. officer was shot at a Panamanian roadblock. By 1:00 a.m. the next morning he was in the air on the way back to Panama. When the conflict began 72 hours later, the troops he and General Stiner had so carefully prepared moved into action throughout the country. By the end of the day, the issue had been decided.

Before and After

Thurman began his active-duty career in 1953 after graduating from an Army ROTC program at North Carolina State University, serving initially in field artillery units. The first of his Southeast Asia tours, spent as an intelligence officer in Vietnam, spanned the years 1961–63. Stateside duties that included attendance at Army Command and General Staff College encompassed the next four years. Thurman then returned to Vietnam in 1967 and commanded a howitzer battalion through the Tet Offensive. Thurman's later duties included instruction at the Army's Field Artillery School and at West Point.

Thurman's most notable assignment—the one that brought him lasting renown among his Army contemporaries—was as commander of the United States Army Recruiting Command. During Thurman's tenure as recruiting service commander, the "Be All You Can Be" campaign was generated. The effort greatly improved the quality of Army recruits. He continues to be credited by many as having saved the all-volunteer army and as being the architect of today's Army.

Thurman's success as commander of the Recruiting Service and his reputation as a master organizer led to postings as Army personnel chief (1981–83), Army vice chief of staff (1983–87), and commanding general U.S. Army Training and Doctrine Command (1987–89). Thurman was in the latter duty, about to retire, when President George H. W. Bush appointed him as SOUTHCOM commander.

General Thurman retired from the Army in 1991, after 37 years on active duty. He died in 1995 at age 64, the victim of leukemia. He is buried at Arlington National Cemetery.

General John Shalikashvili, chairman of the Joint Chiefs of Staff, eulogized Thurman, calling him "a remarkable officer . . . a visionary who carved out a path for the Army of today and, by doing so, showed us courage, talent, intelligence, and strength of character."

Forgotten Leader: Carl W. Stiner

The War Fighter

Stiner was Maxwell Thurman's designated war fighter, responsible for contingency planning and combat operations. Stiner rapidly augmented the existing small staff that he inherited and trained forces from all U.S. services in preparation for combat. In operation he decentralized the command structure, affording on-scene commanders maximum independence and flexibility while enabling him to rapidly identify and shift forces to trouble spots. U.S. ARMY— U.S. ARMY HISTORY AND EDUCATION CENTER

In August 1989, before Thurman officially took command in Panama, he identified Lieutenant General Carl W. Stiner as his operational commander and made him responsible for contingency planning and combat operations. Thurman believed SOUTHCOM's existing Joint Task Force structure was insufficient in size and expertise. Stiner was directed to absorb it, augment it with his own staff, and train forces from all four services. As plans were rewritten, at Thurman's insistence, they specified that Stiner would have tactical command of all units—conventional as well as special operations forces—that would be engaged in the conflict. In Thurman's words, "Carl Stiner is my war fighter and everybody carrying a gun in Panama works for Carl Stiner."

Stiner, a "slow talking country boy from eastern Tennessee," was commander of the XVIII Airborne Corps, the Army's 41,000-strong premier fast-response force. Prior to that posting, he led the Joint Special Operations Command and the 82nd Airborne Division. Aggressive and innovative, he was highly experienced in quick-response warfare. Stiner immediately sent officers to Panama to rework existing plans and prepare for quick-strike, widespread night operations.

Stiner's first command decision occurred before the shooting began. Concerned by the possibility that surprise had been lost and the designated time for H Hour had been compromised by a security leak, Stiner accelerated H Hour to begin operations earlier.

When the fighting began, his thorough preparation and on-scene intensity contributed greatly to a quick and successful result. Stiner had prepared for combat by subdividing his joint conventional and special operations forces into nine separate task forces. The decentralized command below his headquarters level gave his widely dispersed commanders maximum independence and flexibility and allowed Stiner to focus on shifting resources to hot spots and commanders in need.

Before and After

After graduating from the Army ROTC program at Tennessee Polytechnic Institute in 1958, Stiner initially served in infantry-related active-duty assignments, which were interspersed with a tour as commander of a basic training company. His first posting in special operations (1964–66) began duties that would come to define much of his career. After attending Army Command and General Staff College in 1967, Stiner served in Vietnam as a battalion commander in an infantry regiment. Army War College followed, then a tour in Saudi Arabia and later command of an infantry brigade.

In 1980 Stiner was appointed chief of staff of the Rapid Deployment Task Force. That posting was followed by duty as assistant division commander of the 82nd Airborne and a Pentagon tour on the joint staff as assistant deputy for politico-military affairs. In 1984, now a major general, Stiner took command of the Joint Special Operations Command. Nineteen eighty-seven brought duties as Commander of the 82nd Airborne. Stiner was a lieutenant general when Maxwell Thurman named him to command all forces engaged in Operation Just Cause.

Following Just Cause and XVIII Airborne Corps duties, Stiner received his fourth star and was appointed commander in chief, United States Special Operations Command. He was responsible for special operations activities during Operation Desert Storm. Stiner retired from the Army in May 1993.

In his retirement years, Stiner coauthored the book *Shadow Warriors: Inside the Special Forces* with Tom Clancy.

CHAPTER SIX

The Gulf War

THE PATH TO WAR

On August 2, 1990, Iraq overwhelmed Kuwait with a massive attack that posed a threat to the entire Arabian Peninsula. The invasion was a clear violation of international law and presented the world with the looming prospect of affording Iraqi dictator Saddam Hussein with control of a quarter of the planet's oil reserves.

The Gulf War, or Operation Desert Storm, the popular label among the public and media, was the second of three wars waged by Saddam Hussein. In September 1980, several months after seizing power—after years as Iraqi vice president and the power behind the throne—Saddam instigated a war with neighboring Iran. Though Saddam anticipated a quick victory, the conflict deteriorated into an eight-year slaughter that drained blood and treasure from both nations. Little quarter was offered by either side, and Saddam drew the condemnation of much of the world by his use of chemical weapons (mustard gas and nerve agents) on Iranian troops and hydrogen cyanide on more than 60 Kurdish villages in northern Iraq during and after occupation by Iraqi forces. During the prolonged, seesaw struggle, Iraq first captured segments of Iranian territory, then lost that ground and some of its own. Finally, in 1988, Iraq recovered its territory, essentially restoring the boundary between the nations to a status quo antebellum configuration. Losses were severe on both sides. Of Iran's nine million military-age demographic, one million youths were either killed or wounded. Iraq's war dead numbered at least 100,000. More to Saddam's consternation were the accumulated war debts that weakened Iraq's economy. Saddam had borrowed billions from Sunni-governed nations, including the Gulf States, Kuwait, and Saudi Arabia. He had apparently anticipated that repayment would not be burdensome or perhaps even forgiven since he saw himself as having fought Iran—the region's aggressive Shia power—on their behalf. Saddam made it clear that as their protector against Islamic fundamentalism (his view), he intended to recover the costs of the war. The lenders, however, saw no such quid pro quo and wanted the loans repaid.

Particularly as regards Kuwait, long claimed as a historic, integral part of Iraq, Saddam was not about to back down. He had a veteran army, possibly the fourth largest in the world, experienced after eight years of war. The air force was also large and well-equipped.

Saddam also argued that Kuwait was depressing the price of oil by overproducing, thus denying Iraq of its legitimate oil revenues. He also claimed that the Kuwaitis were illicitly extracting oil from fields along the two countries' conjoined boundary.

After a controversial and rather ambiguous July 17, 1980, meeting with the American ambassador, Saddam threatened Kuwait, demanding a stabilization of the price of oil and cancellation of its war loans.

Saddam chose to interpret the emir of Kuwait's response as a refusal. On August 2 Saddam, having earlier positioned large portions of the Iraqi army along the border, invaded Kuwait. The fully mobilized Iraqi force numbered more than a million men configured, at least on paper, in 60 divisions (45 divisions were identified by the coalition forces that would soon confront them). Twelve were armored and mechanized; seven were better trained and supplied Republican Guard formations, and, as regards Saddam Hussein, ideologically pure and politically reliable.

The army was more than adequately equipped, possessing 4,000 tanks, 4,000 infantry fighting vehicles, and 1,000 self-propelled guns. The air force inventory was sizable also: 700 fighter and strike aircraft, although levels of maintenance and serviceability varied from squadron to squadron. The navy was small, but its formidable mine-laying capability would pose a hazard to coalition warships in the coming war. More than 1,200 mines were laid, contact as well as influence types. An extensive clearance effort was required, but the threat was not eliminated before two U.S. naval vessels were heavily damaged.

Opposing the massive force that rolled into the small country was a Kuwait army that numbered only 16,000. Major fighting was over in a day. The Kuwait government and perhaps 200,000 citizens fled the country, opening the way to pillaging on a massive scale.

A series of United Nations resolutions followed. The first, demanding that Iraq withdraw, was passed on the same day the invasion took place. The final one, Resolution 678, passed on November 29, established a January 15, 1991, deadline for Iraq's withdrawal and approved "all necessary means" to expel the invaders.

The United States and Great Britain took the lead in assembling an international force to confront the Iraqis. Eventually, 18 nations would send ground forces. The contributions from Muslim nations (Egypt, which provided two full divisions), Syria, and Pakistan defused Saddam's self-professed claim as champion of Arab nationalism. Additionally, 16 countries sent naval units and 11 provided air combatants. Others contributed financial resources.

Though faced with opposition from some of the world's most formidable military powers, Saddam refused to abandon Kuwait. Asserting himself as an Islamic religious leader, his attempt to justify the aggression on religious grounds was undermined by a September 13 meeting of more than 400 Islamic clerics who authorized Kuwaiti officials to proclaim a holy war against him.

In the days immediately following the invasion, Saddam's military loomed as a realistic, deadly threat to other nations on the Arabian Peninsula. Few forces were available to deter further moves. Saudi Arabia appeared especially vulnerable. The kingdom's military establishment was minuscule compared to Iraq's thousands of troops, tanks, and armored vehicles—all positioned "next door" in Kuwait.

U.S Air Force fighter aircraft began arriving in Saudi Arabia on August 8. However, several weeks of tension remained until sufficient forces could be brought in to repel a potential ground attack. It wasn't until early October that General H. Norman Schwarzkopf, commander in chief, United States Central Command (CENTCOM), and overall commander of coalition forces, reported that "the window of vulnerability" had been narrowed to the point that he could guarantee a successful defense of Saudi Arabia.

On October 11 Schwarzkopf and Army planners formally proposed to combat Saddam with a "one corps" invasion force. Three weeks later, that approach was discarded in favor of an establishment double in size; the entire U.S. Army VII Corps would be brought in from bases in Germany to add strength to the XVII Airborne Corps and other U.S. and allied contingents committed to the fight.

At the outset of the war USAF Colonel John A. Warden, working in a Pentagon office, took the exceptional, unilateral step of drawing together a group of planners, targeteers, intelligence personnel, and weapons experts to devise a plan for an air campaign for the coming conflict. The fruition of their effort, embellished by CENTCOM planners, would come to be regarded as a military masterpiece.

Warden's plan and his interactions with Schwarzkopf and other members of the CENTCOM staff would form an intriguing chapter in the Desert Storm story. Split between U.S. locations and Riyadh, Schwarzkopf was the first senior CENTCOM official to receive Warden's briefing. Even more so than many senior Air Force officers, Schwarzkopf, an Army four-star general, saw the advantages of a strategic air campaign and enthusiastically embraced Warden's proposal.

"That's exactly what I want. Do it," he told Warden and the assembled audience. Schwarzkopf intended to exploit America's control of the skies to the fullest. "Our air power against theirs is the way to go—that's why I called you guys in the first place." The air campaign would lead the offensive against Iraq and set the stage for a later ground attack.

Air operations during Desert Storm would bring three divergent personalities to the forefront. Schwarzkopf was "the most theatrical American in uniform since Douglas MacArthur." Twice wounded in Vietnam, he displayed a legendary concern for the soldiers who served under him, as well as a grasp of essential data and his ability to retain and recall information. He was a holy terror to work for. Nearly everyone on his immediate staff had been subjected to his scathing, volcanic temper, which often came in the form of demeaning verbal assaults delivered in front of colleagues. In the words of historian Rick Atkinson, "During the previous six months, obliquely or directly, he had threatened to relieve or court-martial his senior ground commander, his naval commander, his air commander, and both Army corps commanders. Secretary of Defense Richard B. Cheney had worried sufficiently about Schwarzkopf's temper and his yen for imperial trappings to consider the possibility of replacing him." He would, though, destroy a large and capable enemy army and attain victory at relatively low cost. He made no major strategic errors while waging war with a single-minded intensity. His resolve to lead with an air campaign of the type proposed by Warden was the first of two vital, correct decisions Schwarzkopf made regarding the employment of air power.

The second was to place one individual—USAF Lieutenant General Charles "Chuck" Horner in charge of the air war. "There's only going to be one guy in charge of the air: Horner . . . if you want to fight your inter-service battles, do it after the war." That decision prevented much of the costly, wasteful frittering away of air power so prevalent and so bitterly resented by airmen during the Vietnam War. There would be no "route packages" approach this time around.

On occasion, Horner could be almost as abrasive as Schwarzkopf. And like him, he "took no prisoners" when publicly castigating his staff. Shrewd and intelligent, he was protective of what he saw as his own domain and wary of ideas—like Warden's approach for an air campaign—interjected from outside of his own organization. The "not invented here syndrome"—a disinclination to favorably view ideas generated from the outside—was alive and well on the CENTCOM staff. Horner saw Warden's proposal as a turf issue, an idea that was unwanted and unneeded about an area that was the rightful prerogative of his own organization.

Horner sent Warden home after openly disparaging both the man and the program he advocated. Warden's ideas, though, would prevail thanks to their inherent wisdom and the efforts of officers such as Lieutenant Colonel David Deptula and Brigadier General Buster Glosson. Deptula had accompanied Warden's CHECKMATE group to Riyadh and remained at Horner's request as the principal planner for the air campaign. It was a role that ideally suited both his personality and his extraordinary professional skills. As the plan and the campaign unfolded, he became the conduit for data and ideas funneled to him from Warden and the CHECKMATE staff in Washington.

Horner brought in Brigadier General Buster Glosson to serve as chief targeteer and commander of all USAF units in the Gulf. "Brusque, profane, tireless, and self-confident," Glosson, in the eyes of many, became the engine that drove the air war.

On January 15, 1991, the United Nations deadline for Iraqi withdrawal from Kuwait passed with no action taken. Two days later, allied air assaults began. An operations order published that day set forth allied air war objectives: "Attack Iraqi leadership command and control; gain and maintain air superiority; sever Iraqi supply lines; destroy chemical, biological, and nuclear capability; destroy Republican Guard forces in the Kuwait theater, liberate Kuwait."

The ops order framed a war that would last 42 days. The first 38 consisted almost entirely of an air campaign that, with remarkably few casualties, turned Iraq into darkness and shattered the Iraqi army. In the predawn hours of January 17, a pathway for the 700 air strikes that would be launched against enemy targets that day was torn through Iraqi defenses. Those strikes were the beginning of the 100,876 sorties that would be flown by coalition air forces during the course of the conflict. At its peak, the coalition forces numbered 2,614 aircraft and operated from more than 20 air bases on the Arabian Peninsula.

Tasking orders read like a catalog of major aircraft types resident in the major militaries of the Western world: tankers, reconnaissance, electronic jammers and eavesdroppers, U-2 spy planes, stealth aircraft, A-10s for close air support, F-111s, AWACs, C-130 gunships. B-52 bombers, already 30 years old at the time, shared airspace with the world's premier fighter aircraft: F-14s, -15s, -16s, and -18s from the United States, Tornados from Great Britain and Italy, Rafales from France.

The air campaign unfolded in four phases. Phase One targeted Iraq's military and civil communication systems. Target sets included:

- radar sites, communication towers
- radio, cable, and television stations and networks
- nuclear, chemical, and biological weapons research and development centers
- military production facilities and transportation nodes

- bridges, railway stations, and marshaling yards
- military headquarters, command posts, government ministries, and key offices

F-117A stealth fighters were heavily employed in the Phase One attacks, as were Tomahawk missiles. U.S. Air Force, Navy, and Marine aircraft were joined in the air campaign by British, French, Italian, Canadian, Saudi Arabian, and Gulf State air units.

Phases Two and Three struck Iraqi army positions in Kuwait, focusing on dismembering Iraqi defenses, destroying equipment, and interdicting the enemy's supply chain. At Schwarzkopf's insistence, much of the effort in these phases was carried out by B-52 bombers. The "buffs" flew around the clock, delivering massive amounts of tonnage in carpet-bombing assaults on Iraqi soldiers, equipment, and defensive fortifications. Schwarzkopf had observed B-52 strikes in Vietnam and recalled the destruction they had wreaked and the terror they had induced among enemy forces. Their effect on enemy morale was devastating.

Phase Four was launched in concert with the ground offensive, providing close air support as needed, hitting targets of opportunity, and disrupting the movement of Iraqi forces.

The coalition air effort was massive in scale. U.S. aircraft alone averaged nearly a thousand missions each day. By the end of the war, a quarter of Iraq's electrical generating capacity was in ruins and another half was extensively damaged. Interdiction operations had strangled Iraq's forces in occupied Kuwait. Iraqi forces were restricted to moving at night, and even then they did so at considerable risk. Supplies had been reduced from a sustainment level of 20,000 tons per day to 2,000. When the coalition ground offensive began, allied troops found many Iraqi soldiers on the verge of starvation.

The first few hours of the air offensive set the stage for all that was to follow. The assault was massive in size and scope, a cloud of steel and fire that would persist through the war. The effect would paralyze the Iraqi civilian and military leadership, eroding not only their capability to resist but also their will to do so. The overarching objective of the first few hours—to seize control of the air—exceeded expectations. As squadron after squadron returned, reporting targets struck and almost no losses sustained, the war's result was ordained.

Yankee ingenuity also contributed to the outcome. Joint Stars aircraft, still officially in the test cycle, proved highly useful. Under development as a platform to identify the movement of opposing forces in enemy occupied territory behind the front lines—that is, Warsaw Pact formations in the European Theater—the aircraft surpassed its anticipated capabilities. Iraqi troop movements and armor were pinpointed at distances that amazed allied military planners.

On February 5 American airmen discovered that Pave Tack infrared targeting pods on F-111A aircraft could detect radiation emitted by the engines of Iraqi tanks and armored personnel carriers. Even weak signals could be picked up and converted to visible images, which were then struck by 500-pound laser-guided bombs. Eventually, F-111As were joined by F-15Es equipped with the same Pave Tack technology. The technique, almost immediately labeled as "tank plinking," led to massive destruction of Iraqi armored vehicles. By February 16, one month into the campaign, coalition analysts assessed 1,439 Iraqi tanks—40 percent of the armored forces in Iraq—as having been destroyed. By the time the ground war began, all or nearly all of the Iraqi divisions in Kuwait had been degraded by as much as 50 percent—a threshold established by General Schwarzkopf as a condition for launching the ground assault.

After some initial fits and starts, the targeting of bridges was also predominately shifted to the F-111s using laser-guided bombs. Within a few days, bridges in the Iraq transportation system began falling at the rate of seven to ten each week. In his initial planning, John Warden had anticipated that Phase One and later attacks would knock out about 35 percent of Iraq's electrical grid. Instead, by war's end something close to 95 percent of the country's generated power was destroyed.

One of the few areas that didn't achieve immediate decisive results was the targeting of Scud missiles. On the second day of the war, Saddam Hussein began launching Scuds at cities in Israel. Doing so, he anticipated, would provoke an Israeli response that in turn would draw support to him from sympathetic nations from throughout the Arab world. U.S. officials pleaded with Israel not to retaliate. Patriot missile batteries were quickly dispatched to aid in the nation's defense. Though under considerable pressure from segments of the Israeli civilian and military population, the Israeli government showed surprising restraint.

The Scud offensive destroyed hundreds of apartments and housing units. Dozens of Israelis were wounded or injured in the attacks, but relatively few died as a result of them.

Iraq launched about 90 Scuds during the course of the war. About half of them targeted Israel. The remainder were sent against locations in Saudi Arabia. The most devastating attack occurred in the evening of February 25 when a Scud, aided by an anomaly in a Patriot's software system, avoided the defensive missile and struck a temporary barracks near Dhahran Air Base, killing 28 Americans and wounding 98 others. A significant number were from a single unit—the 14th Quartermaster Detachment—whose members hailed mostly from western Pennsylvania.

Fixed launch sites for Scud missiles had been quickly destroyed. Mobile Scud launchers, though, would prove difficult to find. Most days saw 75–150 sorties devoted to locating and destroying Scuds. On January 28 a Delta Force squadron and an army helicopter unit—400 soldiers in total—were inserted deep into Iraq to search out and destroy Scud equipment, logistics, and command-and-control facilities, as well as the missiles themselves. Their efforts complemented those of a British SAS unit already operating there. Later, a second American unit was added to the mission, increasing the size of the force to 800. Confirmed kills continued to prove difficult—only 16 are known with certainty to have been destroyed—but the intense focus greatly reduced launch activity, which fell from a daily average of five missiles early in the war to only one a day after the first week and a half of the conflict.

Anticipating the coalition attack that was sure to follow the air campaign, Iraqi forces launched a cross-border assault on January 20 that briefly captured the nearby Saudi Arabian town of Khajfi. The attack was intended to disrupt or delay preparations for the major coalition offensive. The Iraqis never achieved a solid hold on the city and by February 1 were driven out by a coalition force mainly composed of Saudi Arabian National Guard units. Other small cross-border incursions met with similar results.

While the air campaign pummeled Iraq and its army of occupation with unremitting fury, allied commanders prepared for the ground offensive. On January 26, at Suqrah Bay, Oman, U.S. Marines conducted a dress rehearsal for a potential amphibious landing on the shores of Kuwait.

Sea Stallion IV, as the exercise was labeled, was the largest amphibious operation since Inchon in the Korean War. More than 17,000 Marines and 11,000 sailors took part. Eventually, General Schwarzkopf chose not to strike Kuwait from the sea. The series of exercises were well publicized, however, and they induced the Iraqis to shift troops and artillery to bolster positions along Kuwaiti beaches in anticipation of Marine landings.

On February 20, in the central portion of the allied line, the 1st Cavalry Division feigned a thrust into Wadi al Batin, a desert gulch in western Kuwait that formed a natural invasion route into the interior. The deception reinforced the Iraqi leadership's predisposed belief that a major attack into Kuwait proper would follow that path. When the actual attack did come 11 days later, it was struck farther west, led by the 1st Infantry Division.

In the closing days of the Phase Four portion of the air campaign, 67 percent of the attacks were focused on fielded Iraqi forces inside occupied Kuwait. Efforts to that point had destroyed large portions of the Iraqi army's combat power, degrading its capability to levels set by Schwarzkopf as necessary precursors to the ground campaign. On February 24, 39 days into the war, he was ready to strike.

When the coalition forces moved against the Iraqis, John Warden's assessment would be proven correct. Contrary to General Horner's narrower view, allied forces so completely controlled the air and so dominated the battle space that only a small number of sorties were required for close air support to assist the rapidly advancing ground forces.

Much as blueprints for the air campaign had evolved as conditions, information, and resources changed, army planners also adjusted their designs as the entire VII Corps arrived in theater. In an extraordinary logistical feat, 146,000 troops in 83 units, 1,400 tanks, and 37,000 pieces of equipment were transferred in the course of two months from one continent to another.

As General Schwarzkopf prepared for the assault, his units faced Iraqi forces concentrated in a narrow portion of Kuwait stretching from the head of the Gulf to the dry water course at Wadi al Batin. Into that section, Iraqi generals had massed 30 or more divisions of the regular army. Six higher-caliber Republican Guard divisions held fortified positions immediately behind them. CENTCOM's concept was to freeze the Iraqis in place while the main "left hook" attack struck behind the Iraqi formations, moving west to east from bivouacs in the Saudi desert.

As the ground war began, allied forces were positioned on Saudi soil, arrayed along more than 300 miles of the kingdom's borders with Kuwait and Iraq. In the southeast, the 1st and 2nd Marines and units of the Joint Forces Command including Egyptian, Syrian, and Gulf State formations were aligned facing the Kuwaiti border. To their left, beginning at the extreme southwest corner of Iraq where its border intersected with Kuwait, Schwarzkopf positioned the powerful VII Corps, whose striking power included the American 2nd Armored Cavalry Regiment, the 1st and 3rd Armored Divisions, the 1st Infantry Division (the "Big Red One"), and the 1st Cavalry Division. Also assigned to the VII Corps was the British 1st Armored Division. To the VII Corps's left, extending another 100 miles farther north, the XVIII Airborne Corps held the left extremity of the allied line. The XVIII Corps, like the VII Corps, was a powerful assemblage of striking power. Both U.S. airborne divisions, the 82nd and the 101st, were part of it, as were the 24th Infantry Division, the 3rd Armored Cavalry Regiment, and the French 6th Division with a component of the Foreign Legion. The Iraqi forces were about to be confronted by an adversary that waged war with power, speed, intensity, and professionalism that far surpassed anything they had experienced in their eight years of war with Iran.

The ground attack was launched on February 24 when the right (southeast) end of the allied line—the two Marine divisions and coalition Arab units—struck Iraqi positions facing them across the Kuwait border.

Schwarzkopf had initially intended to assign U.S. Army Special Forces and Marines to capture Kuwait City. Those plans were altered to allow Kuwaiti and other Arab contingents the privilege of restoring the capital city to Kuwaiti rule. A modest number of U.S. forces assisted in the attack, intervening at times to restrain revenge killings. The Kuwaiti's outrage was understandable. When coalition forces seized control of the city three days later, they were confronted by visible evidence of Iraqi transgressions. More than a thousand Kuwaiti nationals had been killed by Saddam's troops. Many had been tortured in the most heinous ways with electric drills, prods, and acid baths. Others were shot, dismembered, or beaten to death. Rape occurred with a frequency and a number impossible to fully document.

The city itself, one of the most beautiful in the region, was mutilated, sacked, and looted to a degree reminiscent of medieval devastation. Nearly 175,000 homes and apartments were plundered. From most residences *everything* was taken: plumbing, lightbulbs and fixtures, electrical outlets, furniture, curtains, rugs, television sets, appliances, silverware . . . only empty shells remained.

Accounts after the war revealed that as many as half a million private automobiles, trucks, and city buses had been stolen or stripped. Nineteen libraries were looted. Mosques and public buildings were desecrated.

The Marines' role in the campaign, along with that of their Arab allies, was to confront Iraqi formations positioned between the Gulf and Wadi al Batin. Meanwhile, farther north, allied mobile units aligned along the Saudi/Iraq border would strike west to east across the rear of the Iraqi occupying force. As those units advanced toward the interior of Kuwait, they would fix enemy units in place and, if all went well, encircle them.

Early successes across the front caused Schwarzkopf to accelerate the massive attacks elsewhere along the line by 15 hours. On the central portion of the allied line, VII Corps had been in position since February 16. The Corps's strength constituted the largest assemblage of power concentrated for war in a desert setting since British General Bernard Law Montgomery's Eighth Army struck Rommel's forces at El Alamein in World War II. When the attack began, the 1st Infantry Division, followed by the British 1st Armored Division, broke through the Saddam Line, a fortified barrier of minefields, berms, tank emplacements, and fire trenches. The massive force pushed forward, overwhelming in its power, across a 50-mile front. By the next day, February 25, farther west in the XVIII Corps sector, elements of the 101st Airborne had already driven far to the east, cutting Highway 8, a key route for Iraqi reinforcement or retreat. In one of the few instances of Iraqi offensive action, a counterattack briefly slowed the 1st Marine Division's advance.

A day later, in an exodus detected in predawn hours, Iraqi forces began to flee Kuwait City in large numbers. Before sunrise, F-15s bombarded an enormous procession of vehicles streaming out of the city, heading north toward Basra. Working in concert, the Streak Eagles first dropped cluster bombs on Mutlaa Pass, blocking the lead vehicles. Soon after, others in the 12-ship formation bombed the rear of the convoy to prevent a return to Kuwait City. For the next two days American air power—Air Force, Navy, and Marine—ravaged the fleeing vehicles, destroying hundreds of them. The route quickly acquired a name: The Highway of Death.

Almost immediately, POWs in staggering numbers were swept up as coalition forces advanced. Eventually, 70,000–80,000 Iraqi soldiers would be taken captive. Many surrendered in the face of a virtual wall—almost 80 miles in length—of tanks and armored vehicles that pushed east and south across Iraq. Perhaps as many as 100,000 managed to flee to safety. Others, countless in number, were either pushed aside or killed.

On February 26, in perhaps the largest and most notable ground combat of the war, elements of VII Corps, including particularly the 2nd Armored Cavalry Regiment, engaged the Republican Guard Tawakalna Mechanized Infantry Division in the Battle of 73 Easting. The 73 Easting was a geographic coordinate, identifiable via the satellite Global Positioning System. American forces used the system to identify phase lines and boundaries. Needing no surface references, the system was employable even in the most desolate areas of the desert. The Iraqis had no similar capability and had believed that the allies would not be able to accurately locate and maneuver their forces in the trackless terrain.

From its beginning position on the extreme left of the VII Corps area in the center of the allied front, the 2nd Armored Cavalry Division had pushed across the breadth of southern Iraq until eventually coming up against a heavily fortified area about 55 miles long and six miles wide. Unlike at most other barriers, the Iraqis had placed one of their very best formations—the Tawakalna Mechanized Infantry Division—at the front in a position to be the first to engage the approaching allied forces. The division, one of the nation's elite, had more than a thousand Russian-made T-72 tanks and hundreds of fighting vehicles. They were about to be attacked and, as soon would become evident, destroyed by VII Corps's M1A1 Abrams tanks. Perhaps no other battle so clearly demonstrated the Abrams's superiority in every key metric: speed, armor, range, accuracy. Encounters associated with the struggle continued for about six hours, but the most intense, deadly portion lasted only 90 minutes. When it was all over, the Tawakalna Division was essentially wiped out. Hundreds of its soldiers were killed or wounded. Additional hundreds were taken prisoner. Of the 200 tanks directly engaged in the main battle, perhaps two dozen survived. Those numbers paralleled others achieved elsewhere on the battlefield and in other encounters during the conflict. American losses were minimal in comparison: one soldier killed and 12 wounded. One military scholar described 73 Easting as the last great tank battle of the 20th century.

A follow-on battle, about six miles away, would occur shortly after. This engagement, called the Battle of Norfolk, was named after Objective Norfolk, another piece of real estate in the desolate landscape. During the 73 Easting Battle, the British 1st Armoured Division was posted at 75 Easting, about 2,000 meters east, holding VII Corps's right flank. The 1st Armoured would play an important role in the Norfolk battle, attacking and wrecking elements of several Iraqi formations. In a series of encounters, the British unit, commanded by General Rupert Smith, destroyed as many as 200 Iraqi tanks.

In the early evening hours of February 27, the 1st Armoured moved on toward a key objective, the highway near Basra. In the four days since the ground war began, they and several other VII Corps formations had fought their way more than 200 miles across the mostly barren landscape of southern Iraq.

The 1st Armoured's push toward Basra and the movements of other allied units would essentially form the closing ground engagements of Desert Storm. Faced with pressure from the Marine divisions in the south and VII Corps in the west, the Iraqi formations were visibly coming apart.

Perhaps influenced by devastating "Highway of Death" photos on American television (though it appears that sizable numbers of occupants had fled prior to attacks on their vehicles), the Bush administration proposed a ceasefire with the extra stipulation that the Iraqis would fire no more Scud missiles. The Iraqis quickly accepted what was technically a "cessation of hostilities"—fire only if fired upon. The allies would halt offensive operations at midnight February 27/28, 100 hours after the ground war began. The ceasefire would be effective at 0800 hours on the 28th. The Gulf War was over.

The Iraqi army had quite obviously suffered an overwhelming defeat. Still, some dissenters among the allies had hoped that the ceasefire would be deferred for another 24 hours. Doing so, they argued, would have enabled the encirclement of the entire Iraqi force. The opportunity to perhaps replicate one of history's classic battles—Hannibal's "double envelopment" of the Roman armies at Cannae in 216 BC—was not pursued.

Stopping sooner—a "merciful clemency" in the words of one American general—left a "hole" in the allied line that allowed sizable numbers of Iraqi troops and equipment to withdraw in safety. Defense Intelligence Agency estimates suggest that perhaps 70,000–80,000 soldiers, 800 tanks (about one-third of Iraq's Kuwaiti based T-72s), and 1,400 armored personnel carriers escaped.

When Colin Powell, chairman of the Joint Chiefs of Staff, called Schwarzkopf to advise him of the timing of the ceasefire, Schwarzkopf did not object. The administration's decision to halt the war was politically understandable and widely supported by American and allied audiences. Most saw little need to risk additional blood and treasure to further pummel an already defeated foe. The consequences would not be fully apparent until more than a decade later when the equipment that escaped the trap would be used against the allies when they invaded Iraq in 2003. The surviving hardware, when combined with the equipment that had been kept north of the Euphrates River and not used in the Gulf War, provided the Iraq army with substantial continued lethality. Though 90 percent of Iraq's artillery pieces in the Kuwait Theater of Operations had been destroyed, 1,000 remained elsewhere in Iraq, as did 3,000 armored personnel carriers and hundreds of tanks.

The ceasefire did not completely stop the fighting. On March 2, the Hammurabi Division attempted to flee into Iraq. They were struck by the 24th Infantry Division commanded by Major General Barry R. McCaffrey. McCaffrey's soldiers tore into the Hammurabi columns, leaving the mangled hulks of dozens, if not hundreds, of tanks. The next day, Schwarzkopf and his key staff met with senior Iraqi officers at Safwan, Iraq, formalizing the surrender agreements.

The decisiveness of the allied triumph and the decision to end the war were greeted with relief and approval by majority public opinion in the Western world. Those who viewed the outcome in a less favorable light generally argued that the war should have continued until Iraq was totally defeated and the Saddam regime was removed from power.

Doing that would, of course, have meant the invasion of Iraq. The government of President George H. W. Bush concluded that the value of accomplishing those objectives would not justify the price in deaths, dollars, and opinion that would be necessary to attain them. Among other considerations, Bush's representatives noted that the United Nations Resolutions that provided legitimacy for American and allied actions was limited to the liberation of Kuwait. Support, particularly among Arab nations in the region, would likely be lacking as well. Nearly 90 percent of the total cost of the war had been underwritten by the Arab nations, Japan, and Germany. That level of continued support would be problematic if the UN mandate was exceeded.

The administration made the calculation that total victory—invading and occupying Iraq, removing the Saddam regime—would incur further obligations, such as reconstituting a hostile, devastated nation and guiding the transfer to representative democracy in the face of enormously complex internal religious, ethnic, and political differences. Several of the president's key advisors supported that view. Among them, Brent Scowcroft, Bush's national security advisor, strongly urged the president to end the war after expelling Iraq military forces from Kuwait. Continuing the war and pressing on to Baghdad would, he thought "lead to a long, open-ended, and costly occupation that would hurt the U.S. financially and in terms of its international leadership."

Colin Powell also argued in favor of limiting war aims, fearing the possibility of an extended period of American occupation and a potentially long search for Saddam Hussein. In his view, invasion ran counter to the U.S. interests in the Arab world—a postwar vacuum in Iraq would strengthen Iranian and Syrian influence in the region. At any rate, it was widely believed that the Iraqi populace would rise up and unilaterally take care of disposing of Saddam.

Regardless, a residual U.S. presence persisted when "no-fly" zones were later established over northern and southern Iraq. The surrender agreement negotiated by Schwarzkopf at Safwan allowed the Iraqis to operate helicopters inside the nation's territorial confines. Saddam promptly used that capability to suppress the Kurdish population in the north and the "swamp Arabs" in the south who opposed his rule. The "no-fly" zones were established as a counter to the helicopter assaults that devastated entire regions of the country.

"No-fly" zones were not the only actions the allied nations found necessary in response to Iraqi transgressions. Before departing Kuwait, Iraqi sappers sabotaged most of the nation's 1,300 oil wells, collection sites, and production facilities. Experts estimated that more than eleven million barrels spewed from the broken wells every day. The result was an ecological disaster that took months to suppress.

The war had cost the lives of 390 American men and women, 148 of whom had been killed in action. Another 458 had been wounded. By most accounts, casualties among allied nations totaled 510, which included 47 British, 2 French, and 14 Egyptians killed in action.

Estimates of Iraqi losses vary considerably. British sources referenced by historian John Keegan suggest that Iraq may have sustained as many as 60,000 casualties. In Keegan's view, "the most visible Iraqi losses were suffered during the flight from Kuwait over the Mitla Ridge when coalition air and ground attacks on packed masses of armored and soft-skinned vehicles produced devastation."

American sources placed Iraqi losses at 10,000–12,000 killed by allied bombs during the air campaign and another 10,000 killed during the ground offensive. A House Armed Services Committee study assessed Iraqi troop losses at 26,000 killed or wounded during the air campaign with perhaps another 153,000 deserting as a result of the air attacks.

Intelligence estimates regarding the size of the Iraqi force in place in Kuwait when the conflict began also differed considerably. In mid-January, allied planners in Riyadh believed there were as many as 540,000. Later, Schwarzkopf's estimate was 450,000. The House Armed Services Committee study place the force size as somewhere near 362,000 (before the mass desertions took place).

By any standard, the achievements of the U.S. military establishment—the quality of the equipment and the caliber of its personnel—were transcendent. In addition to the professionalism of the men and women who fought the war, "only America could have amassed more than nine million tons of material and hauled it six thousand miles to the Middle East, fought a war and then brought the stuff home again."

For the American military and, indeed, for much of the general populace, the victory in the desert excised the shadows of the Vietnam conflict.
The competence and potency of the American military and the valor of its
soldiers were no longer in question.

The American Army was back.

The masterful ground offensive that followed the devastating air campaign lasted only 100
hours. A ceasefire prevented achievement of a classic double envelopment.

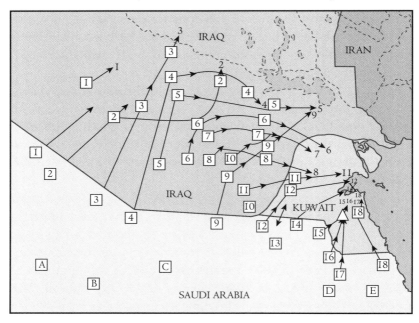

1. French 6th Light Division	10. 1st Cavalry Division
2. 82nd Airborne Division	11. UK 1st Armoured Division
3. 101st Airborne Division	12. Egyptian Force
4. 24th Infantry Division	13. Syrian Armored Division
5. 3rd Armored Cavalry Regiment	14. Saudi-Kuwaiti Joint Force
6. 1st Armored Division	15. 1st Brigade, 2nd Armored Division
7. 3rd Armored Cavalry Regiment	16. 2nd Marine Division
8. 2nd Armored Cavalry Regiment	17. 1st Marine Division
9. 1st Infantry Division	18. Arab Forces

A. XVII Airborne Corps	D. Marine Central Command
B. Army Central Command	E. Joint Force Command East
C. VII Corps	X. Kuwait City

Operation Desert Storm—Liberation of Kuwait

Gulf War—Operation Desert Storm Chronology
1990

August 2: Iraq invades Kuwait.

August 6: Saudi Arabian King Fahd requests U.S. military assistance.

August 8: First U.S. Air Force fighter planes arrive in Saudi Arabia.

August 10: USAF Colonel John A. Warden III presents initial briefing on proposed air campaign to General H. Norman Schwarzkopf.

September 18: Schwarzkopf directs Army planners to begin making preparations for a prospective ground offensive.

October 10: Initial presentation to White House staff proposes attacking Iraqi forces in Kuwait with one U.S. Army corps.

October 31: President George H. W. Bush decides to double the size of U.S. forces in Saudi Arabia. The U.S. VII Corps will be brought to the theater from bases in Germany. The decision will be announced to the public on November 8.

November 19: United Nations Security Council authorizes use of "all means necessary" to expel Iraqi forces from Kuwait. The UN resolution imposes a January 15, 1991, deadline on Iraq to withdraw its forces.

December 6: VII Corps equipment shipped from Germany begins arriving in Saudi Arabia.

1991

January 9: U.S. Secretary of State James Baker meets Iraqi Foreign Minister Tariq Aziz in Geneva, Switzerland, in an unsuccessful attempt to find a peaceful solution.

January 12: By votes of 52–47 in the Senate, and 250–183 in the House of Representatives, the U.S. Congress authorizes the use of force to liberate Kuwait.

January 15: UN deadline to withdraw forces passes without Iraqi compliance.

January 17: Allied air attacks begin with initial strike by Apache helicopters at 2:58 a.m. Riyadh time.

January 18: Iraqi Scud missiles strike targets in Israel.

January 23: Air attacks begin against hardened Iraqi aircraft shelters.

January 26: U.S. Marines in Oman rehearse for a potential amphibious landing on the coast of Kuwait. USAF F-111 aircraft attack oil manifolds at Al Ahmadi to counter the effects of Iraqi sabotage on oil-production facilities.

January 29: Iraqi units attack Khafji, Saudi Arabia, and other border positions. Allied aircraft begin combat patrols to prevent Iraqi aircraft from seeking refuge in Iran.

January 30: American Delta Force units are sent to Saudi Arabia to search for Scud missiles.

January 31: Arab forces composed mainly of Saudi National Guard and Qatari units, assisted by a small U.S. Marine contingent, retake Khafji.

February 1: The last Tomahawk missiles launched during the war target an airfield near Baghdad.

February 3: Gunfire from U.S. battleships is employed for the first time against targets in Kuwait.

February 5: "Tank plinking" missions against Iraqi armor are flown for the first time after it is discovered that Pave Tack infrared targeting systems on USAF F-111 aircraft can detect the faint radiation emitted by the warm engines of Iraqi tanks and armored personnel carriers.

February 6: With the arrival of 3rd Armored Division equipment, the transfer of the entire U.S. VII Corps to the theater is complete.

February 8: Final review of plans for the ground attack takes place in Riyadh.

February 16: VII Corps moves into attack positions.

February 18: Two U.S. Navy vessels, the USS *Tripoli* and the USS *Princeton*, strike mines.

February 20: The U.S. 1st Cavalry division conducts a diversionary strike up the Wadi al Batin to draw attention away from the forthcoming main attack.

February 21: President Bush sets a deadline of noon, February 23, for Iraqi withdrawal from Kuwait.

February 22: U.S. Marines begin infiltrating into the southwest "bootheel" portion of Kuwait.

February 23: Stealth fighters conduct heavy attacks on Iraqi intelligence facilities. Army Special Forces teams are inserted deep into Iraq.

February 24: Ground attack begins. General Schwarzkopf moves up main assault by VII Corps by 15 hours.

February 25: 101st Airborne Division cuts Highway 8 in the Euphrates Valley. Iraqis launch a counterattack against 1st Marine Division units. A Scud missile destroys a barracks in Al Khobar, Saudi Arabia, killing 28 Americans and wounding 98 others.

February 26: Iraqi forces begin fleeing Kuwait City. VII Corps fights Iraqi Republican Guard units in the battle of 73 Easting.

February 27: 24th Infantry Division strikes toward Basra in the Euphrates Valley. 1st Armored Division engages the Iraqi Madinah Division. Kuwait City is liberated. President Bush agrees to halt the war.

February 28: Ceasefire takes effect at 8:00 a.m. Riyadh time.

March 2: 24th Infantry Division engages Iraqi Hammurabi Division as it attempts to flee, destroying 600 Iraqi vehicles.

March 5: General Schwarzkopf meets with Iraqi generals at Safwan, Iraq, to formalize surrender arrangements.

Forgotten Leader: John A. Warden III

A War Plan for the Ages

Warden, an air power visionary, was the major architect of the brilliant plan that visited destruction from the air on Iraq and its army. Warden's "Five Ring Model" targeted Iraqi components such as communications, power, weapons production and storage, and transportation, paralyzing its operating systems. A brief, intense assault at the beginning of the war overwhelmed Iraq's air defenses, degrading them to an extent that allowed air strikes to proceed with near impunity. The 38 days of aerial barrage paved the way for a 100-hour ground campaign that concluded the war. U.S. AIR FORCE—U.S. AIR FORCE HISTORY OFFICE

If the major irony associated with the Gulf War was that the decisive, brilliant air campaign that contributed so much to the allied victory was instigated—indeed, insisted upon—by a "ground-pounding" Army officer, further ironies attend the development of the plan itself and the officer who was mainly responsible for it.

USAF Colonel John A. Warden III commanded no forces, nor was he ever an official member of the Central Command Air Force (CENTAF) planners, the Riyadh-based group that prosecuted the air war during Desert Storm. When Iraq invaded Kuwait, Warden was the director of CHECKMATE, an Air Staff planning cell located in the basement of the Pentagon. He remained in that post throughout the conflict.

When news of the invasion reached Washington, Warden, acting on his own initiative, began developing an encompassing strategic air campaign, expanding the CHECKMATE staff with intelligence personnel, targeteers, weapons and logistics experts, and others drawn from throughout the Air Force.

Warden's sense of urgency was heightened by visits from colleagues such as Lieutenant Colonel David Deptula, a member of the secretary of the Air Force's staff group. Deptula and others were concerned that plans being developed at CENTCOM called for employment of the wrong types of aircraft and gave insufficient attention to considerations such as logistics and the types of munitions best suited to the prospective tasks at hand. CENTCOM planners, Deptula told Warden, were using an outdated, off-the-shelf operations plan that had not kept up with the precision delivery capability of modern aircraft.

Abetted by a call from General Schwarzkopf to the Air Force chief of staff requesting development of an air campaign, Warden received approval to construct a proposal. Working almost nonstop, Warden and his CHECKMATE crew hurried to put together a concept for an air campaign and develop the briefings that would accompany it as it made its way to the highest levels of the Bush administration.

The circumstances associated with Schwarzkopf's request placed Warden in a difficult, somewhat ambiguous situation. Schwarzkopf's request, made at the time he was working from CENTCOM headquarters at Tampa, Florida, went directly to the Air Staff. That approach bypassed Schwarzkopf's own CENTAF staff, most of whom were already in Riyadh. There, in the "Black Hole," a secure room in the deployed headquarters building, Lieutenant General Charles "Chuck" Horner, CENTCOM vice commander, was handling CINC-related duties pending Schwarzkopf's arrival in theater.

John Warden was an air power visionary whose views were likened to those of Billy Mitchell and Giulio Douhet. While Mitchell's and Douhet's ideas had often been disparaged, Warden believed that their basic theoretical premises—most importantly, that air power could be the decisive instrument in war—were fundamentally correct. Missing in the past, though, were essential ingredients such as range, accuracy, and stealth that would make their concepts viable. Those components, he believed, were now resident—in depth—as constituent elements of modern air power. General Michael Dugan, a retired Air Force chief of staff would later say regarding the effect of the precision weapons employed in Desert Storm, "The technology had caught up with the doctrine."

Accuracy was only one facet of the new weapons that made them so effective. Also present was a heretofore unprecedented capability to strike multiple targets with precision from long range. Indeed, in the first 24 hours of Desert Storm more targets were struck than the Eighth Air Force had bombed in all of Germany during the entire years of 1942 and 1943.

Almost from the beginning of aerial warfare there had been a tension between advocates of strategic operations who saw a decisive, potentially war-winning role for air power and those who viewed aerial bombardment more narrowly, as primarily a tactical component focused more prominently on missions such as air defense, interdiction, and close air support. In recent years, high positions in the Air Force hierarchy had been held by a "fighter mafia," a circumstance that in the minds of many experts had tilted the service's emphasis toward tactical considerations.

Warden believed that if used properly, air power could play the determinant role in combat. In Kuwait, that consideration was especially important because it would take months to put sufficient ground forces in place to confront the Iraqi army—fourth largest in the world and "casualty tolerant," as evidenced from its conduct during its recent eight-year war with Iran.

Over the years, Warden had developed what became known as the "Five Ring Model." In his view, enemies should be attacked as if they were living systems that maintain their vitality through inputs such as power, material, food, and other essential means. Cumulative effects from destroying or degrading these sources of sustenance can be just as important or more so than weakening military forces. If well done, an air campaign could induce paralysis in an adversary's operating systems. Every modern nation-state, Warden believed, has 3,000–5,000 strategic area points. Destroying those, he theorized, wins the war—the enemy is rendered prostrate, incapable of undertaking decisive military initiatives.

As with other modern nations, Iraq and its army could be defeated by the selective destruction of target sets within each of the five categories: leadership, production, infrastructure, population, and fielded forces. Attacks on telecommunications and command-and-control facilities could incapacitate Saddam Hussein's regime by eliminating or greatly reducing its ability to communicate with its military formations. Production could be shattered by strikes on power storage and distribution stations, oil storage terminals, and other related facilities. Iraq's oil-production capacity would be mostly spared to enable the nation to pay its bills and ease the process of reconstitution after the conflict ended. Nuclear, biological, and chemical research and production were identified for destruction—a necessary action that would eliminate the threat to the world at large.

In Warden's assessment, railroads were identified as the major target set in the infrastructure category. Saddam's railroads were lucrative targets. Their locations were known and highly visible in the desert landscape. Warden correctly believed that attacks would create enormous bottlenecks as the Iraqis attempted to move supplies to forces in Kuwait. Indeed, the stoppages would make their cargoes vulnerable to destruction as well.

Attacks on population were excluded from Warden's plan. Instead, air power would focus on psychological operations aimed at isolating the Iraqi regime from its people, foreign workers residing in the country, and the draftee soldiers sent to serve in occupied Kuwait. Iraq's military would be subjected to lethal attacks against air defense systems and its offensive air capability. Warden sought massive destruction of Iraq's air component: bombers, fighters, missiles, radar sites, launch centers, and the command-and-control facilities that directed them. Ground forces in Kuwait and other areas near the border would be struck only if they attempted to move into Saudi Arabia—a restriction that would hopefully prevent undue destruction to Kuwait.

Warden called his plan "Instant Thunder," a deliberate twist to contrast it with the gradual, incremental, piecemeal "Rolling Thunder" approach that so frustrated air power advocates during the Vietnam conflict.

Warden's initial concerns dealt mainly with munitions distribution, the availability of sufficient numbers of tankers, and airspace control. His plan would put large numbers of aircraft of various types and capabilities launched from numerous sites in the air at the same time over Kuwait, Iraq, and Saudi Arabia. There would also be language barriers to consider.

Unlike many of his contemporaries, Warden did not believe that the Iraq air defense system would pose a formidable obstacle. Indeed, he thought that the precise, massive strikes planned for the first 15 minutes of the war would overwhelm and paralyze Iraqi air defenses. To a considerable extent those initial attacks would also take the Iraqi air force out of the conflict.

Warden's initial briefing to Schwarzkopf on August 7 met with an enthusiastic response. His introduction to the briefing was decidedly unconventional. The first slide in his presentation specified what the air campaign was *not*. The narrative on the slide read:

What it is—a focused, intense air campaign designed to incapacitate Iraqi leadership capacity in a short period of time. And it is designed to leave basic Iraqi infrastructure intact.

What it is not—a graduated, long-term campaign plan designed to provide escalation options to counter Iraqi moves.

The messages on the slide encompassed two of Warden's most intensely held convictions. One, air power could be the decisive factor in the war. Two, the gradual, incremental approach so costly in Vietnam would not be repeated.

Schwarzkopf's embrace of the proposal surprised some of his Army colleagues and more than a few in the Air Force hierarchy who were initially wary of making air power anything more than an adjunct to ground operations. Seeing it cast as a major element in CENTCOMs war-fighting effort had not been anticipated.

Two days later Warden's briefing was presented to the chairman of the Joint Chiefs of Staff and the service chiefs. A final briefing to Schwarzkopf in Washington, DC, took place on August 17, after which, at Schwarzkopf's direction, Warden and several of his CHECKMATE colleagues flew to Riyadh to present the plan to Lieutenant General Horner and the CENTCOM staff.

When Warden and his party arrived in Riyadh, they were advised by a colleague that CENTAF had given little thought to an air offensive. The existing CENTAF air plan focused almost entirely on an all-out defense against an attack by Iraqi armor and a possible invasion of Saudi Arabia. That narrow focus, defensive in nature, reflected the Tactical Air Command's perception of an air mission that had evolved over decades devoted to supporting the Army against a massive Soviet tank assault across the plains of Germany. To many in the service, the Air Force in recent years had neglected to think of combat in bold, strategic terms. Warden and his team were about to be confronted with that reality.

In appearance, Horner, as described by military historian Rick Atkinson, was "thickset and inelegant, possessed of brawny forearms and an oval face that thrust itself out to the world with fighter pilot assurance." Warden's presentation quickly ran afoul of Horner's temper and his predisposition. Warden and Horner could hardly have been further apart by appearance or temperament. Horner, the hard-partying, hard-charging fighter pilot had no compunction against publicly denigrating subordinates. Warden, by contrast, was slim, finely chiseled, intense, assured of his convictions. In his world facts, ideas, and concepts mattered most—and they could be explained to critics.

Horner, tired and overwhelmed by his duties and acting CINC, reacted antagonistically from the outset. Predisposed to finding fault with a Pentagon "staff puke" whom he regarded as usurping his role, Horner imperiously demeaned Warden's efforts as "academic." Warden, while strong-willed and far from being a "people person," did not share the rudeness or vulgarity prominent in many of his colleagues in the fighter pilot community. Interrupted by Horner's derogatory asides to his staff, Warden struggled his way through the briefing slides. Horner was not an officer accustomed to, or pleased by, opposition to his views. Particularly uncomfortable moments occurred after a Horner tirade that the plan lacked emphasis on addressing the danger from Iraq's armored forces. Warden responded—correctly as results would show—that the threat was overrated. The Iraqis would not be able to function under the U.S. air superiority. Horner, Warden said, was being overly pessimistic. Those were not words that Horner was accustomed to hearing, especially in front of an audience.

When the briefing eventually concluded, Horner kept the members of the CHECKMATE staff who had accompanied Warden in Riyadh to work with CENTAF planners. Warden was not invited to stay. Disconsolate, he was preparing to board the return flight when David Deptula, a member of his team who had been asked to stay in Saudi Arabia, told him, "Don't worry, sir. We'll try to maintain the integrity of the plan."

In the days ahead, that was exactly what happened. Despite the callousness with which Warden's proposal had been greeted, the inherent strength—indeed, brilliance—of the plan shone through. Eventually, its potential became apparent even to the original "Black Hole" planners.

Despite the occasional sniping, Warden's blueprint not only survived but flourished. To Colin Powell and members of the National Command Authority, there was no doubt about the genesis of the plan or the source of inspiration for it. Powell later wrote "His [Warden's] concept remained the heart of the Desert Storm air campaign."

From their workplace in the basement of the Pentagon, Warden and his CHECKMATE group continued to provide ideas and data in a steady flow to Deptula and others at CENTAF (who sometimes disguised the source so as not to provoke Horner's wrath). Warden expanded his contacts with the CIA, NSA, DIA, and other intelligence agencies, further refining the information and proposals sent to Riyadh.

Several changes were made to the basic plan over the next weeks, many of them generated by Warden and his Pentagon team. Target categories were increased from 10 to 12. Strategic targets grew from 84 to 386 by the time air attacks began on January 17, 1991. Eventually, the number would exceed 700.

As the campaign reached its peak, the results played out as Warden had envisioned them: strategic targets were annihilated, neutralized, or degraded, and Saddam's military forces were torn apart. Long after the last bombs had fallen, the brilliance of the air campaign would be the facet of the war most studied and remembered. As author and military theoretician Colonel Richard T. Reynolds concluded regarding the strategic air campaign, "The least that could be said about it was that by so thoroughly destroying the Iraqi capability to conduct warfare, it permitted a war-winning ground campaign. The most that could be said about the air campaign was that it won the war."

Noted commentator David Halberstam echoed those views. It was Halberstam's conviction that "if one of the news magazines had wanted to run on its cover the photograph of the man who had played the most critical role in achieving victory, it might well have chosen Warden instead of Powell or Schwarzkopf."

Before

John Warden graduated from the United States Air Force Academy in 1965. His early interest in strategic matters and high-echelon planning and decision-making was evidenced by his choice of academic major (national security affairs) and by his brief flirtation with transferring to West Point. The latter notion was precipitated by his concern that the nation's air power was being subordinated to the Army in national security considerations. A book by military theorist J. F. C. Fuller, *The Leadership of Alexander the Great*, dissuaded him from pursuing that course and prompted a lifelong interest in strategy and the science of conflict.

As a young officer he flew F-4 Phantom II missions from South Korea during the 1967 *Pueblo* incident. Two years later he completed 266 combat missions in Vietnam as a forward air controller piloting an OV-10 Bronco.

Like many airmen who served in Vietnam, Warden was appalled by the lack of an overarching strategy for combating the war. Likewise, the shifting, conflicting rules of engagement seemed inane and were costly to the air crews constrained by them. He became an advocate for overwhelming force, clear objectives, and a coalescence of military and political objectives. Years later, the introductory slide to his Instant Thunder briefing to General Schwarzkopf would reflect those convictions. It would be Instant Thunder, overwhelming, decisive, immediate, not Rolling Thunder, slow and piecemeal.

A 1975 tour at the Pentagon placed him in the Directorate of Plans with a focus on the Middle East. There, he developed initial ties with the intelligence community and began to attract the attention of senior officers for his astute strategic assessments.

Though still a relatively young officer with but a bit more than a decade of service, "Warden had also become something of a lightning rod in that he was not afraid to forcefully express his views, even to senior officers, and was somewhat impatient with those who disagreed with him. . . . Warden was at this point, and would remain throughout his career, the quintessential air power advocate, and a very controversial figure."

Returned to flying duties after his initial Pentagon tour, Warden moved through a series of flying-related assignments in Europe: wing director of operations; deputy commander for operations, detachment commander, and squadron commander. As a student at National College, Warden wrote an influential book titled *The Air Campaign: Planning for Combat.* The treatise defined his theories of air operations and focused on air power as a determinant factor in warfare in the modern age. The book, though controversial, was widely read throughout the defense establishment. Several of the book's tenets provided the framework for the Desert Storm air campaign and later evolved into the Prometheus Strategy Planning System.

Another tour in Europe, this time at Bitburg, Germany, as commander of a tactical fighter wing, followed his war college assignment. The Bitburg tour was cut short when Warden was again posted to the Pentagon, this time as Director of Warfighting Concepts, which encompassed the CHECKMATE operation. Warden was in those duties when Saddam Hussein invaded Kuwait.

After

Two notable, unique jobs followed Warden's CHECKMATE time. In 1991, in his penultimate assignment, Warden served as special assistant for policy and national security affairs for Vice President Dan Quayle. His final duty left a lasting mark on the Air Force. As commandant of Air Command and Staff College, Warden completely revised the school's organizational structure and curriculum, steering it toward a focus on combat and war-fighting objectives. The school reaped several academic honors during his tenure. Warden retired from the Air Force in June 1995 and has subsequently devoted his time to writing and to development of "Prometheus," a strategic planning concept.

Deeper in the Shadows: David A. Deptula

The Keeper of the Master Plan

Deptula served as the essential liaison between Pentagon planners and the CENT-COM staff in the war room in Riyadh. His easygoing manner disguised an iron will and incisive mind. Rather quickly, he was designated as CENTCOM's principal air offensive campaign planner. Operating in a milieu of prickly personalities and outsized egos, he was the glue that linked the skills of the Pentagon and CENTCOM planners together.
U.S. AIR FORCE—U.S. AIR FORCE HISTORY OFFICE

It is almost without precedent to single out a relatively junior officer as playing a definitive role in constructing and implementing a strategic campaign plan in a major conflict. In Desert Storm, Air Force Lieutenant Colonel David A. Deptula inhabited a role somewhat similar to that played by Major General George Crist during Operation Urgent Fury in Grenada. Deptula was an essential liaison who kept things spliced together between Horner's "Black Hole" staff in Riyadh and Warden's CHECKMATE planners in the Pentagon. But Deptula was far more than a conduit for transferring targeting ideas, analyses, and intelligence data. He, as would soon become apparent, was also a premier strategic planner who possessed one of the Air Force's most incisive minds.

To the prickly personalities that formed the Desert Storm senior hierarchy, he brought an additional special gift: he could "get along" with everyone. One contemporary's character sketch of Deptula described him as "a big teddy bear type of guy with a friendly manner." (Deptula was six feet, two inches, and 215 pounds.) Also, he had worked with both Horner and Warden in the past and was a known, highly regarded commodity.

Underneath the pleasant persona was an iron-willed "give-no-quarter" approach and an extraordinary facility for getting to the heart of key issues. The latter quality was combined with a rare talent for explaining complex matters in simple, easy-to-understand terms.

Deptula was a member of the secretary of the Air Force's staff when the Kuwait crisis developed. He quickly confided his concerns to Warden that the Air Force's initial planning for the prospective war was inadequate and ill-conceived. The CENTCOM staff had pulled material off the shelf from an existing plan that was deficient in several aspects. Deptula was subsequently moved from his work in the secretary's office and placed under Warden on the CHECKMATE cadre. Deptula fully shared Warden's views regarding air power: the enemy structure should be regarded as a system held together by strategic centers of gravity. Those key components should be given priority in the air campaign.

Deptula had accompanied Warden to Riyadh and was one of the CHECKMATE planners that Horner had asked to remain and assist the CENTCOM staff in the "Black Hole." Deptula's qualities were immediately evident to Horner, Glosson, and the rest of the CHECKMATE entourage. He was rather quickly named principal offensive air campaign planner for Operation Desert Storm.

Deptula's work in Riyadh relied on interchanges with Warden's group, who, like the Riyadh staff, worked 24-hour days through the course of the war. His conversations with Warden gave Deptula—and through him the Riyadh planners—an unsurpassed capability to plan and conduct what was to become one of history's most notable campaigns. Working closely with Horner and Glosson on a day-to-day basis, Deptula convinced both men of the efficacy of Warden's Instant Thunder concept and the prospects offered by a strategic air attack. The initial stage of the air war would come to look much like Warden's Instant Thunder proposal.

The CENTCOM plan was transformed from a rather narrowly focused defensive orientation into a full-fledged air campaign against strategic targets as well as Iraqi armor and fielded forces. Deptula said later that he used an "effects-based" approach in building the Desert Storm air campaign targeting plans: "the solution lay in effects-based rather than destruction-based targeting."

John Warden's blueprint for the strategic dismemberment of Iraq and its military forces will likely be the focus of historians for years to come. It is difficult, though, to see how it could have come to full fruition without the assistance and intervention of David Deptula. Throughout the course of the war he was the keeper of the master attack plan.

Before and After

Deptula was a distinguished ROTC graduate from the University of Virginia in 1974. He entered active duty in 1976 after completing work on a master's degree and graduating from pilot training the following year. A series of F-15-related duties—flight lead, instructor pilot, and aerial demonstration pilot—ensued over the next five years.

January 1983 brought his first Washington-area posting as a staff officer in the Air Staff Training Program, Weapon Systems Division, Office of the Secretary of the Air Force for Legislative Liaison. Another tour focused on flying duties preceded attendance at Armed Forces Staff College. Deptula returned to the Pentagon in early 1988, first as an Air Staff action officer in the Department of Warfighting Concepts and subsequently as a policy and issues analyst in the Office of the Secretary of the Air Force. He was in those duties when called first to the CHECKMATE staff and then to Riyadh at the outset of the Gulf War. At CENTCOM he served as principal offensive air campaign planner for the director of campaign plans, and director, Iraq Targeting Group through the remainder of the war.

After

The years following Desert Storm brought a mixture of flying assignments, school attendance (National War College), command billets (Combined Task Force for Operation Northern Watch; General George C. Kenney Warfighting Headquarters, Pacific; vice commander, Pacific Air Forces), and major air command and air staff duties (director of plans and programs, Headquarters Air Combat Command; director of air and space operations, Pacific Air Forces; and deputy chief of staff for intelligence, surveillance, and reconnaissance, Headquarters United States Air Force). Deptula was the first officer to serve in the latter duties.

During his career Deptula was posted to an impressive number of key temporary billets. In addition to his work in Desert Storm, he was a member of the Secretary of Defense Commission on Roles and Missions of the Armed Forces; commander of Operation Northern Watch; director of the Combined Air Operations Center, Operation Enduring Freedom, and component commander of Operation United Assistance, the relief effort that followed the tsunami in South Asia. He also served as Joint Task Force commander for Operation Deep Freeze support for research activities in Antarctica.

Among numerous other honors, he was the recipient of the General H. H. Arnold Award, the Air Force Association's highest honor to a military member in the field of national security.

Deptula retired from the Air Force as a lieutenant general effective October 1, 2010.

Special Mention: William "Gus" Pagonis

"The Animated Greek Logistician"

Beginning with no equipment, facilities, or staff, Pagonis provisioned, fed, billeted, and equipped 650,000 rapidly assembling forces. In late October 1990 a decision was made to send an entire additional corps to the theater—another 146,000 troops, 1,400 tanks, and 37,000 pieces of equipment, along with associated munitions and weapons. His innovative solutions on both occasions have become the source of legends. Only one battlefield promotion was awarded during Desert Storm: it went to Gus Pagonis. U.S. ARMY—U.S. ARMY HISTORY AND EDUCATION CENTER

Major General William "Gus" Pagonis's story perhaps lies even deeper in the shadows than that of other leaders from the Gulf War, or for that matter, most other of the nation's conflicts. In many ways his accomplishments parallel that of Montgomery Meigs, quartermaster general of the Union Army during the Civil War. Though little recalled today, Meigs's contributions, as one member of Abraham Lincoln's cabinet said, were essential to the Union's victory. Like Meigs—who provisioned an army that grew from 16,000 members to two million during the war, exploited the capabilities of available transport, and excelled at supplying armies on the move—Pagonis essentially began with nothing. The first of Schwarzkopf's senior staff to arrive in theater, Pagonis is described in Schwarzkopf's memoir as spending his first two nights in Saudi Arabia sleeping on his poncho on a concrete slab. (In another version, those first nights were spent in the backseat of a rented Chevrolet.) From that meager beginning, he provisioned, fed, and billeted a force that quickly grew to more than 650,000 soldiers. Within a month Pagonis would bed down more troops and hardware than the Saudis had in their entire military establishment. As troops poured in, he used hundreds of Bedouin tents that he found in Saudi Arabia—tents normally used for the hajj, the annual pilgrimage to Mecca—and big Octoberfest beer festival tents, which he hauled in from Germany to provide shade and shelter.

For the duration of the war, Pagonis, in the midst of the turmoil of arriving troops, the shifting positions of major units, and limited available accommodations, provided food, clothing, shelter, transportation, equipment, and munitions for the ever-growing assemblage of American troops. Post offices, clinics, recreation and messing facilities, and other amenities were quickly assembled and made operational.

While the initial cadre of XVIII Airborne Corps personnel were settling in, late October brought orders from the Bush administration to double the size of the American force. The entire U.S. Army VII Corps would be brought in from bases in Germany. The burden again fell on Pagonis and his staff to bed down the huge assemblage. Over a two-month period, Pagonis's organization provided housing, sustenance, and equipment for an additional

146,000 troops in 83 different units. Through his efforts, spaces and provisions for 1,400 more tanks and 37,000 added pieces of equipment were also quickly forthcoming. The enormous logistics exercise involved 21 ships and hundreds of flights of military and civilian contract aircraft.

As the tempo increased and the date of the ground offensive drew near, Pagonis leased nearly every available truck in Saudi Arabia to pre-position dozens of sites far west along the Saudi-Iraqi border. One analyst equated that feat as being equivalent to moving the city of Richmond, Virginia, on short notice. When the shooting began, the ability of American formations to reprovision on the move astounded friends and foes alike.

Only one battlefield promotion was awarded during the Gulf War. It went to Schwarzkopf's "animated Greek logistician." On January 20, 1991, Schwarzkopf promoted Gus Pagonis to lieutenant general.

Before and After

Pagonis was commissioned in 1964 and served in a variety of command and staff positions related to transportation, logistics, and support operations. He commanded a transportation company in Vietnam and used that experience to provide innovative solutions when support difficulties occurred in the austere Saudi Arabian environment. A Pentagon tour in the Office of Legislative Liaison preceded a command billet in a transportation group and chief of staff slots in two infantry brigades. Those duties were followed by service as commanding general, Division Support Command, 4th Infantry Division. Pagonis was assigned to Schwarzkopf's staff while posted to a major function in the Office of the Deputy Chief of Staff for Logistics in Washington, DC.

After Desert Storm, Pagonis was assigned as commanding general, 21st Support Command, Europe, where he served until he retired in 1993. His postretirement career featured influential corporate roles in organizations such as Sears & Roebuck, Rail America, and others. He authored the book *Moving Mountains: Lessons in Leadership and Logistics from the Gulf War*, and for a time was active on the public speaking circuit.

A Familiar Name in a Lesser-Known Role: H. R. McMaster

The Warrior-Thinker

H. R. McMaster is much better known for two things—authoring an influential book titled *Dereliction of Duty*, which chastised senior commanders of the Vietnam era for not confronting administration officials about shortcomings in strategy, and serving for two years as President Donald Trump's national security advisor. Less well known is his leadership as a young officer during a Desert Storm tank battle. In an engagement known as 73 Easting, McMaster's nine tanks destroyed 23 Iraqi tanks in 23 minutes. The battle continues to be studied in the Army's professional schools. McMaster was awarded a Silver Star for his leadership during the encounter. U.S. ARMY—U.S. ARMY HISTORY AND EDUCATION CENTER

Retired Lieutenant General H. R. McMaster is most widely known for two roles during his professional life. The first, as a young officer, was his authorship of the book *Dereliction of Duty*, which challenged American policies and decision-making during the Vietnam War. Most noted for its sharp criticisms of senior officers for their failure to confront President Lyndon B. Johnson and Secretary of Defense Robert S. McNamara regarding the shortcomings of their Vietnam policy—which, in McMaster's view, was inadequate to either pacify the Viet Cong or defeat the North Vietnamese—the book was extensively read in military circles.

The second was his tenure as national security advisor for President Donald J. Trump. McMaster served in that position from March 15, 2017, until March 27, 2018. The cause of his resignation was the source of considerable speculation, varying from conflicts with the Trump staff, most particularly Steve Bannon, and perhaps deteriorating personal relationships with then-Secretary of Defense James Mattis and White House Chief of Staff John Kelly. President Trump was alleged to have been uncomfortable with McMaster's briefing style, which he regarded as "gruff and condescending," and thought McMaster was "aggressive" and "prone to lecture." It is also thought by some that the president took umbrage at McMaster's publicly stated assessment that the Russians had meddled in the 2016 presidential election, and that the two men disagreed on the president's interchanges with the North Koreans.

Much less is known about McMaster's consequential service in the Middle East. Spanning a decade and a half, his duties in the region began as a captain in the Gulf War. He received a Silver Star for leadership during the Battle of 73 Easting on February 26, 1991. In 23 minutes, his troop of nine tanks from the 2nd Armored Cavalry Regiment destroyed 23 Iraqi tanks without sustaining a loss. The battle, and his leadership, continue to be studied in the Army's professional schools.

After

After 73 Easting and the remainder of his time in the Gulf War, McMaster's assignments included instructor duty at West Point, attendance at Army Command and General Staff College, and command of 1st Squadron, 4th Cavalry Regiment. In 2002 McMaster entered into a series of staff positions at CENTCOM that immersed him in planning and operations related to Iraq. As he moved up the CENTCOM hierarchy, he served as executive officer to the deputy commander and subsequently as director of the Commander's Advisory Group—essentially a think tank for the commander in chief.

In 2004 he assumed command of the 3rd Armored Cavalry Regiment and, soon after, deployed with the unit to Iraq. Assigned to secure the city of Tal Afar, a hotbed of insurgent activity, McMaster's innovative approach was the subject of a documentary on PBS *Frontline*, a segment on CBS's *60 Minutes*, and an article in the *New York Times*. In an approach that mirrored the regimen established by David Petraeus and later enshrined in

Army doctrine, McMaster embedded small groups of soldiers in the city, providing a visible presence, 24-hour security, and sources for gathering information. McMaster's extraordinary success led to an invitation from Vice President Dick Cheney to provide a personal briefing.

McMaster commanded the 3rd Armored Cavalry Regiment until June 29, 2006, after which he departed for London to become a senior research associate at the International Institute for Strategic Studies; there he studied issues related to insurgency warfare and developing tactics to combat terrorism. Beginning in August 2007, he spent a year as part of a team established by Petraeus to revise the Army's Counterinsurgency Field Manual. Assignment with the Army's Training and Doctrine Command followed. After a posting to Kabul, McMaster was promoted in 2012 to major general and assigned to Fort Benning, Georgia, as commander of the Army's Maneuver Center of Excellence. Three-star rank came in 2014, and with it his penultimate assignment in the military as deputy commanding general of the U.S. Army Training and Doctrine Command and Director of the U.S. Army's Training and Doctrine Command's (TRADOC) Army Capabilities Integration Center.

McMaster retired from the military on May 18, 2018, two months after resigning as national security advisor. He subsequently published a memoir and accepted a position as visiting fellow at Stanford University.

References to the extraordinary caliber of McMaster's military service have continued to surface in recent years. A colleague from the war in Afghanistan called him "the architect of the future U.S. Army" and "the 21st century's pre-eminent warrior." General Jack Keane, former Army vice chief of staff, recalled McMaster's "sheer brilliance as a wartime brigade commander."

CHAPTER SEVEN

Afghanistan/Iraq/Global War on Terrorism

SETTING THE STAGE

For many in the American audience, the wars in Afghanistan and Iraq seemed to merge like the channels of a river flowing, sometimes at flood tide, through the early decades of the 21st century. What began in Afghanistan in September 2001 as a national payback for the 9/11 attacks on the United States later morphed into a countrywide operation in Afghanistan and all-out invasion of Iraq. In the years ahead, the two wars would be prosecuted in tandem, and at times portions of the forces sent to the region would be employed interchangeably.

Though the conflicts had certain elements in common, the major objectives that inspired each of them varied considerably. Afghanistan was driven by vengeance—retribution for the assaults on the American homeland. The focus, at least at the outset, was fairly narrow—to capture or kill Osama bin Laden and neutralize or destroy the al-Qaeda terrorist group responsible for the attacks.

The invasion of Iraq aimed at eliminating weapons of mass destruction thought by the George W. Bush administration to be in possession of the Iraqi regime. Bush's staff argued that destroying the stockpiles, munitions factories, and research laboratories that sustained the weapons programs would concurrently rid the world of a tyrant who abused his own people and posed a threat to other nations in the region. The administration also sought to establish a link between bin Laden and the regime of Saddam Hussein.

Of the two wars, the one in Iraq was far more controversial.

231

Whereas the 9/11 attacks stunned and outraged much of the world—in the following days, students shouting "We are all Americans" marched in the streets of *Tehran*—the invasion of Iraq drew far less support from around the globe.

In Afghanistan members of the international community, led by nations from the NATO alliance, contributed troops to support the effort. In Iraq the Bush administration cobbled together a modest "coalition of the willing," to which only the United States, Great Britain, Australia, and to a lesser extent Poland contributed combat forces. A few other countries deployed medical units or sent only token contingents and restricted their employment and locations.

Concurrent with the dual wars in Afghanistan and Iraq, under the Global War on Terrorism rubric initialed by President George W. Bush and expanded by President Barack Obama, American Special Forces, trainers, and specialists were deployed to dozens of countries around the globe. The animating concept of the global war was to seek out and destroy terrorist cells and remove their threat to the American homeland. The terrorists were regarded as stateless military combatants and thus subject to attack regardless of physical location or domicile. It was a contentious legal doctrine that was used to support controversial kill/capture operations.

In varying degrees, the U.S. involvement in Afghanistan and Iraq continued for two decades. Focusing mostly on Iraq, critics suggest that hardliners in the Bush administration "cherry-picked" intelligence data in an attempt to justify the war. Lieutenant General H. R. McMaster, who criticized Vietnam-era American military and political leadership of deception in *Dereliction of Duty*, concluded that in Iraq there was not a deliberate effort to deceive the American public. Rather, McMaster said, "the planning for the war was inadequate. There was an intellectual failure, more than deception."

Advocates of the war argued that deposing Saddam Hussein and prospectively setting Iraq on the road to democratic government were in themselves signal achievements for the Middle East.

The costs to the United States in blood and treasure in what some came to label the "forever wars" was substantial. As of May 2021, casualty figures for Afghanistan were 2,218 deaths (1,833 killed in combat) and 20,093 wounded. Comparable figures for Iraq were 4,418 deaths (3,481 killed in combat) and 31,994 wounded. Other actions in the Persian Gulf region resulted in 74 deaths (38 killed in combat) and 288 wounded.

In total, more than 2.7 million American military personnel were deployed to Afghanistan and Iraq. More than half served more than one tour. Troop strength in Afghanistan peaked at 99,800 in 2012. In Iraq the highest total, 165,607, occurred in 2008. Dollar costs of the Global War on Terrorism for the same period were estimated at $5.5 trillion, with another trillion spent on care for veterans.

While the tandem conflicts continued in Afghanistan and Iraq, the growth of new and ongoing terrorist incidents elsewhere in the region continued generally unabated. Eventually, al-Qaeda and ISIS offshoots, as well as other militant organizations such as al-Shabaab were spawned in Yemen, Syria, Somalia, and other locations in the Middle East and Africa. The Global War on Terrorism followed.

THE PATH TO WAR

Although Osama bin Laden had been linked to bombings throughout the Mideast region, few Americans through much of the 1980s and 1990s, other than a small number of military and intelligence officials, were aware of him or his al-Qaeda organization. Even events on U.S. soil—the 1990 slaying of Rabbi Meir Kahane and the 1993 bombing of the World Trade Center—did not draw major attention. Nor, to a surprising degree, did two fatwas that, now viewed in context, posed clear declarations of war against the United States. The first, in August 1996—"Declaration of War Against American Occupying of the Two Holy Places"—focused on U.S. personnel based in Saudi Arabia while maintaining the "no-fly zone" (Operation Southern Watch) over portions of neighboring Iraq.

The second fatwa, in February 1998, was broader and more ominous. "Killing Americans," bin Laden's edict said, was an "individual duty for every Muslim." Bombings of the American embassies in Kenya and Tanzania followed soon after.

For much of this period, U.S. policy vacillated between treating bin Laden and al-Qaeda as a law enforcement problem or as a military opponent. In 1999 an American grand jury returned an indictment. However, the Taliban government in Afghanistan, where bin Laden was then sheltering, refused requests for extradition. In August the Clinton administration authorized the firing of cruise missiles against bin Laden's base in Afghanistan. Bin Laden was not at the encampment at the time, and the strikes were generally ineffective.

On October 12, 2000, al-Qaeda operatives struck the USS *Cole* while it was refueling in port at Aden, Yemen. The attack killed 17 sailors and wounded 37 others. On this occasion, near the transition point between the Clinton and Bush (43) administrations, the U.S. took almost no outwardly visible action in response. Some analysts have conjectured that the indecisive shifts in policy and, particularly, the rather tepid retaliatory efforts might have added further encouragement—if any was needed—for bin Laden's decision to carry out the 9/11 attacks.

The attacks, and the 3,000 American deaths that resulted from them, would define the presidency of George W. Bush and guide the nation's political and military actions around the globe for years to come.

Afghanistan

Two days after 9/11, President George W. Bush authorized the CIA to launch operations against al-Qaeda and its Taliban adherents in Afghanistan. President Bush's order called for the CIA to "collect real-time actionable intelligence to help shape the battlefield and to use all means to target al-Qaeda." Congress also acted quickly to provide the Bush administration with a legal basis for action against Afghanistan, where bin Laden was known to have established his operating base. On September 14 the Senate and House of Representatives gave the president unprecedented latitude to wage global war. The wide sweep of the authorization allowed Bush, and later Obama, to extend its scope far beyond Afghanistan, eventually transforming the focus of operations to locations around the globe.

The Authorization for Use of Military Force stated: "The President is authorized to use all necessary and appropriate force against those nations, organizations, or persons he determines planned, authorized, committed, or aided the terrorist attack . . . or harbored such organizations or persons."

Three days later, on September 17, the president signed a secret directive—code-named "Greystone"—that granted the CIA authority to capture and hold militants across the globe. The document provided the auspices for the controversial "black sites" program and "kill/capture" operations.

The initial CIA team deployed to Afghanistan within days of the attack on the World Trade Center. Most were established and in place by September 27. The initial unit was small—about 60 members—former Delta Force veterans, former SEALs, and other personnel with Special Ops backgrounds. On October 19 they were joined by a Special Forces commando team, the first American military to arrive "in country."

The combined U.S. military and CIA paramilitary force quickly struck at the Taliban regime and al-Qaeda terrorist cadres. They were soon joined by American and British air units that hammered targets over a wide area. The campaign progressed rapidly: success was achieved at a pace not anticipated by planners. By November 9 the first Taliban stronghold, Mazar-e-Sharif, was taken by Afghani Northern Alliance forces allied with American units. Two days later Kabul fell. Kandahar, the spiritual home of the Taliban, was taken on December 7, effectively smashing the Taliban regime and ending the organization's grip on national power. The government's fall deprived al-Qaeda of its sanctuary, eventually forcing bin Laden and other key officials to seek refuge elsewhere.

The most noted and controversial engagement was fought December 6–17 at Tora Bora, a complex of caves in a mountainous region along the Afghanistan-Pakistan border about 90 miles east-southeast of Kabul. Osama bin Laden and considerable numbers of al-Qaeda militia were believed to have taken refuge in the cave system, which had been used as a stronghold during Russia's invasion of Afghanistan. U.S. officials, then and later, assessed the operation—code-named "Jawbreaker"—as providing the best chance to kill or capture bin Laden.

As the units assembled, air strikes saturated the base area, dropping tons of laser-guided and enormous "daisy-cutter" bombs on the cave complex. In early December personnel from the CIA's military component, the National Clandestine Service Special Activities Division and the 5th Special Forces Group, with assistance from contingents of British commandos and a German Special Forces cadre, began moving toward the complex.

On December 5 Northern Alliance troops seized the ground below and adjacent to the caves in an attempt to block potential al-Qaeda escape routes. The allies finished clearing the complex on December 17, killing an estimated 200 al-Qaeda fighters while sustaining few casualties. An extensive search uncovered no trace of bin Laden or other members of the al-Qaeda leadership.

Though the outcome was a clear tactical success, the handling of the battle continues to spark controversy. The leader of the CIA contingent wanted to deploy additional numbers of Army Rangers, a request that was turned down, possibly in the belief that if bin Laden had escaped, he would be captured by the Pakistanis and turned over to U.S. officials. General Tommy Franks, commander, CENTCOM, asserted that "bin Laden was never within our grasp."

Based on documents recovered at the scene and interviews with fighters captured during the battle, a Senate investigation concluded that bin Laden had in fact been at Tora Bora and that he and other senior leaders had escaped. General Franks's actions during the operation and others in the defense hierarchy, including Secretary of Defense Donald Rumsfeld, have subsequently been called into question. Some critics have judged Franks as being inattentive to the battle, not comprehending the importance of killing or capturing bin Laden. One analyst labeled Franks's refusal to deploy 800 additional Rangers from nearby bases to assist in the assault on Tora Bora as "one of the greatest military blunders in recent U.S. history."

In retrospect, it appears that U.S. officials perhaps overvalued Pakistan's enthusiasm and effectiveness in guarding the country's frontier with Afghanistan. Similarly, the allies likely placed too much reliance on Northern Alliance and other native forces who, either by inattention or bribery, or some combination of both, may have abetted bin Laden's escape.

In the years subsequent to Tora Bora, Afghanistan continued to be a battleground. The size and intensity of the encounters ebbed and flowed; manpower surges were followed by drawdowns, and at times America's commitment to the Afghan struggle took a backseat in men, money, and material to the conflict in Iraq.

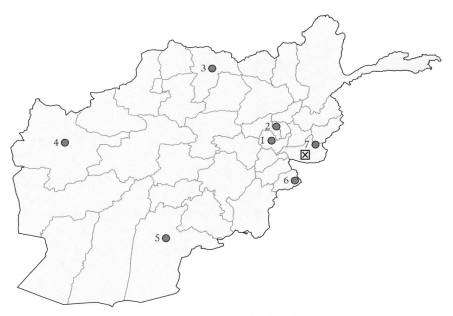

1. **Kabul:** Taken by U.S./allies Nov 13, 2001; taken by Taliban Aug 14, 2021
2. **Bagram:** Primary U.S. base, vacated July 2, 2021
3. **Mazar-e-Sharif:** Taken by U.S./allies Nov 9, 2001; taken by Taliban Aug 2021
4. **Herat:** Taken by U.S./allies Nov 12, 2001; taken by Taliban Aug 13, 2021
5. **Kandahar:** Taken by U.S./allies Dec 7, 2001; taken by Taliban Aug 13, 2021
6. **Khost:** Taken by U.S./allies Nov 2001; taken by Taliban Aug 15, 2021
7. **Jalalabad:** Taken by U.S./allies Nov 14, 2001; taken by Taliban Aug 13, 2021
X. **Tora Bora:** Battle fought Dec 6–17, 2001

Afghanistan

Forgotten Leader: Gary Berntsen

The Storming of Tora Bora—the First of the "What-Ifs"

An officer with the CIA's National Clandestine Special Activities Division, Berntsen led a coalition of CIA personnel, special operations contingents, and Northern Alliance allies in ousting the Taliban from Afghanistan. He also guided the storming of Tora Bora, a complex of caves and bunkers where Osama bin Laden and key followers were thought to have taken refuge. Berntsen's request for 800 Rangers to help seal Tora Bora escape routes was refused by the CENTCOM commander, a decision that some analysts believed may have enabled bin Laden to escape into Pakistan.

PENGUIN RANDOM HOUSE: CROWN PUBLICATIONS

A CIA officer, Gary Berntsen led a unit of the CIA's National Clandestine Special Activities Division (the CIA's military arm) during the taking of the Tora Bora stronghold in December 2001. Though not a uniformed member of the United States military, Berntsen and his team played a key role in the successful storming of the al-Qaeda redoubt. The defeat of the Taliban and al-Qaeda forces removed any vestiges of Taliban control and deprived al-Qaeda formations of their fortress-sanctuary in Afghanistan.

Berntsen's team arrived at Jalalabad, Afghanistan, on December 3, 2001. Two days later, after Northern Alliance troops had gained control of areas near the cave complex, Berntsen's team of CIA and Special Ops forces began calling in nonstop air strikes that lasted for three days, causing al-Qaeda fighters to move to prepared positions higher on the mountainsides. A few days later additional numbers of U.S. Special Forces, British Commandos, and German Special Forces arrived to augment Berntsen's group. Under pressure from Berntsen's units and Northern Alliance formations, al-Qaeda representatives talked the Northern Alliance commander into a temporary truce—a unilateral decision on his part—ostensibly for the purpose of surrendering weapons. The pause in action provided a window of opportunity that, some have conjectured, might have enabled bin Laden and other al-Qaeda leaders to escape into Pakistan.

Heavy fighting broke out again on December 12. Berntsen's contingent and Northern Alliance and tribal militias numbering about 2,000 fighters attacked caves and bunkers, sweeping over outposts and training areas embedded throughout the huge complex. The last caves were cleared on December 17.

As the allied units approached the Tora Bora area, Berntsen had seen a developing opportunity to kill or capture bin Laden who, along with key functionaries, was believed, based on solid intelligence, to be at Tora Bora. The prospect of eliminating the threat presented itself to the United States from the al-Qaeda organization. To Berntsen, the door appeared open to bring the war on terrorism to a rapid conclusion. To increase the chances for success, he requested additional Rangers be sent to aid in the attack and help seal escape routes. As noted, that request was refused by the CENTCOM commander, General Tommy Franks.

The uncertainty remains. Strategically, a major opportunity may have been missed. Certainly that was no fault of Berntsen's, who sought to eliminate bin Laden and foreclose the possibility of al-Qaeda's survival.

Tactically, the battle was handled exceptionally well. Coalition forces suffered minimal casualties, and no U.S. personnel were known to have been killed. Al-Qaeda elements were believed to have suffered 200 killed from the ground assault and air attacks. Sixty operatives were captured, some of whom were later incarcerated at the U.S. military prison at Guantanamo, Cuba.

Before and After

Berntsen's career as a member of the armed forces consisted of four years enlisted service in the United States Air Force, during which he devoted large amounts of time to study, physical training, and skydiving. After his discharge, he attended college, where he focused on political science and Russian studies. He was preparing for a commission in the United States

Marines when, in October 1992, he was recruited into the CIA, where he would spend the duration of his career in the Directorate of Operations.

In August 1998 Berntsen led the CIA team that responded to the U.S. Embassy bombing at Dar es Salaam, Tanzania. His actions led to the capture of at least 21 individuals responsible for planning and carrying out the attack.

Berntsen was initially sent to Afghanistan on a subsequently aborted mission in March 2000. Three months after 9/11, in November 2001, he was assigned as commander of CIA forces in eastern Afghanistan. He was serving in that role when he led the operation against the Tora Bora stronghold.

After

Berntsen left the CIA in June 2005. In his postretirement career he worked as an analyst for various news outlets and civilian and government agencies in addition to authoring works of fiction and nonfiction. His book *Human Intelligence, Counterterrorism, and National Leadership: A Pocket Guide* was published in November 2008 as a working guide for members of the incoming Obama administration.

In 2010 Berntsen was defeated in a primary election while running for a senate seat from New York State.

Iraq

To audiences around the globe, the Iraq War began on March 21, 2003, when at 6:00 a.m. Baghdad time, U.S. and allied forces moved across the Kuwait border into Iraq. Those units were not the first inside the ancient country, however. For varying lengths of time perhaps as many as 31 special forces teams from the U.S., UK, Australia, and Poland had been operating behind the lines seeking out Scud missile sites, seizing bridges and transportation nodes, securing oil fields, and capturing oil platforms. A CIA team had in fact been operating in northern Iraq (Kurdistan) since February 20 of the preceding year, paving the way for potential introduction of additional forces.

Controversy surrounding the war had begun before the first shots were fired and would continue for years to come. At times the intensity of the debate was discernable even among senior players inside the White House and State Department.

Propelled to a considerable degree by Vice President Dick Cheney, the George W. Bush administration attempted to leverage the considerable power granted it after 9/11 to expand operations beyond Afghanistan. Though the link was problematic, the administration argued that al-Qaeda had a center of support in Iraq, a threat made more ominous by a companion belief that Saddam Hussein's regime possessed weapons of mass destruction.

Numerous skeptics inside and outside the government took issue with the alleged tie between bin Laden and Saddam Hussein. Brent Scowcroft, former national security advisor to President George H. W. Bush, was perplexed by the suggested connection, writing that "the only thing that Osama bin Laden and Saddam Hussein have in common is that they both hate the United States. Saddam is an anti-cleric socialist." The latter remark referenced bin Laden's immersion in an intensely fanatical branch of the Muslim religion. In a soon-to-follow op-ed piece (*Wall Street Journal*, April 15, 2002), Scowcroft wrote that there is "scant evidence to tie Saddam Hussein to terrorist organizations and even less to the September 11, 2001 attack. Indeed, Saddam's goals have little in common with the terrorists who threaten us, and there is little incentive for him to make common cause with them."

Among other notables, General Hugh Shelton, chairman of the Joint Chiefs of Staff, concurred with Scowcroft's view. In Shelton's opinion, "there was not one shred, one iota of evidence that would say 9/11 was linked into Iraq."

The global consensus opposed an attack on Saddam Hussein, narrowing greatly the number of partners the U.S. could rely on for assistance. The Bush regime continued to look for evidence to justify stronger actions against Iraq, suggesting that aluminum tubes were possible centrifuges for use in enriching uranium. The assessment was disputed within the administration with Vice President Cheney and Secretary of Defense Rumsfeld taking a hard line, opposed by State Department officials including Secretary Colin Powell. Powell and the State Department noted that of the five surrounding countries, only Kuwait and Jordan acquiesced to military actions against Iraq.

In the end, the hardliners prevailed. A draft NSDD set forth U.S. intentions quite clearly: the U.S. goal was to "free Iraq in order to eliminate

Iraqi weapons of mass destruction and associated programs—to prevent Iraq from breaking out of containment and becoming a more dangerous threat to the region and beyond."

For the international community, the weapons of mass destruction issue had festered since the end of the Gulf War almost a decade earlier. A series of United Nations resolutions had initially resulted in an inspection system that imposed measures against Iraq for weapons of mass destruction–related infractions. That system had worked effectively for some years. Inspectors leveraged denials for entry to questionable locations and countered instances of Iraqi noncooperation by denying oil sales on the international market. In 1999 Saddam refused further access to facilities and expelled inspectors from Iraq. The inspection regime was replaced by a softer program that essentially allowed oil sales in return for humanitarian aid. Saddam, however, played fast and loose with aid intended for distribution among his hungry populace. Called into accounting, he once again refused to allow access to inspectors.

On November 8, 2002, a further United Nations Resolution, 1441, provided Iraq with "a final opportunity to comply with the disarmament obligations" that had been set by previous sanctions. Resolution 1441 broadened previous resolutions beyond the weapons of mass destruction issue, identifying explicit additional violations such as production of prohibited missiles and other armaments, refusal to compensate Kuwait for looting the nation during its period of occupation in 1990–91, and making false statements. Failure to comply would result "serious consequences." The latter term was agonizingly arrived at after three of the five members of the Security Council—France, Russia, and China (with France and Russia being most viscerally adamant)—opposed any wording that would connote automatic resort to armed conflict in the event of Iraq's noncompliance.

In response to the resolution, on November 27, Iraq once again allowed inspectors to return and released thousands of pages of documents, many of which had previously been made available, asserting that no weapons of mass destruction remained.

The United States, no longer willing to let the issue go unresolved, insisted that Iraq was in material breach of the United Nations Resolution. The majority of the permanent members of the Security Council and substantial numbers of the General Assembly continued to oppose the direct linkage of noncompliance with military intervention.

On March 16, 2003, President Bush met in the Azores with the prime ministers of Great Britain, Spain, and Portugal, the host country. The group established a March 17 deadline—the following day—for complete compliance with the United Nations' provisions. That response was not forthcoming. Four days later, the allied coalition went to war.

As shown in the comparison below, the Iraqi army that the allies would face was not as formidable as the force that had waged war in Desert Storm a bit more than a decade earlier.

	Desert Storm	2003
Republican Guard Divisions	7	6
Regular Army Divisions	27	17
Tactical Aircraft	815	310
SAMs	100	60
Tanks	5,000	2,000
Self-Propelled Artillery	500	150
Towed Guns	3,000	2,000
Armored Personnel Carriers	7,000	2,000

Altogether, the Iraqi military establishment consisted of about 400,000 members. The Republican Guard divisions were the most professional and the best trained and equipped. The regular army was composed mostly of conscripts and varied greatly in quality. Interestingly, as the fighting progressed, large numbers of irregular forces—fedayeen (martyrs)—proved to be particularly difficult opponents. Though most had but minimal training and were not especially well equipped, Iraq's homegrown anti-Western fanatics were joined by like believers from other Islamic nations—Syria, Egypt, Saudi Arabia, Morocco, and Pakistan foremost among them—in engaging in aggressive, self-sacrificing warfare.

At CENTCOM headquarters, planning for a potential attack had been ongoing for the better part of a year. General Tommy Franks had worked through several war plan iterations, and over time Secretary of Defense

Rumsfeld had shuffled additional troops into the area in packet sizes small enough to be inconspicuous. By the time the allies crossed the border into Iraq, 241,500 American servicemen and -women were deployed in the region. They were joined by 41,000 British, 2,000 Australians, and 200 Poles. Ground forces, from all allied nations, numbered 183,000.

Special Forces teams were already busy behind the scenes. The Polish unit captured oil platforms, and other special operators prevented the destruction of oil fields. Perhaps as many as 25 percent of Iraq's western desert was at least partially controlled by special ops personnel sent to the area to prevent Scud missile launches.

At six a.m. on March 21 the 1st Marine Division, soon to be followed by the 3rd Infantry Division, crossed the border, moving north into Iraq. (Kuwait, alone among Arab nations, provided the invaders with a place to assemble.) The 1st Marine Division was officially a component of the 1st Marine Expeditionary Force, which also consisted of Task Force Tarawa (a reinforced brigade) and the 3rd Marine Aircraft Wing. The 3rd Infantry was a component of V Corps, part of the Third Army. In addition to the division, its elements also included a portion of the 101st Airborne, a brigade of the 82nd Airborne, the 173rd Airborne Brigade, and elements of the 4th Infantry Division. The assault units met only light resistance. By the end of the day lead elements were as much as 60 miles inside Iraq and already in control of a sizable portion of Iraq's oil fields.

A British component, part of the 3rd Commando Brigade, accompanied the U.S. Marines' thrust. A second major British force, a mixed unit containing some U.S. troops, was launched by sea and captured the port of Umm Qasr and the Rumaila oil field. Soon after, while the bulk of U.S. forces moved toward Baghdad, the British unit set out to seize Basra, the nation's second-largest city.

The second day was a reprise of the first. Some elements of the 3rd Infantry Division closed the day 150 miles deep into Iraq. Officers reported that much of the Iraqi army seemed almost to be melting away. Particularly for recruits from the local area, "thousands of them are just taking off their uniforms and going home."

As the Americans moved deeper into the Iraqi heartland, pockets of intense fighting erupted. At Najaf, two days of street-by-street combat were required to clear the city. One of the few instances of heavy organized resistance took place at Hillah and the surrounding area on April 2–10. There the Iraqi Hammurabi Republican Guard Division engaged units of the U.S. 101st Airborne. When the battle was over, the way to Baghdad was open.

After fighting off waves of fedayeen attackers on April 3 and an assault by Republican Guard tanks on the next day, Marine units pushed into eastern Baghdad by April 7. Opposition was light at first, then increasingly heavy on April 9 as the fighting carried through university grounds where the Marines were faced by aggressive fedayeen defenders. By the end of that day the campus area was cleared and the Marines took Paradise Square, toppling the massive statue of Saddam Hussein.

As the Marines pressed through the city, spearheads of the 3rd Infantry were also moving against Baghdad after having reached the outskirts of the city on April 2. Meanwhile, U.S. paratroopers had created a second front, albeit a small one, in northern Iraq, where they had linked up with Kurdish fighters. CENTCOM assessed that two Republican Guard divisions had been rendered combat ineffective.

A week later U.S. Army forces were on the banks of the Tigris River, and Marines had moved into downtown Baghdad. On April 9 the Iraqi government collapsed, marking the end of Saddam Hussein's regime.

Allied casualties during the course of the fighting numbered 122 Americans and 33 British. The numbers of Iraqi casualties are not known. Highest numbers were among the fedayeen irregulars, and there were also considerable losses among those Republican Guard divisions that chose to engage in a major way. Large portions of the conscript regular army simply drifted away. Surprisingly few prisoners were taken, and most of those who were captured were soon set free.

After a lengthy search, on December 13, 2003, Saddam Hussein was captured near Tikrit. He was hanged on December 30, 2006, after being convicted by an Iraqi tribunal.

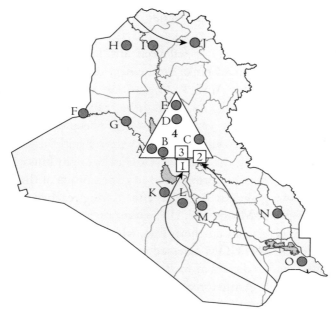

INVASION ROUTES—SITES OF MAJOR BATTLES AND INSURGENT ATTACKS

1. Major axis of attack (March 21–April 9)   3. Baghdad
2. Supporting axis of attack   4. Sunni Triangle

A. Ramadi   I. Mosul
B. Fallujah   J. Bashur
C. Baqubah   K. Karbala
D. Samarra   L. Najaf
E. Tikrit   M. Diwaniyah
F. Husaybah   N. Amarah
G. Haditha   O. Basra
H. Tal Afar
    Invasion of Iraq—2003

A Familiar Name in a Lesser-Known Role: David H. Petraeus

The Godfather of Counterinsurgency Doctrine

David Petraeus's primary notoriety comes from successfully combating the insurgency that began later in the struggle for Iraq. Less well known is his generalship as commander of the 101st Airborne Division during the initial invasion and the subsequent capture of Baghdad. In Northern Iraq, his work in aiding the populace, improving living conditions, and accelerating the political process was widely lauded, heralding his later work in confronting the widespread uprising. U.S. ARMY—U.S. ARMY HISTORY AND EDUCATION CENTER

David Petraeus is widely known nationally and internationally for his role in quelling the massive terrorist violence that engulfed Iraq following the allied victory in 2003. Far less known is that Petraeus, then a major general, commanded the 101st Airborne Division during the conflict and led it through some of the heaviest fighting. After succeeding as a combat leader, his postwar administration of the complex, fragmented Mosul region provided a beacon for others to follow and informed later development of the Army's counterinsurgency doctrine.

Petraeus led the 101st during V Corps's drive across Iraq. Though victory came soon and without severe losses, it was a campaign that tested men, equipment, and leaders. As the "Screaming Eagles" neared Baghdad, their major opponent was a Republican Guard formation, the Hammurabi Division, one of the elite units in the Iraqi Army. Sandstorms, a harsh climate, and, at times, a difficult landscape presented additional challenges.

A key initial objective of the 101st was the fortified city of Najaf. Standing at the nexus of Highways 8 and 9, the town was a major stop on the way to Baghdad. Compensating for his lack of armor with air support from Army helicopters and fixed-wing aircraft from the Air Force and Navy, Petraeus approached from the south with three battalions of the 1st Brigade supported by a tank battalion while the 2nd Brigade covered routes near the city. Using a helicopter screen as a reconnaissance platform, Petraeus and the 101st assaulted Najaf block by block. After three days of fighting during which more than 200 enemy vehicles were destroyed, the city was secured on April 1.

The 101st then pushed farther north toward Hillah. The assault on that city supported two objectives. The first was to cover a force of U.S. Marines as the unit crossed the Tigris River. The second was to shield the 3rd Infantry Division's coming attack on Baghdad by foreclosing Iraqi units from moving from positions farther north near Karbala. The combat around Hillah brought the 101st up against the Hammurabi Division. Replete with armor, artillery, and veteran infantry, the division guarded Baghdad's southern approaches.

The resulting fight escalated into an intense, eight-day battle in and around the city. The 101st used the full panoply of American weapons—artillery, tanks, and air strikes—as the unit eliminated resistance in the city. Nearly 300 Iraqi armored vehicles, 800 other vehicles, and dozens of bunkers and strongpoints were destroyed as the 101st pushed street by street through the city.

After a theaterwide pause to replenish supplies and ride out a sandstorm, elements of the 101st joined other formations in operations in the Karbala Gap, an area southwest of Baghdad bordered on one side by a large lake and on the other by the Euphrates River. The gap was dissected by Highway 8, the main road into the southwestern suburbs of the metropolis.

After a notable fight, U.S. forces led by U.S. Marine and 3rd Division formations took the city. The capture of Baghdad freed Petraeus and the 101st to push far to the north. They moved quickly, making the longest heliborne assault in military history. The unit established its base of operations in the Nineveh Governorate, a large, geographically and ethnically diverse region home to the ancient city of the same name. The present-day

Governorate has Mosul as its capital and hosts the major cities Erbil and Kirkuk; names later familiar to many Americans from war-related news broadcasts. The population is made up of an amalgam of Arabs, Assyrians, Kurds, Yazidis, Shabaks, and Turkmen.

The chaotic environment that followed the allies' triumph on the battlefield was notable for the variety of conditions that confronted the victorious units and the radically different ways their leaders responded to them. Perhaps the harshest approach was wielded by the 4th Infantry Division operating in north-central Iraq. In and around Tikrit the unit rounded up thousands of "military-age" males, likely radicalizing large numbers of them. In Anbar Providence in the west, the 3rd Cavalry Regiment and the 82nd Airborne also employed especially stringent measures. Circumstances in Baghdad varied almost block to block in a complex jumble of religious, political, and clan-based orientations.

Conditions were calmest in the northern part of the country, where Petraeus was based with the 101st. Petraeus, like many other commanders, often discarded guidance—such as it was—from Lieutenant General Ricardo Sanchez, commander, Multi-National Force-Iraq and his headquarters staff. Petraeus focused on getting rapid aid to the population, employing civic action programs that visibly improved living and working conditions. He went so far as to negotiate with the Syrian government to provide electricity to Mosul.

One of Petraeus's more significant adjustments was to pull troops from large main bases and put them in teams of 35–75 soldiers who lived and circulated among the local population. Negotiations with insurgent cadres by subordinates were approved—indeed, welcomed. Petraeus ranked protecting the Iraqi populace as the 101st's number-one mission. More than other commanders, he saw the utility of employing former members of the Baath Party. At considerable risk, Petraeus reached out to Sunni insurgents, providing money and other incentives for them to change sides.

Drawing on his previous nation-building experiences in Haiti and Bosnia, Petraeus jump-started the local political process—city council elections were held within weeks—and generated more than 4,000 public works and reconstruction projects. When Petraeus left Iraq, it was widely accepted that the forces under him had done an excellent job of "winning the hearts and minds" of the Iraqi people.

The 101st's departure from Iraq in 2004 brought an end to Petraeus's first major leadership role in Iraq and the Middle East. In the years ahead, others would follow.

Before and After

Petraeus graduated from West Point in 1974. Lean and sharp-featured, he possessed an intellect and energy that stood out in an assemblage of scholars and Type A personalities. Following completion of Ranger School as a distinguished graduate, Petraeus served in a variety of positions—a mixture of command and staff billets in light infantry, mechanized, and infantry units at progressively higher organizational levels—in rapid succession. In 1981 he was chosen as aide-de-camp to the commander of the 24th Infantry Division. In 1982–83, he attended Command and General Staff College, graduating at the top of his class. He spent the following two years earning a PhD from Princeton before returning to West Point as an instructor.

After serving as military assistant to the supreme allied commander, Europe, he returned to field duty (1988–89) as operations officer with the 3rd Infantry Division (Mechanized), 3rd Infantry Regiment. The end of the decade saw him posted to the Pentagon as aide and assistant executive officer to the chief of staff of the U.S. Army.

By then a lieutenant colonel, Petraeus followed the Washington, DC, billet with a 1991–93 tour as commander of the 101st Airborne Division (Air Assault) 3rd Battalion, 187th Infantry Regiment at Fort Campbell, Kentucky. Still with the 101st in 1993–94, Petraeus moved up to assistant chief of staff for plans, operations, and training (G-3).

Petraeus's first experience with nation-building took place in 1995, when he was posted to the United Nations mission in Haiti as chief operations officer during Operation Uphold Democracy. Another command billet followed, this time (1995–97) with the 1st Brigade, 504 Parachute Infantry Regiment of the 82nd Airborne Division. From 1997 to 1999, Petraeus was back in the Pentagon as executive assistant to the director of the joint staff and subsequently, to the chairman of the Joint Chiefs of Staff.

Petraeus was promoted to brigadier general on January 1, 2000. He returned to the 82nd Airborne the following year as assistant director for operations and briefly served as division commander. He led elements of the 82nd to Kuwait as combat formations were rotated through the theater. Promotion to major general came January 1, 2003.

For ten months during 2001–2, Petraeus served in Bosnia-Herzegovina, dual-hatted as NATO Stabilization Force chief of staff for operations and commander of the U.S. Joint Interagency Counterterrorism Task Force.

After

Following his outstanding performance during the Iraq War, Petraeus pinned on his third star on May 16, 2004. His sojourn stateside did not last long. Concurrent with his promotion to lieutenant general he was named commander of a newly created organization—the Multi-National Security Transition Command–Iraq. The mission statement of the infant unit was daunting in its scope and difficulty. Petraeus's troops were tasked with training, equipping, and mentoring Iraq's army, police, and associated security forces as well as building the organization and physical structure—military bases, police stations, and border-protection sites—to sustain them. It was a compliment to Petraeus's leadership that he successfully brought the unit to life in the midst of a particularly difficult period marked by heavy fighting in places such as Fallujah, Mosul, and Najaf. Still, by the time Petraeus completed his assignment 15 months later, more than 100,000 security personnel had been trained and associated equipment had been distributed.

Petraeus returned to the United States to become commandant of the Army Command and General Staff College at Fort Leavenworth, Kansas. While serving in that position, he assembled a broad-based group of civilian and military experts and employed them to help develop U.S. Army Field Manual 3-24, *Counterinsurgency.* The document remains the Army's "bible" for combating insurgent warfare.

In the meantime, during Petraeus's three years at Fort Leavenworth, conditions inside Iraq were markedly deteriorating. Nationwide insurgent attacks had increased from 26,456 in 2004 to 34,131 in 2005. By the middle of the following year an average of 1,000 roadside bombs per week spread chaos and death across the nation. Two million Iraqis—mostly Sunnis—fled the country.

As conditions inside Iraq spiraled downward in 2006, President George W. Bush called in a panel of experts to discuss the conflict and make recommendations on how to proceed. The group strongly urged the president to place Petraeus in command. He was, by most accounts, not the choice of the Army establishment. Some of his colleagues regarded him as an outsider—a Princeton PhD, more comfortable than most with reporters and politicians. And his success in leading the 101st during the war and in pacifying Mosul later had placed him in the spotlight. Petraeus and the staff he surrounded himself with took risks, introducing innovative programs that addressed unique, changing operating circumstances. It was an environment for which few senior officers had been trained and many were decidedly uncomfortable with.

President Bush acceded to the panel's advice. Petraeus was appointed as commanding general of the Multinational Force–Iraq. Promotion to four-star general followed immediately. Petraeus returned to Iraq in 2007 during one of the darkest periods of the war. Baghdad was characterized as a dying city under siege. During the final few days of the "surge," which generally coincided with Petraeus's arrival, U.S. troops were subjected to attacks on an average of 180 times a day. In May 126 Americans were killed. Slowly, though hardly visible at first, like the turning of a huge ship, conditions began to change. One hundred thousand Sunni insurgents changed sides. U.S. casualty figures began to decline: 93 killed in June, 60 in July, 55 in August, 14 in December.

In recognition of the progress being made and the increasing capability of Iraqi forces, Petraeus recommended late in the year that surge forces be drawn down and U.S. military efforts be focused more on countering threats from Shiite militia groups. With U.S. deaths at their lowest point since 2003 and life returning to Baghdad, "surge" units deployed to Iraq were withdrawn in early 2008 without replacement.

Petraeus's accomplishments during the period have been generally acclaimed. Military historian Victor Davis Hanson declared that "without David Petraeus, the American effort in Iraq—along with the reputation of the U.S. military in the Middle East—would have been lost long ago."

October of that year brought another Iraq/Middle East–focused appointment for Petraeus, this time as commander, United States Central Command. The job placed Petraeus in charge of 20 countries and two ongoing conflicts—Operation Enduring Freedom in Afghanistan and Operation Iraqi Freedom. He again stressed the need for his troops to live among the people—"You can't kill your way out of an insurgency"—interact with them, and convince the population that morally, physically, and economically they would be better served by supporting the U.S. rather than aiding the insurgents.

In mid-2010 President Barack Obama appointed Petraeus to replace General Stanley McChrystal when McChrystal was removed on short notice as commander of U.S. Forces in Afghanistan. Petraeus assumed command on July 4, focusing, as always, on the civilian population. From the first, guidance to his soldiers stressed that "the people of Afghanistan are the center of gravity in the struggle"; ultimately, it was they who would determine the fate of the Afghan nation.

After serving in Afghanistan for a year, Petraeus ended a 37-year military career on August 31, 2011. His time in the Army is remembered for his energy, aggressiveness, and willingness to take measured risks. As an instructive devise, Petraeus himself sometimes recalled a sign he had observed during his service in Iraq. The note had been posted by a young company-grade officer: it read, "In the absence of orders and guidance, figure out what they should have been and exercise vigorously."

Several of Petraeus's personal observations found a place in the Army's *Counterinsurgency* manual. Among them were "Don't try to do too much with your own hands," and "Money is ammunition" (i.e., exploit the use of discretionary funds in civic action programs). The manual emphasizes that ultimate success depends on local leaders, and stresses the need to find and employ flexible, adaptable leaders who set the right tone.

Two months after his retirement, he was chosen as director of the Central Intelligence Agency, having been nominated for the position prior to his retirement. After receiving generally good marks during his one-year tenure, Petraeus resigned his position on November 9, 2012. His departure came in the aftermath of publicity associated with an extramarital affair and a related misdemeanor charge of mishandling classified information for which he pled guilty and was fined.

Subsequent to his retirement, Petraeus has been the recipient of several honorary awards and positions and has served on several academic and corporate boards in directorial and advisory capacities. He is a senior official on the governing bodies of more than 25 philanthropic, scholastic, historic, and charitable organizations.

GLOBAL WAR ON TERRORISM

Two days after 9/11 President George W. Bush announced the beginning of a "Global War on Terrorism," declaring, "We are supported by the entire world. The attack took place on American soil," he acknowledged, "but it was an attack on the heart and soul of the civilized world. And the world has come together to fight a new and different war. . . . A war against all those who seek to export terror, and a war against those governments that support or shelter them." President Bush's speech was followed by military, diplomatic, financial, law enforcement, humanitarian, and homeland security measures aimed at combating and forestalling actions by terrorist organizations. In a quickly following ancillary move, on October 26 the passage of the Patriot Act expanded the search and surveillance powers of federal agencies.

In the coming months and years a series of Enduring Freedom operations were initiated in several regions around the globe. Conducted under the auspices of the Global War on Terrorism, each involved in varying degrees the commitments of U.S. forces (though not always or often in combat roles), trainers, equipment, and resources. Foremost among these were Operation Enduring Freedom–Kyrgyzstan (2001); Philippines (2002); Horn of Africa (2002); Trans Sahara (2007); and Caribbean and Central America (2008).

The locations and frequency of many of Global War on Terror actions will likely remain in the shadows. Indeed, when Admiral McRaven spoke to President Obama during the Special Forces raid on Osama bin Laden's compound, he noted almost in passing that such actions routinely took place several times each night throughout the region.

Forgotten Leader: William H. McRaven

Mission: Bin Laden

McRaven directed the raid on Osama bin Laden's compound that resulted in bin Laden's death. Operating from Jalalabad, Afghanistan, McRaven's team of 24 SEALs and Special Operations personnel flew 100 miles into Pakistan where bin Laden was thought to have taken refuge. When a problem developed with one of the specially modified MH-60 helicopters, McRaven's troops responded coolly, moving to a well-rehearsed backup plan. The team was on the ground for only 38 minutes, two minutes less than in extensive rehearsals. U.S. NAVY—U.S. NAVAL HISTORY AND HERITAGE COMMAND

It seems unusual that too much of the American public, the name of the officer who led the successful search for Osama bin Laden is not widely known. Indeed, that officer, who guided the operation that eliminated the figure most Americans regarded as the great villain of the 21st century, is quite probably better recalled for a speech titled "Make Your Bed" that he delivered to a university commencement audience. Widely disseminated on YouTube—the presentation has received more than 12 million views—the speech is often used in training sessions, motivational seminars, and leadership forums. Delivered in a relaxed, conversational style, the speech maintains an impact that is enhanced by McRaven's appearance. More than one member of the university audience noted that in the ribbon-bedecked uniform of a four-star admiral, the lithe former cross-country runner looked like someone out of central casting.

In February 2011 McRaven, then a vice admiral, was serving as commander of the Joint Special Operations Command when he was summoned to CIA Headquarters at Langley, Virginia. There, CIA Director Leon Panetta gave him details regarding bin Laden's suspected location and assigned operational control of the prospective kill-or-capture mission to him.

After a decade spent searching, including an early near-miss effort at Tora Bora, Afghanistan, the CIA had developed what was thought to be solid intelligence indicating bin Laden had taken refuge in a compound at Abbottabad, Pakistan. The location was a considerable distance inside that country, about 100 miles from the Afghan border. Thus, the question of how best to get in and get out was a major consideration. That was but one of several issues that required resolution. McRaven assembled what was later described as a "dream team" of special operators, assigning members of the Navy's vaunted SEAL Team 6 to work with CIA specialists. Planning began immediately.

Three possibilities received consideration. One, a strike by B-2 Stealth bombers, was discarded because bin Laden's remains might be difficult or impossible to identify. Family members and other nonbelligerents might be harmed or killed as well. Then, too, the optics of dropping bombs on the territory of an ostensibly friendly country could be politically damaging both regionally and internationally.

A second alternative was to use the SEAL/CIA team in concert with Pakistani forces who would be brought into the plan a short time before the raid was carried out. While more defensible politically, there was little confidence that the details would be kept secret. A brief phone call would allow bin Laden to flee. A third option was eventually agreed upon; a small

American-only force would strike quickly, "service the target," and get out. If things went well, time on the ground would be minimal. Pakistani officials would be notified immediately afterward. Hopefully that, and the surgical nature of the raid, would keep repercussions at a manageable level. The sovereignty issue—flying over more than 100 miles of Pakistani airspace—was regarded as the biggest issue. McRaven was confident that the technical aspects of the raid could be handled: the SEALs flew similar missions in Afghanistan almost every night.

Using satellite imagery and local information, experts constructed models that duplicated bin Laden's compound. McRaven's combined SEAL/CIA team used them as they prepared at training sites in North Carolina and Nevada for the raid. Eventually, 28 special operators, including an explosive expert and an interpreter, along with a dog, were selected for the mission. Four of the team members were alternates in the event injuries to the primary members were sustained during the rigorous preparations.

The SEAL team arrived in Jalalabad, Afghanistan, on April 27, three days prior to the scheduled date for the mission. The Jalalabad location would serve as the SEALs' base for the mission. Other decisions were finalized at the time: bin Laden would be designated "Geronimo"; the mission itself would be called Operation Neptune Spear.

The raid, originally planned for April 30, a moonless night, was delayed one day by McRaven because of extensive cloud cover. The following night, May 1, at about 11:30 p.m., 24 men, including 22 special operations personnel, the explosive expert, the translator, and the dog, left Jalalabad on two specially modified MH-60 Black Hawk helicopters. The strike team was composed of SEAL Team 6 members and CIA specialists from that organization's Special Activities Division. Flying the Black Hawks were aircrews from the 160th Special Operations Aviation Regiment (Airborne)—the "Night Stalkers." McRaven ran the mission from Jalalabad. Monitoring it from various locations were officials who essentially constituted America's National Command Authority. The president and key staff were watching from the White House. CIA Director Leon Panetta was online from CIA Headquarters. In Kabul, Afghanistan, General David Petraeus stood ready to launch U.S. air assets in the event Pakistani warplanes attempted to intercept the strike force's helicopters. General James Cartwright followed the action from the Pentagon's Operations Center. All watched as the helicopters lifted off from Jalalabad.

The helicopters that carried the raiders were highly classified variants of the MH-60 filled with advanced technology that suppressed the sound of the rotors and greatly reduced the size of their radar signatures. Their flight profile was designed to further exploit their stealth characteristics—they would fly very fast and very low.

The Black Hawks were not the only U.S. helicopters in the air that night. Three MH-47 Chinooks were also part of the mission. One, carrying additional SEALs, settled into a position on the Afghan side of the border. Two others flew to an isolated, uninhabited location 50 miles north of the target compound. They carried a Quick Reaction Force that would respond if the SEALs on the ground at Abbottabad ran into trouble. Elsewhere in the area, Air Force fighter aircraft and search-and-rescue helicopters stood poised to intervene as conditions dictated.

As the two MH-60s approached bin Laden's hideout, the lead Black Hawk carrying SEALs assigned to rappel into the compound encountered a major problem. Abbottabad's warm temperature and high altitude combined with the weight of the full load and extra tonnage from the stealth technology affected the craft's stability and lift capacity. In training sessions conducted at high altitude in the U.S., chain link fences had been used to simulate the compound's walls, which were actually made of concrete. Twelve feet high, the solid barriers combined with Abbottabad's thin air and other factors to disrupt the Black Hawk's airworthiness to an extent unforeseen in practice runs. Over the compound, the craft spun 90 degrees to the right and dropped suddenly. In a remarkable feat of airmanship, in conformance with the operation's contingency plan, the pilot managed to control the Black Hawk sufficiently to bring it down in the compound's outer courtyard. In a soft but jarring landing, the helicopter's nose dug into the ground and the tail section tilted upward against the perimeter wall. The rotors did not strike the ground, thus preventing further damage. No SEALs were injured beyond bruising. The bad news was that any hope of surprise was gone. The SEALs reacted to the altered situation by blowing open the entrance to the inner compound and making their way to the main house.

McRaven, by all accounts, responded coolly. Recollections have him advising the officials who were tuned in that "we will be amending the mission . . . as you can see, we have a helicopter down in the courtyard. My men have prepared for this contingency and will deal with it."

Inside the compound, SEALs from the crashed helicopter and the second MH-60 disposed of a threat from a guesthouse near the main building. Two more hostiles were dispatched as the SEALs neared the primary residence. Ten minutes into the mission, team members entered the larger house after blowing aside a security gate that barricaded the entrance to the interior stairwells. SEALs moved up the steps, clearing each floor room by room. On the second floor, bin Laden's 23-year-old son was killed when he peeked around a corner after a SEAL had whispered his name.

Bin Laden was found on the third floor. He was killed by SEALs who confronted him in the darkness after having caught a glimpse of a tall man who peered out of a doorway and then entered a room down the hallway. Other members of the team then entered the room. DNA samples were quickly taken, and the body was photographed from various angles, including several in profile. The Arabic-speaking SEAL questioned women and children in the residence, who confirmed that the slain individual was bin Laden.

Events continued to move quickly. Operation Neptune Spear's senior on-scene SEAL came into the room. After gathering information and examining the body, he advised McRaven "Geronimo E.K.I.A." (enemy killed in action). At this point, the SEALs had been on the ground for about half an hour. Orders were given to prepare the crashed MH-60 for demolition.

A Quick Reaction Force helicopter, summoned to carry out SEALs who had arrived in the downed Black Hawk, was soon hovering overhead. Fuel was becoming a consideration, as was the increasing volume of curiosity seekers, puzzled by a mysterious electricity failure that darkened parts of the nearby area, brought to the scene by the series of explosions and helicopter activity. SEALs speaking Pashto (which caused some onlookers to conclude they were Afghans) told the assembled audience to depart the area and return to their homes.

There was a sizable Pakistani military presence in and around Abbottabad—indeed, the Pakistani Military Academy was less than a mile away—and the SEALs were worried that elements of Pakistan's military could arrive in force at any time.

Meanwhile, in the remaining few minutes available to them, SEALs moved through the compound gathering documents, cassette tapes, computers, and other items of potential intelligence value. Despite their limited time, they managed to retrieve an enormous amount of material that they lugged to the helicopter in duffel bags, mesh containers, and other convenient containers immediately at hand, including at least one gym bag. The SEALs left Abbottabad in 38 minutes, two minutes shorter than their practice time. Much of the action, including the killing of bin Laden, had taken place in the first 15 minutes.

Because of its higher probability of making it back to Afghanistan, the remaining stealth Black Hawk received bin Laden's body for transport. DNA samples and duplicate photos were distributed between the helicopters to provide greater assurance that evidence of his demise would reach American authorities and the international audience. As the helicopters lifted off, demolition charges were detonated, incinerating the damaged MH-60 and its stealth equipment. The surviving Black Hawk and the Chinook carrying the SEALs left otherwise ride-less by the initial mishap flew separate routes back to Jalalabad. All aircraft arrived safely, although the Black Hawk had to refuel at a location inside Pakistan.

At 3:00 a.m. local time Admiral Mike Mullen, chairman of the Joint Chiefs of Staff, called his Pakistani counterpart to advise him of the Neptune Spear operation. From Jalalabad bin Laden's body was flown to Bagram, where further DNA samples were extracted and additional tests, including facial recognition analyses, were conducted. The corpse was then taken via helicopter to the USS *Carl Vinson*, positioned in the Arabian Sea. There, in conformance with Islamic customs, the body was washed and placed in a white sheet. After religious rites and prayers translated into Arabic, the body was buried at sea.

Late in the evening of May 1, in remarks televised to a national audience, President Obama informed the American public of bin Laden's death. The news was greeted enthusiastically. At two major league baseball games, crowds spontaneously erupted into chants of "USA, USA," and sang "God Bless America."

The success of Operation Neptune Spear was a tour de force for McRaven, who was highly lauded for the obvious skill that had gone into the planning and preparation and for the cool, unruffled leadership during the course of the mission.

Before and After

McRaven was commissioned as an officer in 1977 through the Naval ROTC program at the University of Texas at Austin. He went immediately into SEAL training and would remain in special operations–related duties almost through the entirety of his 37-year military career. Soon after completing Basic Underwater Demolition/SEAL Training courses, he was sent to the Philippines—the first of many deployments and assignments that placed him in key billets at every echelon in the Navy special operations world.

Located in Abbottabad, Pakistan, bin Laden's compound was assaulted on May 2, 2011, by a team of SEALs and Special Operations personnel. Bin Laden was located at the rear of the building on the top floor and killed during the first 15 minutes of the raid. There were no casualties to the assault force during the 38-minute operation.
CREATIVE COMMONS

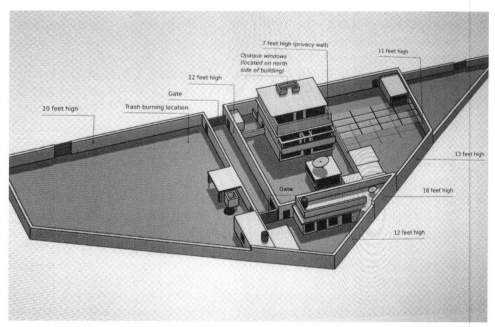

The compound in Abbottabad served as bin Laden's hideaway for many years. He communicated only by courier and stayed in seclusion, avoiding satellite and other means of detection.
CREATIVE COMMONS

As a young officer, he collided with Commander Richard Marcinko, a profane, charismatic near-legend in the special ops community. McRaven objected to Marcinko's questionable (later determined to be illicit) actions as leader of SEAL Team 6. Marcinko, who was later removed from command and sentenced to prison, relieved McRaven of his duties. The dismissal action was reversed, and McRaven was returned to his previous position as squadron commander.

A list of McRaven's subsequent duty titles reads like a compendium of the most critical, demanding duties in the special ops world. He was a UDT platoon commander, squadron commander of Naval Warfare Development Group, SEAL Team 1 executive officer, a task unit commander during Desert Storm, a CENTCOM task group commander, commander of SEAL Team 3, and deputy commander for operations at the Joint Special Operations Command. As a student at the Naval Postgraduate School, McRaven helped establish a special operations/low intensity conflict curriculum. He was the first graduate of the course. His thesis, "The Theory of Special Operations," is considered a seminal document in the evolution of the career field.

From 1999 to 2001 he was commander of the Joint Special Operations Command. In the summer of 2001 McRaven was severely injured during an exercise-related parachute drop. When he had sufficiently recovered, he was called to duty in Washington, DC, to serve as deputy national security advisor and director for strategic planning in the National Security Council Staff's Office of Combating Terrorism. He was the principal author of the government's National Strategy for Combating Terrorism.

Billets as assessment director of the U.S. Special Operations Command and staff duty in the Office of the Chief of Naval Operations and Chief of Staff Naval Special Warfare Group complemented a career that, by this time and for the remainder of his career, was devoted almost entirely to special operations. From the outset of the Global War on Terrorism, McRaven was deeply immersed in duties associated with the conflict. His GWOT postings included assignments in Afghanistan and Iraq before engagements in the wider war and the Operation Neptune Spear mission that killed bin Laden.

At Headquarters, Joint Special Operations Command, McRaven initially served as deputy to General Stanley McChrystal. McRaven aided McChrystal in directing the organization's metamorphosis from an establishment that conducted planning, training, and exercises, and developed tactics and standardized equipment. Under McChrystal and McRaven,

JSOC evolved into the most closely guarded secret force in America's national security apparatus. Among all the components of the nation's military establishment, only JSOC reports directly to the president of the United States.

As McChrystal's deputy, McRaven commanded the task force responsible for High Value Targeting operations—identifying targets, planning the raids, and carrying out the operations. As the war progressed, under McRaven's oversight, the target list grew from a dozen or two to significantly higher numbers. With McRaven as a driving force, the organization was restructured to carry out global manhunts. Inside Iraq, McRaven led the search for Saddam Hussein. In December 2003, his men, accompanied by troops from the U.S. 4th Infantry Division and Iraqi militia, captured the dictator on a farm near Tikrit. In 2006 McRaven was assigned as the first director of NATO's Special Operations Command.

In June 2008, as a newly minted three-star admiral, McRaven took command of JSOC from McChrystal. In that position McRaven further intensified the search for bin Laden, advocating increased latitude for his forces to operate inside Pakistan. A month later, President Bush approved special guidance authorizing kill-or-capture operations. Bush's order superseded earlier arrangements made with Pakistan's then-President Pervez Musharraf that U.S. forces would seek permission for raids beforehand and would operate in concert with Pakistani units.

Under the broadened rules, McRaven expanded operations inside the country. When President Obama assumed the presidency, he further extended the war, increasing the use of drones and expanding the global kill/capture program. Obama was determined, as was McRaven, to not merely respond to attacks but to take the fight to al-Qaeda and its affiliates, seeking out and destroying individual operatives, bases, and training areas. Numbers of commando raids reached 2,500 per year—averaging seven per night—although at times as many as 15 were conducted in a single evening. The size of the special operations force was increased, as was the number of countries to which they were deployed. The operations were not always without controversy, and legality of the raids and the guidance that authorized them have sometimes been called into question.

After

On August 8, 2011, McRaven was promoted to four-star admiral. He took command of the United States Special Operations Command on the same day. During his tenure, he accelerated the use of drones, missiles, and special operations raids in the quest to deny sanctuary to terrorist groups across the globe.

When McRaven retired from the Navy effective September 1, 2014, he had held command positions at every echelon in the special operations hierarchy. He left a multifaceted legacy. History will probably recall the most visible of those achievements, the bin Laden raid. But equally substantial in its impact was the work he shared, and later expanded, with General McChrystal in devising full-spectrum operations against al-Qaeda, the Taliban, and other terrorist organizations. The system of developing intelligence and reacting quickly to it became a model for actions that followed elsewhere. In *National Strategy for Combating Terrorism* McRaven wrote, "We will not triumph solely or even primarily through military might. We must fight terrorist networks . . . using every instrument of national power—diplomatic, economic, law enforcement, financial, information, intelligence, and military."

McRaven's concepts continue to characterize the special operations approach to war fighting. In *The Theory of Special Operations* McRaven wrote that "a simple plan, carefully constructed, realistically rehearsed and executed with surprise, speed, and purpose," would provide "relative superiority." With that advantage, success would result even against long numerical odds. Operation Neptune Spear, launched in the face of large numbers of opposing forces in close proximity, would seem to validate McRaven's thesis. The operative part of the raid on the compound took 15 minutes; 23 minutes later the SEALs were on their way home, mission accomplished.

McRaven served as chancellor of the University of Texas System from January 2015 until May 2018, before stepping away from his second career for reasons of ill health. His name has subsequently surfaced at times as a possible nominee for key positions. Following the 2020 presidential campaign, McRaven was considered for the post of secretary of defense.

Special Mention: Afghanistan, Iraq, and the Global War on Terrorism

The long and often winding road that has characterized American involvement in the Global War on terrorism in general and Afghanistan and Iraq in particular adds complexity to the task of leadership assessment. Driven at times by conditions on the ground and at others by changes in administration, adjustments in policy and troop levels have resulted in a seesaw pattern of surges and drawdowns. In some key positions, the military has seen fit to shuffle senior officers with considerable frequency, making it difficult to assign ultimate responsibility for achievements and shortcomings.

The individuals identified in the following paragraphs are regarded by most colleagues and scholars as having served with distinction, often in a variety of roles, in Afghanistan or Iraq (often both), as well as CENTCOM and other nearby hotspots. Their presence "in theater" was made notable by the breadth of their responsibilities and the diverse nature of the duties they performed.

Special Mention: John F. Mulholland Jr.

The Shadow Warrior

Mulholland was one of the American military's most renowned and highly experienced special operators. He commanded Special Operations Forces in Afghanistan (Operation Enduring Freedom) and Iraq (Operation Iraqi Freedom), and he also held key Special Ops positions in organizations based on the Arabian Peninsula and Kuwait. U.S. ARMY—U.S. ARMY HISTORY AND EDUCATION CENTER

In both Afghanistan and Iraq, Lieutenant General Mulholland commanded some of the first special ops units dispatched to those conflicts. In Operation Enduring Freedom, he led Special Operations Task Force–North (Task Force Dagger) through the initial stages of America's involvement, working skillfully with CIA cohorts and Afghan militia units.

In Operation Iraqi Freedom, he served as commander of the Combined Joint Task Force–West, and subsequently as commander, Coalition Joint Task Force Arabian Peninsula, again seeing service in the earliest days of the campaign prior to the arrival of conventional units.

Mulholland's involvement in the region did not end with the abatement of initial hostilities. He later served as chief, Office of Military Cooperation–Kuwait.

After beginning his career with service in infantry and airborne units, Mulholland graduated in 1983 from the Special Operations Qualifying Course. He spent the remaining 32 years of his 37-year career in special operations units. Mulholland's assignments included many of the premier positions in that unique career field: commanding general, United States Army Special Forces Command (Airborne); deputy commanding general, Joint Special Operations Command; commanding general, Special Operations Command Central; commanding general, United States Army Special Operations Command; and deputy commander, United States Special Operations Command. In 2015 he concluded his career as associate director of the CIA for Military Affairs. He retired as a lieutenant general.

It is indicative of the caliber of soldiers and the nature of the services these "shadow warriors" performed during his tenure that in a single 2008 awards ceremony Mulholland presented 19 Silver Stars, two Bronze Stars for Valor, five Commendation Medals for Valor, and four purple hearts to members of the 3rd Special Forces Group (Airborne).

Special Mention: William S. Wallace

Victory in the Desert

William Wallace commanded V Corps, the largest allied formation, during the invasion of Iraq. The corps achieved great success, moving 300 miles into enemy territory and defeating an army of half a million soldiers while sustaining remarkably few casualties. U.S. ARMY—U.S. ARMY HISTORY AND EDUCATION CENTER

General Wallace led V Corps during the invasion of Iraq. The largest of the two major allied formations, V Corps initially consisted of the 3rd Infantry Division, parts of the 101st Airborne (Air Assault) Division, and a brigade of the 82nd Airborne. Later added to its striking power were components of the 4th Infantry Division and the 173rd Airborne Brigade. The Corps possessed a formidable array of armor—U.S. infantry divisions fielded 270 Abrams tanks complemented by ample numbers of Bradley fighting vehicles. Air cover and close air support for Wallace's battle groups—typically made up of a Bradley and a tank battalion—were supplied by helicopter units including an integral unit of Apache gunships. Though not under Wallace's command, V Corps could also call upon Navy and Air Force assets for close air support.

The coalition's victory in Desert Storm a dozen years earlier had significantly attenuated Iraq's Republican Guard and regular army formations as well as its strength in tanks, artillery, and air power. Thus, the army that Saddam Hussein fielded in 2003 was not as formidable as its Gulf War counterpart. Still, the remaining numbers were not inconsequential—the Iraqi army considerably outnumbered the attackers—and Wallace's troops had a larger stage to deal with. Baghdad was 300 miles from the nearest jump-off point on the border of Kuwait. This time the entire land mass of Iraq was in play, and the nation itself was the objective.

Wallace commanded V Corps until June 14, 2003, when he left for a new assignment as commanding general of the United States Army Combined Arms Center at Fort Leavenworth, Kansas. The timing of his move meant that, during his tenure, units under his command were mainly opposed by conventional main-force Iraqi formations. Although fedayeen cadres had made their presence known, widespread civil disorder and terrorist incidents did not erupt until after his departure. Thus, how he would have handled those situations and what degree of success he might have attained must remain a matter of conjecture. What is "measurable" are the results of V Corps's campaign during the period of March to June 2003.

In a three-week campaign, V Corps and its companion formation, the 1st Marine Expeditionary Force, pushed 300 miles over at-times-difficult terrain, defeated an army of half a million men, and sustained remarkably few casualties in doing so. Mitigating circumstances aside, it was a remarkable achievement.

Any discussion of Wallace would not be complete without noting that he led V Corps during its deployment on short notice from its base in Germany to the Iraqi theater. All available air and sea assets were called upon. Confusion occurred as entire unit sets were sometimes separated out of necessity to secure available transportation. Ultimately, the Corps components arrived intact in theater, and its constituent parts were quickly reassembled.

Before and After

A West Point graduate (1969), Wallace began his career as an armor officer. After a tour in Vietnam, he served with the 82nd Airborne Division as a company commander, battalion adjutant, and battalion operations officer. Schooling followed—the Armor Officer Advanced Course and the Naval Postgraduate School—before an assignment in Germany with the 2nd Armored Cavalry Regiment. In 1991, he took command of the 11th

Armored Cavalry Regiment, patrolling the vital Fulda Gap, the Soviet Army's anticipated invasion route in event of conflict.

Promoted to General, Wallace then commanded the 4th Infantry Division (Mechanized). A later career move placed him as Director of Joint Training at the United States Joint Forces Command. He was in the position before taking over as V Corps in July 2001.

After

Wallace left V Corps in June 2003 to assume command of the United States Army Combined Arms Center, serving in that position until October 2005. Wallace's final assignment was as commanding general, United States Army Training and Doctrine Command. He retired as a four-star general on December 8, 2008.

Special Mention: Sean MacFarland

The Soldiers' General

Widely respected by his soldiers, MacFarland, of all of America's senior military commanders who saw service in Afghanistan and Iraq, probably served longest and had the most varied duties. During the initial invasion of Iraq, he led the 1st Armored Division Brigade Combat Team through several difficult battles and was credited with helping facilitate the "Sunni Uprising" that caused many in that influential group to change sides. He later led forces that recovered much of the extensive territory in Syria controlled by ISIS, paving the way for their final defeat soon after. U.S. ARMY—U.S. ARMY HISTORY AND EDUCATION CENTER

When viewed over a period of a decade and a half, Lieutenant General Sean MacFarland's service was among the longest and his duties among the most varied of any American officer who saw action in Afghanistan and Iraq.

MacFarland led the 1st Armored Division Brigade Combat Team through Iraq War battles at Tal Afar, Sinjar, Hit, and Ramadi. When the fighting subsided, he was most notably credited by many as aiding the "Sunni Awakening," which induced Sunni partisans to aid coalition forces in combating terrorist activities. In Ramadi, his efforts were recalled for introducing counterinsurgency principals and for his exceptional commitment to enhance the safety of the populace and improve their living conditions.

MacFarland was widely respected by his soldiers—and that feeling was strongly reciprocated. Historian Thomas Ricks quotes him as saying: "One of the reasons we were able to hold on despite a failing strategy and turn the situation around was that the soldiers continued to be led by highly competent, professional junior officers and non-commissioned officers whom they respected. And they gave us senior officers the breathing space we needed, but probably didn't deserve, to properly understand the fight that we were in."

In intervals over later years, he served in Kuwait during Operation Desert Thunder; as chief of staff for operations for the International Security Assistance Force in Afghanistan; and as deputy commanding general for operations for U.S. Forces in Afghanistan.

From 2015 to 2016 MacFarland commanded III Corps and Combined Joint Task Forces–Operation Inherent Resolve and led those forces against the Islamic State in Iraq and Syria. Under his leadership, coalition forces reconquered nearly half of the territory overrun in the preceding months by Islamic State fighters. The final defeat of the Islamic State that followed in the months ahead was attributable in large measure to the conditions established by MacFarland's operations.

Before and After

MacFarland's career was primarily spent in armor and cavalry units. He served as troop leader, commander, and executive officer, as well as in staff positions from company level to the Pentagon. His assignments took him to various locations in Germany and, while there, to ancillary duties in Bosnia-Herzegovina and Macedonia.

Interestingly, MacFarland's acquaintance with Iraq and the Middle East preceded the Iraq War and other Global War on Terrorism operations.

A decade earlier he was deployed to the region during Operation Desert Shield/Desert Storm. MacFarland's career was notable for the number of consequential command billets he held and for the scope of responsibilities associated with them. Command positions at higher-echelon levels included III Corps (and Coalition Joint Task Force–Operation Iraqi Freedom), XVII Airborne Corps, 1st Armored Division, and Joint Task Force–North (Fort Bliss). Additionally, he served as deputy commander for leader development and education, and deputy commandant of the Army's Command and General Staff College.

He was serving as deputy commander and chief of staff for the United States Army Training and Doctrine Command when he retired from active duty in February 2018.

An example—one of many—of MacFarland's compassion for his soldiers occurred in Anbar Province, Iraq, in 2006. MacFarland was at an airstrip with a group of soldiers when the body bag containing the remains of a recently killed young soldier was carried to the helicopter. MacFarland asked the name of the soldier. Told that it was "Terry Lisk," MacFarland said, "I don't know if this war is worth the life of Terry Lisk, or ten soldiers, or 2,500 soldiers like him. What I do know is that he did not die alone. A Greek philosopher said that only the dead have seen the end of war. Only Terry Lisk has seen the end of this war."

RETROSPECTIVE: AFGHANISTAN, IRAQ, AND THE GLOBAL WAR ON TERRORISM

Afghanistan

In Afghanistan the initial postwar period began well for the allied coalition. On June 13, 2002, a traditional Afghan Loya Jirga council elected Hamid Karzai as transitional head of state. Two years later, Karzai became Afghanistan's first democratically elected president.

In the years that followed, the focus of U.S. and coalition operations changed somewhat as adjustments were made to address shifting circumstances, availability of resources, and other considerations.

Through the Tora Bora operation at the outset, a first brief phase was aimed at toppling the Taliban government, thus eliminating the sanctuary provided to the al-Qaeda combatants. That segment of the war was over by the end of 2001.

A second period, generally encompassing the years 2002–9, sought to defeat remaining Taliban cadres and rebuild Afghanistan's core institutions. Sporadic violence continued as the Taliban regenerated forces from across the border in Pakistan. By late 2002 some al-Qaeda and Taliban elements began adopting guerilla techniques as they carried the fight to coalition forces. The Western public may not be familiar with battles fought at Takur Ghar (March 2002), Shok Valley (April 2008), Wanat (July 2008), Ganjgal (September 2008), Operation Khanjar (July 2009), and Kamdesh (October 2009), for example, but at those locations and many others coalition troops in large numbers fought, bled, and died in combat that was as brutal and violent as any in recent history.

As the war in Iraq grew in size and intensity, attention was increasingly focused on that conflict. The transfer of forces to that arena caused some members of the coalition to view Afghanistan as an "orphan headquarters." In Thomas Ricks's words, "The Afghan War did not thrive on neglect." During the period 2004–9, suicide bombings and other security problems increased ninefold. Troop withdrawals and periodic discussions of drawdowns did little to improve morale.

Over the years, as coalition forces settled in, operations throughout the country (as in other Global War on Terrorism venues) were often distinguished by fluctuating levels of intensity dictated by conditions on the ground, forces available, and the extent and immediacy of the insurgent threat. Though other instances could be cited, Operation Khanjar in Afghanistan provides an illustrative example of the periodic activity spikes that came to characterize the struggle.

After several years of generally stable troop levels and anti-insurgent activities, a major operation was mounted in the summer of 2009, aimed at clearing Helmand province of Taliban forces. Located in southern Afghanistan, the province had become a Taliban stronghold accessible to volunteers from throughout the Muslim world eager to enlist in the insurgents' cause. In response to widespread and increasing violence, President Barack Obama authorized a 21,000 increase in U.S. force size. The first contingent, 10,000 Marines, arrived in Helmand in June.

Operations commenced with actions in the Helmand River valley on July 2 and officially lasted through August 20. Operation Khanjar achieved some degree of success in improving conditions in the province, although coalition officials acknowledged that many Taliban fighters vacated the area and shifted to other parts of the country. Some allied officers at the time expressed the concern that the movement of Taliban forces was abetted by stringent rules of engagement aimed at minimizing civilian casualties. The troop surge associated with the campaign involved the largest offensive airlift of Marine forces since the Vietnam War.

Coincident with the surge in 2009, commanders adopted a more classic counterinsurgency regimen. Exploiting the temporary increase in troop strength, the U.S. and NATO allies sought to provide better protection for civilian populations and energize the attempt to induce insurgents to reenter Afghan society. The animating notion was to create conditions that would allow U.S. and NATO forces to gradually withdraw, enabling a phased, nationwide takeover of military and police functions by the Afghan government.

On May 1, 2012, a U.S.-Afghan Strategic Partnership Agreement was signed. Despite the pact, the strategic situation deteriorated, eventually inducing the Obama administration to return General David Petraeus to the region to serve as commander, International Security Force–Afghanistan. On October 13, 2013, President Obama declared the War on Global Terrorism to be over, replacing the "global" emphasis with a focus on specific hostile groups such as al-Qaeda, the Islamic State in Iraq and the Levant, and others. For U.S. forces stationed in Afghanistan, the wording was essentially cosmetic. Obama declared an end to the combat role in Afghanistan effective December 20, 2014, though widespread violence continued and eventually necessitated another temporary troop surge aimed in part at targeting opium labs and other major sources of the insurgents' revenue.

The upsurge in violence in the middle of the decade was fomented in considerable measure by ISIS-K, an affiliate of the Islamic State government operation in Afghanistan. Founded in January 2015, the ISIS-K acronym is derived from the organization's formal title: Islamic State Khorasan Province. Violent and aggressive, the group by 2018 was assessed by major intelligence services as being one of four of the world's deadliest terrorist organizations.

Initially, ISIS-K drew much of its strength from the Nangarhar Province and the Tora Bora region. Abetted by millions of dollars, training programs, and advice provided by ISIS core organizations in Syria and Iraq, the group rather quickly spread throughout the country. Focused on creating conditions of panic and instability, ISIS-K sought to undermine national authority by casting doubt on the government's ability to provide security and care for its citizens. Interestingly, these objectives frequently made ISIS-K a strategic rival of the Taliban. ISIS-K's ultimate goal is a global caliphate, whereas the Taliban, in the view of ISIS-K leaders, is an organization whose more benign ambitions are limited to Afghanistan. As fighting became more widespread, the U.S. and its allies occasionally found themselves in an unusual informal partnership with Taliban forces, sometimes providing air support and other assistance to Taliban operations against ISIS-K.

For a time circa 2019–20, it appeared that these actions and others by the Afghan Army and coalition allies were achieving success. One operation resulted in the mass surrender of 1,400 ISIS-K fighters. Eventually, though, the number and intensity of ISIS-K operations increased coincident with a nationwide resurgence in Taliban operations.

Three events may have influenced the insurgents' calculus.

On February 29, 2020, the Trump administration signed a peace agreement with Taliban officials. Among other provisions, the pact called for U.S. and coalition forces to be withdrawn within 14 months (May 2021) and for the release of Taliban prisoners held by Afghan and coalition forces. The arrangement was conditions based, contingent on a reduction in violence and the exclusion of al-Qaeda and Islamic State affiliates from territory controlled by the Taliban. Raids, ambushes, and bombings of civilian establishments continued, however, although Taliban-affiliated groups denied responsibility for them. Afghanistan government officials were not represented in these talks, which were held in Doha, Qatar. Their exclusion from negotiations drew criticism from many analysts who argued that their absence signaled a lack of support from their American allies.

On July 2, 2021, in an operation that sparked considerable controversy in America, the U.S. vacated Bagram Air Base, its primary operating base throughout the nation's two-decade involvement in Afghanistan.

On July 8 President Joseph R. Biden announced that U.S. forces would depart the country on August 31, ahead of the previously announced September 11 date.

Possibly aided by the visible drawdown of American and allied troop strength, the declared intention to leave by a date certain, and the weakness and corruption of the Afghan government, the Taliban offensive gathered momentum with a speed that took allied and Afghan officials—and the Taliban—by surprise. In June 2021, A U.S. intelligence estimate had assessed that Kabul could hold out for six months. A follow-on estimate in August reduced that projection to late fall.

It all happened much faster than that.

Zaranji, the first provincial capital, fell on August 6. More than 20 others followed in the next nine days. In the north, Mazar-e-Sharif, thought to be an anti-Taliban stronghold, fell on August 14. Jalalabad was lost overnight. By August 15 Kabul was isolated.

As conditions deteriorated, U.S. officials sought Afghan President Ashraf Ghani's support for an approach brokered between U.S officials and the Taliban. The agreement called for the Taliban to remain outside Kabul. Ghani would step down, paving the way for the formation of an inclusive interim government that would include the Taliban and other parties. With some reluctance, Ghani agreed. For a brief time, it appeared that a path, though precarious, might be open to a peaceful transition.

That prospect was short-lived. Perhaps misled by staff members who, alarmed by the presence of Taliban troops at the city's gates, misrepresented the threat to his personal security, President Ghani fled the country without advising the U.S. or many of his own officials. Ghani's route took him first to Uzbekistan and then to the United Arab Emirates, where he eventually found refuge. Soon after, other government officials sought sanctuary in Pakistan and the UAE. By the end of the day, Afghanistan's government had disintegrated. In Kabul, looting and violence began soon after.

The government's collapse prompted hurried talks in Doha, Qatar, where key officials, including U.S. Marine General Kenneth "Frank" McKenzie, commander CENTCOM; American Ambassador Ross Wilson; and Abdul Ghani Baradar, chief of Taliban's political wing, had assembled. According to sources, Baradar told McKenzie, "We have a problem. We have two options to deal with it. You [U.S. military] take responsibility to secure Kabul or you have to allow us to do it."

McKenzie, aware of President Biden's official mandate and personal determination to withdraw all U.S. forces, told Baradar that the U.S. mission was to safely extract American citizens, Afghan allies, and others at risk—and that the U.S. would need the airport to do that. An agreement was immediately reached: the Americans could have the airport until August 31; the Taliban would control the city.

The first contingent of U.S. Marines arrived on August 14 to provide security for round-the-clock withdrawal actions. On August 26 an ISIS-K suicide bomber killed 13 U.S. servicemen and -women guarding access to the airport and 170 Afghans awaiting entrance to the grounds. The U.S. retaliated with a drone strike that killed the alleged perpetrator. A few days later a second drone attack blew up a vehicle mistakenly believed to be carrying explosives to the airport to carry out a second attack. Several civilians were killed. When the evacuation efforts concluded, 5,500 Americans amid a total of 124,000 at-risk persons had been flown to safe-haven areas.

At one minute before midnight on August 30, U.S. Army General Christopher Donohue—the last American serviceman from a force that at its peak (2012) numbered nearly 100,000—stepped aboard an aircraft and left Afghanistan.

The narrative of America's military involvement in Afghanistan closes with General Donohue's departure. It seems clear, though, that the final chapter in Afghanistan's story has yet to be written. Many analysts predict an extended period of unrest, arguing among other things that Taliban leaders do not have the skills necessary to run the country. Some see the possibility of civil war, perhaps initially between the Taliban and ISIS-K, or of a split into several areas controlled by rival tribal groups or warlords. Indeed, though ultimately it gained little traction, an incipient opposition movement, the National Resistance Front, quickly formed in the Panjshir Valley region, an hour northeast of Kabul, under the leadership of Amrullah Saleh and Ahmad Massoud. Massoud is the son of Ahmad Shah Massoud, a legendary guerilla fighter who successfully fought Soviet forces and was assassinated by Taliban/al-Qaeda operatives two days prior to 9/11.

Military considerations aside, it appears problematic that the political climate, at least initially, will be conducive to attracting the foreign investment necessary to extract the nation's extensive mineral resources. At the same time, the $10 billion in assets held abroad by the Afghan central bank may be difficult for a Taliban-dominated government to access and exploit. In early 2022 U.S. President Biden proposed allocating $7 billion of the $10 billion to Afghanistan for relief efforts. His decision to award the remaining $3 billion to victims of the 9/11 attacks was immediately disputed by Taliban officials. It appears that for the foreseeable future Afghanistan will be dependent on foreign aid. International agencies assess that hunger affects one-third or more of the country's 38 million citizens.

In the longer term, demographic considerations among those 38 million may play a consequential role in determining Afghanistan's future. Some commentators have asserted that it may not be easy for the Taliban to reverse the changes to modern life that the movement finds distasteful. Citing considerations such as that 65 percent of the population is less than 25 years old (the median age is 18), the literacy rate among members of that generation is about 75 percent, and most of them have access to cell phones and media, it is the view of these analysts that it may turn out that "the Taliban cannot make time run backward." The validity of that conjecture remains to be demonstrated.

A final "lessons learned report" issued by the special inspector for Afghanistan reconstruction the day after Kabul fell to the Taliban cited the absence of a consistent, clear U.S. strategy as a major reason for the lack of success in Afghanistan. "At various points, the U.S. government hoped to eliminate al-Qaeda, decimate the Taliban movement that hosted it, deny all terrorist groups a safe haven in Afghanistan, build Afghan security forces so they could deny terrorists a safe haven in the future, and help the civilian government become legitimate and capable enough to win the trust of Afghans." After years of escalating operational intensity, the U.S., beginning in about 2011, reversed course, shrinking its footprint and cutting its spending. The effect of the drawdown highlighted the vulnerability of the Afghan government and revealed its dependency on American assistance. The report assessed that from the beginning of the U.S. involvement there was a general lack of understanding about Afghanistan and the amount of resources that would be required to succeed. Further issues—a series of overstated objectives and an overreliance on military solutions—compounded those initial shortcomings. The eventual result was an Afghan government that could not sustain progress or provide for its own security.

Iraq

When viewed through the lens of time and distance, the fluctuating nature of the warfare and type of conflict faced by American forces in Iraq becomes more apparent. On December 11, 2011, American combat forces were withdrawn after engaging in what had been, in large measure, conventional combat. That stage of the conflict was followed by a cycle of insurgent warfare (2011–13) as militants transformed operations to a type more closely resembling historic guerilla tactics. As ISIL, a new, more powerful militant group, achieved widespread success, an international military coalition led by the United States intervened in 2014 to bolster Iraqi government forces. A civil war phase then occurred from 2014 to 2017, followed once again by a considerable reversion to insurgent warfare. As conditions on the ground changed, the combinations of forces that formed temporary coalitions to oppose militant operations also shifted as needed to adjust to the circumstances at hand.

As analyzed by military historian John Keegan, the approach that guided America's deposing of Saddam Hussein and, in its aftermath, its policy toward Iraqi governance was ideological in nature. In Keegan's view, the Bush administration had reached two conclusions. The first was that the only way to get rid of a despot like Saddam Hussein was through military action. The second was that it was possible to move from tyranny to representative government in a relatively short period of time. As American forces took control, procedures developed by the State Department to systematically introduce democratic functions were discarded in favor of a process intended to provide Iraqis with a representative government in a short period of time—the most ambitious goal being 90 days.

Initially a retired Army general, Jay Garner, was put in charge. Garner proved inadequate to the task and was replaced by Paul Brenner, a State Department counterterrorism expert, supported by a cadre of short-term and generally untrained staff members.

Both Garner and Brenner and their staffs made egregious mistakes. One of the first, and most serious, was to disband the Iraqi army. The effect was to put thousands of unemployed, discontented youngsters, many with weapons, on the streets. Similarly, the national police force was also eliminated. Both actions were taken under the assumption that their continued existence would, in effect, perpetuate the residue of

Saddam's despotic regime. It is not possible to assess that possibility, but what is certain is that their absence was catastrophic. Rampant looting began immediately, melding quickly into organized attacks, which further gave way to full-blown insurgency.

U.S. forces were immediately caught up in the violence. Numbers of killed and wounded through violent actions increased on a daily basis. By the end of the year more than 500 had been slain. Though polls showed that as much as 80 percent of the Iraqi population was pleased that Saddam was no longer in charge, that consideration proved to be only one piece of the jigsaw that formed internal Iraqi politics. Indeed, the Sunni-Shiite split, along with the support of major groups for individual religious and political leaders, proved to be dynamic factors in the chaotic environment.

In an atmosphere of confusion and turmoil, another decision by Brenner's Provisional Authority compounded the effects of the dissolution of the army and police. Brenner's determination to remove Baath Party members from government employment instantly deprived the nation's new regime of enormous numbers of experienced experts and administrators. There was comparatively less violence and chaos in the portion of the country under British administration. British officials governed with a more pragmatic view that the most essential priority was to reestablish law and order and restore essential services—water, electricity, gas, and medical care.

In January 2004 a report by David Kay, head of the Iraqi Survey Group, indicated that no weapons of mass destruction had been found. The document stated that while it was doubtful that any would be located, the possibility could not be totally ruled out. None were ever found. In April of that year the allied cause suffered a setback when CBS News, soon followed by other major media outlets, released photos of prisoners being abused at the Abu Ghraib prison. The photos sparked worldwide condemnation.

Meanwhile, the situation inside Iraq continued to deteriorate. By as early as February 2004 the struggle had become a military and political negative for the United States. Operations in Iraq rather quickly absorbed 100,000 U.S. troops (the number eventually peaked at more than 160,000 in country), a major stretch for an Army tasked with fighting three simultaneous wars: Iraq, Afghanistan, and the Global War on Terrorism.

The escalating numbers of incidents reached alarming proportions. On October 13, 2005, a press briefing by Major General Rick Lynch, spokesman for the Multi-National Force–Iraq cited the following figures: "The total number of attacks on Americans and Iraqis for the week ending October 7, 2005: 743. Average number of attacks per day, for the week ending October 7, 2005: 106."

Conditions began to change for the better with innovations introduced by Generals David Petraeus and Ray Odierno whose efforts were aided by a superb ambassador, Ryan Crocker. Concurrent with a major surge in troop size in 2007, the Army's adaptations markedly improved its capability to conduct counterinsurgency operations.

In succeeding years force sizes fluctuated, generally trending downward though interspersed with temporary spikes when forces were ratcheted up in response to local conditions. In August 2008 the Iraqi Parliament prohibited the presence of U.S. forces in cities by the following summer and advocated their total removal by the end of 2011. Troops were out of the cities by June 2009, and combat operations ostensibly ceased by August 2010. When the Obama administration and the Iraqi government failed to conclude a Status of Forces Agreement, most U.S. troops were withdrawn, leaving only 700 trainers in country.

As the American involvement in Iraq continued into its second decade, the emergence and burgeoning strength of an ISIS offshoot known as the Islamic State of Iraq and the Levant (ISIL) and other groups associated with it caused the conflict to spill into nearby countries. Eventually, Operation Inherent Resolve, the name given to the international campaign against ISIL forces, placed U.S. forces in action not only in Iraq but also in Syria and, in a related campaign, Libya as well.

In June 2014 ISIL declared a caliphate after having overrun large portions of Syria and perhaps as much as a quarter of Iraq. At the height of its power, the self-proclaimed caliphate controlled more than 40,000 square miles of territory in Iraq and Syria inhabited by more than seven and a half million people. The Libyan branch, headquartered in Sirte, controlled a sizable swath of that country as well.

Meanwhile, ISIS- and ISIL-sponsored attacks and violence perpetrated by groups affiliated with them permeated much of the Islamic world. Egypt, Turkey, Saudi Arabia, Yemen, Bangladesh, and Lebanon were among targeted nations. Concurrently, terrorist groups extended the scope of their attacks, striking London, Paris, Madrid, and other locations in the west.

President Obama responded to the crisis by returning 5,000 troops to help the Iraqi Army defeat insurgents who appeared to be on the verge of further advances. Beginning in mid-2015, a formidable international military force was assembled to reclaim territory controlled by large and generally well-equipped ISIL units. The U.S. Army's III Armored Corps led the combined task force for the first three and a half years before being replaced by the XVII Airborne Corps. U.S. Special Forces and artillery units were most often employed in support of Iraqi infantry and Syrian Democratic Forces. The full panoply of American airpower—U.S. Air Force fighters, bombers, tankers, gunships, helicopters, transports, reconnaissance, ground attack, and unmanned aerial vehicles—as well as naval air units from several carrier strike forces and Army helicopters, visited destruction on ISIL formations and fortifications. It was an international endeavor: American air units were joined in the effort by air forces from twelve other nations. Interestingly, at times Russian and Syrian air assets were also employed against ISIL targets. Almost 35,000 air strikes were conducted. Defeat of ISIL in Iraq was proclaimed on December 9, 2017.

In the years 2014–15 the war in Iraq had begun to extend beyond that nation's boundaries. In neighboring Syria, conditions had become especially chaotic. Already rent by a civil war that began early in 2011, the new wave of violence added another dimension to the ongoing struggle between pro-regime forces and democratic groups trying to overthrow it. Both sides received significant amounts of external support. In addition to political backing, Iran, Russia, and Hezbollah funneled military and economic aid to the regime of Bashar al-Assad and the Syrian Armed Forces. The anti-Assad Free Syrian Army received sustenance from the CIA and was generally aligned with Kurdish-dominated Syrian Democratic Forces. The latter group's Autonomous Administration of North and East Syria was backed by the United States.

Complicating the situation for America and its allies was the presence in increasing strength of jihadist groups and ISIL forces who, in their quest for additional territory, also generally opposed the Assad regime. Thus, the very groups whose actions formed the motivation for America's having launched the Global War on Terrorism were, as part of their repertoire of violence, at times engaging a foe shared with the United States.

Coalitions shifted as conditions on the ground changed and disputes regarding philosophy and territory caused alliances to shatter or reshape. Relationships between major jihadist leaders were also sometimes fractious, causing groups to separate or temper their support. Nonetheless, by mid-decade jihadist cadres led by ISIL controlled significant territory in both Iraq and Syria. A caliphate was declared with Raqqa as its capital. The caliphate imposed Sharia law on the territories it controlled and regarded most nonaffiliated groups as being apostate.

The major intervention launched by the United States and its international partners in response to the rising tide of ISIL conquests succeeded after a four-and-a-half-year struggle. On March 23, 2019, fifteen months after the defeat of ISIL in Iraq, the defeat of ISIL in Syria was announced. Both were considerable achievements, victories that drew surprisingly little attention in the West and at best modest coverage in Western media.

Although estimates vary widely, ISIL casualties in Inherent Resolve operations were thought to be enormous, numbering by almost all accounts in the multiple thousands. U.S. sources believed as many as 80,000 may have been killed. British estimates placed the figure at around 25,000. Additional numbers were claimed by Iraqi and Syrian ground forces. Several ISIL political leaders, military commanders, and other high-value targets were thought to have been among the casualties.

An operation similar to Inherent Resolve, this one called Operation Odyssey Lightning, was conducted in Libya during the period of August–December 2016. A major focus was the capture of Sirte, the capital of the Libyan branch of ISIL. The major U.S. involvement consisted of precision air strikes in support of allied advances on the city. The air campaign included the use of U.S. Air Force B-2 bombers, which struck ISIL camps located south of the city.

Foremost perhaps in Syria, the lingering effects of these conflicts remain with us. As time drew on, the long and tortuous struggle in that country increased in its uniqueness and complexity. The Assad regime's attempt to push jihadist forces from its territory caused Turkey to intervene more directly in the fighting. Already stressed by the presence of perhaps as many as three million refugees from the conflict, the Turkish government was alarmed by the prospect of another two to three million seeking sanctuary as they were driven toward its border by Assad's forces. Turkey reacted forcefully, stopping the Syrian Army's advance, stabilizing the front, and halting the flow of refugees. Eventually, on December 8, 2024, the Assad regime was overthrown by Syrian National Army forces supported by Turkey.

In Lebanon, most especially during the years 2011–17, parts of that fragile country also became a battleground as forces on both sides of Syria's civil war brought their conflict to Lebanon's soil.

A further offshoot of the war was fraught with special danger. In southwest Syria, along that nation's border with Israel, the presence of nearby Iranian and Hezbollah cadres drew periodic exchanges of fire as Israeli units responded to the perceived threat by striking sharp blows against areas dominated by Iranian and Hezbollah forces.

Global War on Terrorism

The wide sweep of operations associated with the Global War on Terrorism is made evident by the fact that in addition to forces in country, troops in support of Operation Enduring Freedom (Afghanistan) were based in Uzbekistan, Kyrgyzstan, Tajikistan, and Pakistan, with additional small numbers in Yemen, Oman, Ethiopia, Kenya, and Egypt. Operation Iraqi Freedom was directly supported by supplementary troops posted in Turkey, Saudi Arabia, Kuwait, Pakistan, Qatar, and the United Arab Emirates.

Over the years, media coverage tended to focus on Afghanistan and Iraq as the major venues in the Global War on Terrorism struggle. There should be no mistaking, however, that the war on terrorism was indeed "global" in nature. Significant efforts—all initially under the Operation Enduring Freedom rubric—were ongoing, sometimes for years, at other locations around the world.

Operation Enduring Freedom–Trans Sahara

American forces, in concert with allies and indigenous units, have operated over wide stretches of the Sahara/Sahel region of Africa, including Algeria, Burkina Faso, Chad, Mali, Niger, Nigeria, Senegal, and Tunisia. The emphasis on specific programs has varied by country depending on local conditions. Generally, though, U.S. teams have been engaged in combating terrorism, training national forces, countering drug trafficking, and assisting in border security as well as opposing and denying sanctuary to extremist groups. More recent years have witnessed a shift toward a broader operational focus.

Operation Enduring Freedom–Horn of Africa

The official area for the Horn of Africa establishment encompasses Sudan, Somalia, Djibouti, Ethiopia, Eritrea, Kenya, and Seychelles. Operations have extended to other nations as well, sometimes touching Mauritania, Comoros, Liberia, Rwanda, Uganda, and Tanzania.

On the ground, U.S. troops have operated as part of a Combined Joint Task Force. Afloat, components of the U.S. Navy's Fifth Fleet have sailed as part of a combined international naval force.

Americans have served as advisors and provided equipment and material for what has for the most part been a noncombat role that has avoided long-duration operations by permanently assigned troops. Strikes by drones, cruise missiles, and air units have, however, been employed with some frequency. Most have been focused on the al-Shabaab terrorist organization active in many parts of the region.

U.S. naval units actively combat the rampant piracy that has long plagued the shipping lanes that skirt the tip of the continent. The area off the coast of Somalia has been struck with particular intensity over the years.

Inside Somalia, al-Qaeda-linked terrorist groups have vexed long-standing efforts to quell violence and move the nation to a more benign environment.

Operation Enduring Freedom–Philippines (Later, Operation Freedom Eagle)

Muslim-predominant areas in the southern Philippines—in particular, Mindanao and the nearby islands of Jolo and Basilan—have long been terrorist trouble spots. Underlying unrest can be traced back to the Philippine Insurrection at the turn of the 20th century. Though the Philippine national government ostensibly has sovereignty over the region, parts of it have been categorized at times in the past as "ungoverned."

Beginning in January 2002, U.S. Special Forces were deployed to the region to assist Philippine Army units in attaining control. The military's special operators were later joined by personnel from the CIA's Special Activities Division in combating al-Qaeda units and its Abu Sayyaf offshoot. The struggle has been waged with particular intensity on the island of Basilan, the location of the Abu Sayyaf's stronghold. The Battle of Marawi (May 23–October 17, 2017) featured urban warfare on a major scale before Philippine forces eventually prevailed.

In recent years, about 250 American military members are thought to have been assigned to operations in the Philippines.

Around the Globe

Since al-Qaeda began operations in the early 1990s, almost no nation or region of the world has been spared attack by that organization or the numerous offshoots it has spawned. In the Western world, headline-inducing attacks have struck at London, Paris, Madrid, and Brussels among many other locations. In the United States, the World Trade Center was targeted in 1993 and destroyed in 2001. On October 12, 2000, the USS *Cole* was attacked while in port at Aden, Yemen. More recently, "homegrown" terrorists inspired by al-Qaeda or linked to it killed 14 Americans and wounded 22 at San Bernardino, California (December 2, 2015). Another 49 were killed and 53 wounded at a nightclub in Orlando, Florida (June 12, 2016).

Recent assessments of worldwide terrorist activities generally conclude that while the number of terrorist incidents has declined in recent years (the Global Terrorism Index reported a total of 3,350 in 2023), the attacks have become deadlier—the 3,000 occurrences accounted for more than 8,000 deaths. The same period also saw a shift in the epicenter of attacks from the Middle East to the Central Sahel area of sub-Saharan Africa. In 2023 more than half of all terrorist-related deaths worldwide took place in that region.

In January 2018 Secretary of State James Mattis announced that competition between great powers has replaced global terrorism as the primary international security focus of the United States. The struggle continues, although often not at the forefront of public interest or media attention.

Author's note: While this book was in process, on December 8, 2024, the regime of Bashar al-Assad was overthrown by Syrian forces supported by Turkey.

References

The Cold War
The Path to War
11 "Geography, demography, and tradition contributed . . ." Gaddis, John Lewis. *We Now Know: Rethinking the Cold War.* New York: Oxford University Press, 1997, p. 25.

William H. Tunner
12 "[If] Berlin falls . . ." Sutherland, Jon, and Diane Cranwell. *The Berlin Airlift: The Salvation of a City.* Gretna, LA: Pelican Publishing Company, 2008, p. 179.

17 "as inflexibly systematic as a metronome . . ." Collier, Richard. *Bridge Across the Sky.* New York: McGraw-Hill, 1978, p. 101.

20 "Berlin blockade backfired . . ." Sutherland and Cranwell, p. 133.

26 "The most spectacularly successful failure . . ." Owen, Robert C. "The Hearings That Revolutionized Airlift." *Air Force Magazine* (November 2014): p. 67.

Bernard A. Schriever
31 "brigadier general of unusual competence . . ." Sheehan, Neil. *A Fiery Peace in a Cold War: Bernard Schriever and the Ultimate Weapon.* New York: Random House, 2009, p. 222.

32 "[Schriever] has excellent staying qualities . . ." Sheehan, p. 260.

32 "nationally supported effort of the highest priority" Sheehan, p. 274.

35 "I will not fire you . . ." Sheehan, p. 395.

37 "he was not afraid of anything . . ." Sheehan, p. 142.

40 "This is the most capable officer known to me" Sheehan, p. 44.

41 "If you can find someone who is knowledgeable . . ." Sheehan, p. 157.

43 "known as a man with complete integrity" Stine, G. Harry. *ICBM, the Making of the Weapon That Changed the World.* New York: Crown Publications, 1991.

Korea
Walton Walker
51 "If we had not pressured the United Nations . . ." Truman, Harry S. *Autobiography of Harry S. Truman.* Columbia: University of Missouri, 2002, p. 102.

52 **"a squat, plump, square-jawed Texan . . ."** Boyle, Hal. "Late General Walker Was Key in South Korea." Associated Press, July 31, 1955.

54 **"We are fighting a battle against time . . ."** Halberstam, David. *The Coldest Winter: America and the Korean War.* New York: Hyperion, 2007, p. 167. For an extended version of the speech, see Toland, John. *In Mortal Combat: Korea 1950–1953.* New York: Harper, 1991, p. 121.

56 **"They expended more ammunition . . ."** Toland, p. 205.

59 **"home for Christmas"** Patterson, James E. "Some Never Made It Home for Christmas." *Los Angeles Times*, June 28, 1986.

61 **"Bullshit"** Toland, p. 282.

61 **"if he smells Chinese chow . . ."** Halberstam, p. 202.

63 **"It is difficult to believe that any other general . . ."** Toland, p. 373.

63 **"a short, chunky, nice looking fellow . . ."** "Walton Walker—Forgotten Hero." http://www.oocities.org/generalwalktonwalker/11walkerbio.html. Retrieved March 29, 2018.

65 **"If American military history . . ."** Halberstam, p. 254.

66 **"He was the forgotten commander . . ."** Halberstam, p. 255.

Oliver P. Smith

66 **"The Marine breakout from the Chosin Reservoir"** Halberstam, David. Interview. *Proceedings.* The Naval Institute. Annapolis, MD, 2003.

67 **"quiet, reserved"** Toland, John. *In Mortal Combat: Korea 1950–1953.* New York: Harper, 1991, p. 176.

70 **"Don't let a bunch of Chinese laundrymen stop you"** Toland, p. 384.

70 **"barrel through"** Halberstam, David. *The Coldest Winter.* New York: Hyperion, 2007, p. 433.

72 **"What casualties?"** Halberstam, *The Coldest Winter,* p. 434.

72 **"Almond's greatest weakness . . ."** Halberstam, *The Coldest Winter,* p. 428.

73 **". . . the plan left "wide gaps" in his left flank . . ."** Halberstam, *The Coldest Winter,* p. 433.

77 **"Retreat, hell, we're simply advancing in another direction"** Shaara, Jeff. *The Frozen Hours.* New York: Ballantine Books, 2017, p. 457.

79 **"The breakout from the Chosin Reservoir . . ."** Halberstam, *The Coldest Winter,* p. 468.

80 **"a narrow, frightening shelf . . ."** Halberstam, *The Coldest Winter,* p. 435.

81 **"The campaign is perhaps the most brilliant . . ."** Shaara, p. 504.

83 **"one of the special, quiet heroes . . ."** Halberstam, *The Coldest Winter,* p. 430.

VIETNAM
Robin Olds

96 **"We weren't allowed to dogfight . . ."** Kuhn, Tom. "Robin Olds: An Unconventional Man's Fight for Conventional Warfare." *Airman Magazine* (October 2006).

101 **"mindless, soul-searing, thankless . . ."** Olds, Christina, Robin Olds, and Ed Rasimus. *Fighter Pilot: The Memoirs of Legendary Ace Robin Olds.* New York: St. Martin's Press, 2010, p. 231.

102   "With all due respect, the way to end the war . . ." Olds et al., p. 344.

103   "challenging and interesting . . ." Olds et al., p. 37.

104   "They can't even bomb an outhouse without my approval" Boot, Max. *The Savage Wars of Peace*. New York: Basic Books, 2003, p. 287.

104   "Prior to Linebacker II [the bombing campaign], the North Vietnamese . . ." Parks, W. Hays. "Linebacker and the Law of War." *Air University Review* (January–February 1983). See also Kissinger, Henry K. *White House Years*. New York: Little, Brown and Company 1979, pp. 1458–61.

The Tet Offensive

109   "We have too often been disappointed by the optimism of American leaders . . ." Stephan, Brad. "American Honor." *Wall Street Journal*, January 23, 2008, p. 18.

110   "If I've lost Cronkite, I've lost the average citizen" Boot, Max. *The Savage Wars of Peace*. New York: Basic Books, 2002, p. 309.

110   "Tet became a stunning manifestation of an important truth . . ." Hastings, Max. *Vietnam: An Epic Tragedy, 1945–1975*. New York: HarperCollins, 2018, p. 434.

110   "one of the most critical tactical decisions of the war" Palmer, David Richard. *Summer of the Trumpet: The History of the Vietnam War from a Military Man's Viewpoint*. New York: Ballantine, 1978, p 235.

Frederick C. Weyand

111   "often hailed as the only senior officer who prepared for trouble . . ." Hastings, Max. *Vietnam: An Epic Tragedy, 1945–1975*, New York: HarperCollins, 2018, p. 443.

113   "Crack the Sky, Shake the Earth" Dougan, Clark, and Stephen Weis et al. *Nineteen Sixty-Eight*. Boston: Boston Publishing Company, 1983, p. 10.

114   "I've destroyed a single division three times . . ." Fromson, Murray. Editorial. *The New York Times*, December 11, 2008.

114   "One of the agonies you'd go through . . ." Hastings, p. 328.

114   "the key to success in Vietnam . . ." Salter, Mark, and John McCain. *Hard Call: The Art of Great Decisions*. New York: The Hachette Group USA, 2007.

114   "our air is going to be the glue that holds all this together . . ." Hastings, p. 599.

115   "the American Army is really a people's army . . ." Karnow, Stanley. *Vietnam: A History*. New York: The Viking Press, 1983, p. 16.

116   "slow-spoken Californian" Hastings, p. 443.

118   "He was arguably the best American general of the Vietnam War" Zabecki, Maj. Gen. David T. (ret.). "Farewell to General Frederick C. Weyand." HistoryNet. https://www.historynet.com/farewell-to-general-frederick-c-weyand/. Retrieved February 20, 2025.

Orlinto Mark Barsanti

119   "the 101st Airborne Division is present for duty" Patterson, Michael Robert. "Orlinto Mark Barsanti, Major General, United States Army." Arlington National Cemetery. http://arlingtoncemetery.net/ombarsanti.htm. Retrieved August 19, 2016.

120 **"During the [Tet] holiday period, we need to be especially watchful . . ."** Bleistein, Sadie. "101st CAB TET Offensive Historical Article," November 2, 2008. https://www.army.mil.article/29698/101st_tet_offensive_historical_article. Retrieved March 30, 2019.

121 **"The man has an almost inconceivable amount of energy"** Patterson, http://arlingtoncemetery.net/ombarsanti.htm.

123 **"preparing all necessary systems and facilities . . ."** Olinto Mark Barsanti, Major General, United States Army." Retrieved August 19, 2016.

THE DISSENTERS
John Paul Vann

126 **"the closest the U.S. came in Vietnam to having a Lawrence of Arabia"** Sheehan, Neil. *A Bright Shining Lie: John Paul Vann and America in Vietnam.* New York: Random House, 1988, front matter narrative.

126 **"outspoken professionally and fearless in battle"** Sheehan, front matter narrative.

126 **"a wire-thin stick of ferocious energy and aggression"** Hastings, Max. *Vietnam: An Epic Tragedy 1945–1975.* New York: HarperCollins, 2018, p. 159.

127 **"tendency to play down the real picture"** Karnow, Stanley. *Vietnam: A History.* New York: Viking Press, 1983, p. 302.

127 **"irreverent candor was a refreshing antidote . . ."** Karnow, p. 260.

128 **"a miserable damn performance"** Hastings, p. 159. See also, Boot, Max. *The Road Not Taken: Edward Lansdale and the American Tragedy in Vietnam.* New York: Liveright Publishing Corporation, 2018, p. 402.

128 **"smart, determined, [with] reverse-slanting eyes . . ."** Hastings, p. 187.

128 **"small man with an outsize command presence"** Boot, p. 553.

128 **"He wanted to know everything about anything . . ."** Hastings, p. 187.

129 **"He was one guy I would have trusted with my life"** Hastings, p. 187.

131 **"rendered invaluable assistance in stopping the offensive"** Boot, p. 554.

132 **"Vann treated Vietnam as if the struggle was his personal property . . ."** Hastings, p. 613.

133 **"If the war is to be won, it must be done by the Vietnamese . . ."** Sheehan, p. 526.

Edward Lansdale

134 **"I've met a handful of people . . ."** Boot, p. 358.

134 **"What I respected [about Lansdale] was that . . ."** Hastings, p. 107.

135 **"one of the most unconventional . . ."** Boot, p. xlvii.

135 **"do what you did in the Philippines"** Sheehan, p. 134.

135 **"to undertake paramilitary operations . . ."** Millett, Allan R., ed. *A Short History of the Vietnam War.* Bloomington: Indiana University Press, 1978, p. 18.

136 **"People don't just pull up . . ."** Karnow, p. 222.

138 **"show [Diem] by deeds . . ."** Karnow, p. 248.

138 **"General Lansdale is the most highly qualified . . ."** Boot, p. 360.

139 **"It was morally wrong . . ."** Boot, p. 415.

140   "upon their doing their utmost . . ." Boot, p. 537.
141   "damn hard for guerillas . . ." Boot, p. 599.
141   "Communist guerillas hide among the people . . ." Karnow, p. 221.
142   "We [the U.S. military] mostly sought to destroy . . ." Boot, p. 599.
142   "One of the tragedies of the whole thing . . ." Boot, p. 572.

Victor H. Krulak
145   "won the war for us" Coram, Robert. *Brute: The Life of Victor Krulak, U.S. Marine.*
      New York: Back Bay Books, 2010, p. 71.
145   "was so smart, so assertive, so *right* . . ." Coram, p. 145.
146   "For your information, the Marine Corps is the Navy's police force . . ." Coram,
      p. 203.
147   "[the U.S.] would force the peasants . . ." Hastings, p. 131.
148   "nameless villages and hamlets . . ." Coram, p. 266.
148   "protection is the most important thing you can bring" Coram, p. 266.
148   "the shooting war is still going ahead at an impressive pace" Karnow, p. 293.
148   "You two did visit the same country, didn't you?" Karnow, p. 293.
149   "notoriously unsuccessful" Sheehan, p. 374.
149   "the essential ingredients for success have been assembled" Sheehan, p. 304.
150   "he was a rarity in the U.S. military . . ." Sheehan, p. 629.
150   "could be described without exaggeration as genius" Sheehan, p. 293.
151   "Your way will take forever . . ." Coram, p. 290.
152   "design for victory . . ." Sheehan, p. 631.
154   "You cannot win militarily . . ." Sheehan, p. 637.
156   "In Vietnam, it was the job of active duty senior officers . . ." Coram, pp. 315–16.

GRENADA
158   "serious problems in the ability of the Services to cooperate jointly" Senate Armed
      Services Committee Staff Report "Operation Urgent Fury, October 1983." Wash-
      ington, DC: Government Printing Office, p. 10.
158   "one of the perhaps dozen most militarized states in the world . . ." Adkin, Major
      Mark. *Urgent Fury: The Battle for Grenada.* Lexington, MA: Lexington Books, 1989,
      p. 21.
165   "only Marxist regime in modern times to suffer invasion and military destruction
      . . ." Adkin, p. XV.
166   "It [the invasion] was the first time ever I was glad to see an American" Adkin,
      p. 313.

George B. Crist
168   "a visible but completely safe role" Joint History Office of the Joint Chiefs of Staff.
      Operation Urgent Fury. Washington, DC, 2014, p. 3.
168   "close coordination with the Caribbean community forces at the appropriate
      time" Joint History Office of the Joint Chiefs of Staff, p. 36.

Panama

174 **"shortcomings in service cooperation and interoperability"** Joint History Office, Office of the Chairman of the Joint Chiefs of Staff. *Operation Just Cause: Panama.* Washington, DC: Government Printing Office, 2020, p. 1.

178 **"a small-framed man of average height . . ."** Woodward, Bob. *The Commanders.* New York: Simon & Schuster, 1991, p. 92.

175 **"maximum leader for national liberation"** Woodward, p. 185.

177 **"bodies of our enemies will float down the Panama Canal"** Joint History Office, p. 27.

178 **"Our strategy in going after this army . . ."** Powell, General Colin. Pentagon Press Conference, December 20, 1989.

182 **"We are plainly convinced that the population of Panama . . ."** Donnelly, Thomas, Margaret Roth, and Caleb Barker. *Operation Just Cause: The Storming of Panama.* New York: Lexington Books, 1991, p. 390.

Maxwell Thurman

187 **"a sequence of subtleties and innuendos"** Woodward, Bob. *The Commanders.* New York: Simon & Schuster, 1991, p. 92.

187 **"uncommon vigor, aggressiveness, and determination"** Joint History Office, Office of the Chairman of the Joint Chiefs of Staff. *Operation Just Cause: Panama.* Washington, DC: Government Printing Office, 2020, p. 3.

187 **"a bachelor workaholic . . ."** Woodward, p. 94.

189 **"caused Noriega to believe the U.S. was trying to intimidate him"** Joint History Office, p. 25.

190 **"a remarkable officer . . ."** "Maxwell Reid Thurman: General—United States Army." Arlington National Cemetery Website. Retrieved September 19, 2020.

Carl W. Stiner

191 **"Carl Stiner is my war fighter . . ."** Donnelly, Thomas, Margaret Roth, and Caleb Barker. *Operation Just Cause: The Storming of Panama.* New York: Lexington Books, 1991, p. 89.

191 **"slow talking country boy"** Chen, Edwin. "Panama: The Road to Victory." *Los Angeles Times,* December 26, 1989.

The Gulf War

195 **"the window of vulnerability"** Atkinson, Rick. *Crusade: The Untold Story of the Gulf War.* New York: Houghton Mifflin Company, 1993, p. 54.

196 **"That's exactly what I want. Do it."** Reynolds, Colonel Richard T. *The Heart of the Storm: The Genesis of the Air Campaign against Iraq.* Maxwell Air Force Base, AL: Air University Press, 1995, p. 56.

196 **"Our air power against theirs is the way to go . . ."** Reynolds, p. 110.

196 **"the most theatrical American in uniform . . ."** Atkinson, p. 1.

196 **"During the previous six months . . ."** Atkinson, p. 3.

197 "There's only going to be one guy in charge of the air . . ." Atkinson, p. 217.
198 "Brusque, profane, tireless, and self-confident" Atkinson, p. 64.
198 "Attack Iraqi leadership command and control . . ." Atkinson, pp. 20–21.
207 "merciful clemency" Atkinson, p. 468.
208 "lead to a long, open-ended, and costly occupation . . ." Tirpak, Frank A. "Lieutenant General Brent Scowcroft, 1925–2020." *Air Force Magazine,* September 20, 2020, p. 42.
209 "the most visible Iraqi losses were suffered during the flight from Kuwait . . ." Keegan, John. *The Iraq War.* New York: Alfred A. Knopf, 2004, p. 82.
209 "only America could have amassed more than nine million tons of material . . ." Atkinson, p. 492.

John A. Warden III
215 "The technology had caught up with the doctrine" Kelly, Michael. "The American Way of War." *The Atlantic Monthly* (January 2002).
218 "What it is—a focused, intense air campaign . . ." Atkinson, Rick. *Crusade: The Untold Story of the Persian Gulf War.* New York: Houghton Mifflin, 1993, p. 60.
218 "thickset and inelegant, possessed of brawny forearms . . ." Atkinson, p. 39.
219 "Don't worry, sir . . ." Atkinson, p. 62.
219 "His [Warden's] concept remained the heart of the Desert Storm air campaign." Powell, Colin, and Joseph E. Persico. *My American Journey.* New York: Ballantine Books, 1995, p. 460.
220 "The least that could be said . . ." Reynolds, Colonel Richard T. *Heart of the Storm: The Genesis of the Air Campaign against Iraq.* Maxwell Air Force Base, AL: Air University Press, 1995, p. xii.
220 "if one of the news magazines had wanted to run on its cover . . ." Halberstam, David. *War in the Time of Peace: Bush, Clinton, and the Generals.* New York: Little, Brown and Company, 2002, pp. 47–49.
221 "Warden had also become something of a lightning rod . . ." Olson, John Andrews. *John Warden and the Renaissance of American Air Power.* Washington, DC: Potomac Books, 2007, p. 37.

David A. Deptula
223 "a big teddy bear type of guy" Reynolds, Colonel Richard T. *Heart of the Storm: The Genesis of the Air Campaign against Iraq.* Maxwell Air Force Base, AL: Air University Press, 1995, p. 22.
224 "'effects-based' approach in building the Desert Storm air campaign . . ." Correll, John T. "The Assault on EBO." *Air Force Magazine* (January 2013), p. 52.

William "Gus" Pagonis
227 "animated Greek logistician" Atkinson, Rick. *Crusade: The Untold Story of the Persian Gulf War.* New York: Houghton Mifflin Company, 1993, p. 2.

H. R. McMaster

229 **"gruff and condescending," "aggressive," "prone to lecture"** "Why Did Trump Drop National Security Advisor?" BBC World News. March 22, 2018. Retrieved June 29, 2019.

230 **"the architect of the future U.S. Army," "the 21st century's pre-eminent warrior-thinker"** "Gen McMaster Makes *Time*'s '100 Most Influential.'" *Military Times*, April 27, 2014.

230 **"sheer brilliance as a wartime brigade commander"** Gertz, Bill. "Iconoclast Army General to Get Third Star: Army Maj. Gen. H. R. McMaster Receives Promotion." *The Free Beacon*. Retrieved February 18, 2014.

AFGHANISTAN/IRAQ/GLOBAL WAR ON TERRORISM

232 **"the planning for the war was inadequate . . ."** Kreishner, Otto. "Army General Calls Decision to Invade Iraq an 'Intellectual Failure.'" *Air Force Magazine* (February 2015), p. 4.

233 **"Killing Americans . . ."** Copinger-Symes, Major T. R. "Is Osama Bin Laden's Fatwa Urging Jihad against Americans Dated 23 February 1998 Justified by Islamic Law?" *Defense Studies*, October 19, 2007.

234 **"collect real-time actionable intelligence to help shape the battlefield . . ."** "On the Front Lines: The CIA in Afghanistan." CIA website. Extracted May 25, 2022.

234 **"The President is authorized to use all necessary and appropriate force . . ."** Scahill, Jeremy. *Dirty Wars*. New York: Norton Books, 2013, p. 19.

236 **"bin Laden was never within our grasp"** Kerry, John. "Tora Bora Revisited: How We Failed to Get bin Laden and Why It Matters Today." *Report to the Members of the Committee on Foreign Relations: United States Senate. John Kerry, Chairman. One Hundred Eleventh Congress, First Session, November 30, 2009*. Washington, DC: Government Printing Office, 2009.

236 **"one of the greatest military blunders . . ."** Bergen, Peter. "The Battle for Tora Bora: The Definitive Account of How Osama Bin Laden Escaped Our Grasp." *New Republic*, 2009.

241 **"the only thing that Osama bin Laden and Saddam Hussein have in common . . ."** Woodward, Bob. *Plan of Attack*. New York: Simon & Schuster, 2004, p. 159.

241 **"scant evidence to tie Saddam Hussein to terrorist organizations . . ."** Woodward, p. 159.

241 **"there was not one shred, one iota of evidence . . ."** Scahill, p. 14.

241 **"free Iraq in order to eliminate Iraqi weapons of mass destruction . . ."** Woodward, p. 154.

244 **"thousands of them are just taking off their uniforms and going home"** Woodward, p. 403.

David H. Petraeus

252 **"without David Petraeus, the American effort in Iraq . . ."** Hanson, Victor Davis. *The Savior Generals: How Five Great Commanders Saved Wars That Were Lost—From Ancient Greece to Iraq*. New York: Bloomsbury Press, 2013, p. 237.

252 **"you can't kill your way out of an insurgency"** Bergen, p. 286.

252 **"the people of Afghanistan are the centers of gravity . . ."** Bergen, Peter L. *The Longest War: The Enduring Conflict between America and Al-Qaeda.* New York: Free Press, 2011, p. 286.

253 **"We are supported by the entire world"** President George W. Bush, presidential address, September 11, 2001, Washington, DC.

253 **"In the absence of orders and guidance . . ."** Ricks, Thomas E. *The Generals.* New York: Penguin Books, 2012, p. 460.

William H. McRaven

257 **"we will be amending the mission"** Scahill, p. 446.

263 **"We will not triumph solely or even primarily through military might . . ."** Gellman, p. 100.

263 **"a simple plan, carefully constructed"** Gellman, Burton. "The Admiral." *Time,* December 16, 2011–January 2, 2012, p. 100.

Sean MacFarland

270 **"one of the reasons we were able to hold on . . ."** Ricks, p. 421.

271 **"I don't know if this war is worth the life of Terry Lisk . . ."** Ricks, p. 329.

Retrospective

272 **"orphan headquarters"** Ricks, p. 439.

272 **"The Afghan War did not thrive on neglect."** Ricks, p. 439.

275 **"We have a problem. We have two options . . ."** George, Susannah, Missy Ryan, Tyler Pager, Pamela Constable, John Hudson, and Griff White. "Surprise, Panic, and Fateful Choices: The Day America Lost Its Longest War." *Washington Post,* August 28, 2021.

277 **"the Taliban cannot make time run backward."** Ignatius, David. "News in a New Afghanistan." *Washington Post,* October 2, 2021.

277 **"At various points, the U.S. government hoped to eliminate al-Qaeda . . ."** Sopko, John F. *What We Need to Learn: Lessons from Twenty Years of Afghan Reconstruction.* Special Inspector General for Afghan Reconstruction, Arlington, VA: 11th Report, August 16, 2021.

280 **"The total number of attacks on Americans and Iraqis . . ."** Filkins, Dexter. *The Forever Wars.* New York: Vintage Books, 2009, p. 234.

Bibliography

The Cold War

Ambrose, Stephen E., and others. *The Cold War: A Military History*. New York: Random House, 2006.

Berg, Thomas. *The Clash of Titans: The Cold War*. Seminar. University of Nebraska-Lincoln, Osher Lifelong Learning Institute, 2019.

Butler, Susan. *Roosevelt and Stalin: Portrait of a Partnership*. New York: Knopf, 2015.

Dallek, Robert. *The Lost Peace: Leadership in a Time of Horror and Hype, 1945–1953*. New York: Harper, 2011.

Fink, Carole K. *Cold War: An International History*. Boulder, CO: Westview Press, 2013.

Gaddis, John Lewis. *The Cold War: A New History*. New York: Penguin Books, 2006.

———. *The United States and the Origins of the Cold War*. New York: Columbia University Press, 1972.

———. *We Now Know: Rethinking the Cold War*. New York: Oxford University Press, 1997.

Harper, John Lamberton. *The Cold War (Oxford Histories)*. New York: Oxford University Press, 2009.

McMahon, Robert J. *The Cold War: A Very Short Introduction*. New York: Oxford University Press, 2003.

Roberts, Geoffrey. *Stalin's Wars: From World War to Cold War, 1939–1953*. New Haven, CT: Yale University Press, 2006.

Wettig, Gerhard. *Stalin and the Cold War in Europe*. Lanham, MD: Rowman & Littlefield, 2008.

William H. Tunner

Collier, Richard. *Bridging the Sky*. New York: McGraw-Hill, 1978.

Hoppe, Billy J., Lt. Col., USAF. *Lieutenant General William H. Tunner in the China-Burma-India "Hump" and Berlin Airlift: A Case Study in Leadership in Development of Airlift Doctrine*. Maxwell AFB, AL: Air Command and Staff College, 1995.

Knight, Clayton. *Lifeline in the Sky*. New York: Morrow, 1957.

Owen, Robert C. "The Hearings That Revolutionized Airlift." *Air Force Magazine* (November 2014).

Patterson, Michael Robert. "William H. Tunner—Lieutenant General, United States Air Force." Arlington National Cemetery Website. March 3, 2024. http://www.arling toncemetery.net/whtunner.htm. Retrieved February 21, 2025.

Sutherland, Jon, and Diane Cramwell. *The Berlin Airlift*. Gretna, LA: Pelican Publishing Company, 2007.

Tunner, William H. *Over the Hump*. New York: Duel, Sloan, and Pearce, 1964.

United States Air Force Biography. *Lieutenant General William H. Tunner*. http://www .af.mil/information/bios. Retrieved July 31, 2020.

Bernard A. Schriever

Boyne, Walter J. "The Man Who Built the Missiles." *Air Force Magazine* (October 2000).

"General Bernard Adolph Schriever." United States Air Force Biography Display. http:// www.af.mil/AboutUs/Biographies/Display/tnbid/215/Article/104877/general-ber nard-adolph-schriever-aspx. Retrieved June 10, 2020.

Patterson, Michael Robert. "Bernard Adolph Schriever—General, United States Air Force." Arlington National Cemetery Website. March 1, 2024. http://www.arling toncemetery.net/baschriever.htm. Retrieved February 21, 2025.

Sheehan, Neil. *A Fiery Peace in a Cold War: Bernard Schriever and the Ultimate Weapon*. New York: Random House, 2009.

Stine, G. Harry. *ICBM, the Making of the Weapon That Changed the World*. New York: Crown Publications, 1991.

Stout, David. "Gen. Bernard Schriever, 94, Air Force Missile Chief, Dies." *New York Times*, June 24, 2005.

KOREA

Blair, Clay. *The Forgotten War: America in Korea 1950–1953*. New York: Crown Publishing, 1987.

Brady, James. *The Coldest War: A Memoir of Korea*. New York: Thomas Dunne Books, 1990.

Cumings, Bruce. *The Korean War: A History*. New York: Modern Library Chronicles, 2010.

Futrell, Robert F. *The United States Air Force in Korea*. Washington, DC: Office of Air Force History, United States Air Force, 1983.

Halberstam, David. *The Coldest Winter*. New York: Hyperion, 2007.

Hastings, Max. *The Korean War*. New York: Simon & Schuster, 1987.

Ridgway, Matthew. *The Korean War*. New York: Doubleday, 1967.

Toland, John. *In Mortal Combat: Korea 1950–1953*. New York: Harper, 1991.

Truman, Harry S. *Autobiography of Harry S. Truman*. Columbia: University of Missouri, 2002.

Walker

Appleman, Roy E. *South to Naktong, North to the Yalu*. Washington, DC: Government Printing Office, 1961.

Blair, Clay. *The Forgotten War: America in Korea, 1950–1953*. New York: Times Books, 1987.

Halberstam, David. *The Coldest Winter: America and the Korean War*. New York: Hyperion, 2007.

Haynes, R. S. "Walter Harris Walker." *Dictionary of American Military Biography.* Santa Barbara, CA: Greenwood Publishing Group, 1984, pp. 1153–56.

Heefrier, Wilson Allen. *Patton's Bulldog: The Life and Service of General Walton H. Walker.* Shippensburg, PA: White Mane Publishing Company, 2002.

The General Walton Walker Society. "Walton Walker—Forgotten Hero." http://www .oocities.org/generalwaltonwalker/11walkerbio-html. Retrieved April 21, 2015.

Toland, John. *In Mortal Combat: Korea 1950–1953.* New York: Harper, 1991.

Zabecki, David T. "Stand or Die—1950 Defense of Korea's Pusan Perimeter." HistoryNet, May 1, 2009. https://www.historynet.com/stand-or-die-1950-defense-of-koreas -pusan-perimeter/. Retrieved February 21, 2025.

Zimmerman, Dwight Jon. "Lt. Gen. Walton Walker Defied General of the Army Douglas MacArthur." *Defense Media Network*, October 24, 2014.

Oliver P. Smith

Encyclopedia Britannica. "Oliver P. Smith. http://www.britanica.com/EBchecked/topics /1743817/Oliver_P_Smith. Retrieved April 20, 2015.

Frank, Ben. "General O. P. Smith Interview." Marine Corps Research Center, Quantico, VA, June 1969.

"General Oliver P. Smith (USMC) (Deceased)." United States Marine Corps History Division. http://www.mcu.usmc.mil./historydivision/Pages/Who's%Who/S-U /Smith_op.aspx. Retrieved August 20, 2015.

Halberstam, David. *The Coldest Winter.* New York: Hyperion, 2007.

———. Interview. *Proceedings.* Annapolis, MD: Naval Institute Press, 2003.

La Bree, Clifton. *The Gentle Warrior: General Oliver Prince Smith, USMC.* Kent, OH: The Kent University Press, 2001.

"O. P. Smith Collection Highlights—Record of Military Service of General O.P. Smith, USMC." Marine Corps Archives & Special Collection. https://www.tecom.marines .mil/Portals/90/Docs/Archives/O.P.%20Smith%20Collection%20Highlights.pdf. Retrieved February 21, 2025.

Ricks, Thomas E. "O. P. Smith: The Most Underrated General in American History?" *Foreign Policy,* September 21, 2016.

Shaara, Jeff. *The Frozen Hours.* New York: Ballantine Books, 2017.

Shisler, Gail B. *For Country and Corps: The Life of General Oliver P. Smith.* Annapolis, MD: Naval Institute Press, 2009.

Toland, John. *In Mortal Combat, Korea 1950–1953.* New York: Harper, 1991.

VIETNAM

Boot, Max. *The Road Not Taken: Edward Lansdale and the American Tragedy in Vietnam.* New York: Liveright Publishing Corporation, 2018.

———. *The Savage Wars of Peace.* New York: Basic Books, 2002.

———. "The War over the Vietnam War." *Wall Street Journal,* October 8, 2011, p. C5.

Bowden, Mark. *Hue 1968: A Turning Point of the American War in Vietnam.* New York: Atlantic Monthly Press, 2017.

Broughton, Jack. "The Vietnam War That Wasn't." *Air Force Magazine*, August 2014, pp. 68–72.

Butler, David. *The Fall of Saigon*. New York: Simon & Schuster, 1985.

Correll, John T. "Encounter in the Gulf of Tonkin." *Air Force Magazine*, January 2012.

———. "Into Son Tay." *Air Force and Space Digest*, October/November 2018, pp. 74–77.

———. "Vietnamization." *Air Force Magazine*, August 2017, pp. 60–64.

Editors of Boston Publishing Company. *The American Experience in Vietnam*. Boston: Boston Publishing Company, 2014.

Emerson, Stephen. *Air War over North Vietnam: Operation Rolling Thunder*. Barnsley, UK: Pen and Sword Military, 2018.

———. *North Vietnam: 1972 Easter Offensive*. Barnsley, UK: Pen & Sword, 2020.

Grandolini, Albert. *The Easter Offensive Vietnam 1972*. Warwick, UK: Helion & Company, 2015.

Hastings, Max. *Vietnam: An Epic Tragedy, 1945–1975*. New York: HarperCollins, 2018.

Kann, Peter R., and Francis Fitzgerald. "Reporting from Vietnam: American Journalism 1959–1969," cited in *Bookmarks: Stories in American History*. Public Affairs, 2001, p. 414.

Karnow, Stanley. *Vietnam: A History*. New York: The Viking Press, 1988.

Millett, Allen R., ed. *A Short History of the Vietnam War*. Bloomington, IN: Indiana University Press, 1978.

Morrison, William H. *Twentieth Century American Wars*. New York: Hippocrene Books, 1993.

Niles, Douglas. *A Noble Cause: American Battlefield Victories in Vietnam*. New York: Berkley Caliber, 2015.

Nolan, Keith W. *The Battle for Saigon: Tet 1968*. New York: Pocket, 1968.

Phillips, Thomas D. "Vietnam: A Retrospective." In *A Pilgrim in Unholy Places*. Westminster, MD: Heritage Books, 2006, pp. 150–62.

Schemmer, Benjamin F. *The Raid: The Son Tay Prison Rescue Mission*. New York: Ballantine Books, 2002.

Schlight, John. *The United States Air Force in Southeast Asia: The War in South Vietnam—The Years of the Offensive 1965–1968*. Washington, DC: Office of Air Force History, 1988.

Schmitz, David F. *The Tet Offensive: Politics, War, and Public Opinion*. Lanham, MD: Rowman & Littlefield, 2005.

Sheehan, Neil. *A Bright Shining Lie: John Paul Vann and America in Vietnam*. New York: Random House, 1988.

Sorley, Lewis. *A Better War: The Unexamined Victories and Final Tragedy of America's Last Years in Vietnam*. New York: A Harvest Book, Harcourt, Inc., 1999.

Summers, Harry G., Jr. *Vietnam War Almanac*. New York: Books on File Publications, 1985.

Tucker-Jones, Anthony. *The Vietnam War: The Tet Offensive 1968*. Barnsley, UK: Pen & Sword, 2014.

Wilbanks, James H. *The Battle of An Loc*. Bloomington: Indiana University Press, 2005.

———. *The Tet Offensive: A Concise History*. New York: Columbia University Press, 2008.

Willensen, Kim. *The Bad War: An Oral History of the Vietnam War*. New York: The New American Library, 1987.

Williams, William Appleman, Thomas McCormick, Lloyd Gardner, and William LeFeber, eds. *America in Vietnam.* New York: W. W. Norton & Company, 1989.

Robin Olds
Boot, Max. *The Savage Wars of Peace.* New York: Basic Books, 2003.
Emerson, Stephen. *Air War over North Vietnam: Operation Rolling Thunder.* Barnsley, UK: Pen and Sword Military, 2018.
Futrell, R. Frank, et al., eds. *The United States Air Force in Southeast Asia, 1965–1973: Aces and Aerial Victories.* Washington, DC: Office of Air Force History, 2012.
Grier, Peter. "The Chappie James Way." *Air Force and Space Digest*, October/November 2018.
Kissinger, Henry K. *White House Years.* New York: Little, Brown and Company, 1979.
Kuhn, Tom. "Robin Olds: An Unconventional Man's Fight for Conventional Warfare." *Airman Magazine* (October 2006).
Losey, Stephen. "Mustache March: Robin Olds' Mustache Is Just a Sliver of His Story." *Air Force Times*, March 4, 2019.
Michel, Marshall L. *Clashes: Air Combat over North Vietnam.* Annapolis, MD: Naval Institute Press, 1997.
Olds, Christina, Robin Olds, and Ed Rasimus. *Fighter Pilot: The Memoirs of Legendary Ace Robin Olds.* New York: St. Martin's Press, 2010.
Parks, W. Hays. "Linebacker and the Law of War." *Air University Review* (January–February 1983).
Schlight, John. *The United States Air Force in Southeast Asia: The War in Vietnam—The Years of the Offensive 1965–1968.* Washington, DC: Office of Air Force History, 2015.

Frederick C. Weyand
Dougan, Clark, and Stephen Weis et al. *Nineteen Sixty-Eight.* Boston: Boston Publishing Company, 1983.
Fromson, Murray. Editorial. *The New York Times*, December 11, 2008.
Hastings, Max. *Vietnam: An Epic Tragedy, 1945–1975.* New York: HarperCollins, 2018.
Karnow, Stanley. *Vietnam: A History.* New York: The Viking Press, 1983.
Salter, Mark, and John McCain. *Hard Call: The Art of Great Decisions.* New York: The Hachette Group USA, 2007.
U.S. Army Official Biography. "General Frederick Carlton Weyand, U.S. Army."
Zabecki, Maj. Gen. David T. (ret.). "Farewell to General Frederick C. Weyand." HistoryNet. https://www.historynet.com/farewell-to-general-frederick-c-weyand/. Retrieved February 20, 2025.

Orlinto Mark Barsanti
Bleistein, Sadie. "101st CAB TET Offensive Historical Article." U.S. Army. https://www.army.mil/article/29698/101st_cab_tet_offensive_historical_article. Retrieved March 30, 2019.

Gonzales, Mary L. "101st Combat Record in Vietnam 'Unmatched.'" https://web.archive
.org/web/20181002174246/http://fortcampbellcourier.com/news/commentary/arti
cle_bcd86ea2-06b8-11df-a6f1-001cc4c03286.html. Retrieved March 30, 2019.

History of the 101st Airborne Division (Air Assault) Division History. https://scream
ingeagle.org/division-history/. Retrieved March 30, 2019.

Patterson, Michael Robert. "Orlinto Mark Barsanti, Major General, United States
Army." Arlington National Cemetery. http://arlingtoncemetery.net/ombarsanti.htm.
Retrieved August 19, 2016.

John Paul Vann

Boot, Max. *The Road Not Taken: Edward Lansdale and the American Tragedy in Vietnam.*
New York: Liveright Publishing Corporation, 2018.

Halberstam, David. *The Making of a Quagmire: America and Vietnam during the Kennedy
Era.* New York: Rowman & Littlefield, 2008.

Hastings, Max. *Vietnam: An Epic Tragedy 1945–1975.* New York: HarperCollins, 2018.

Karnow, Stanley. *Vietnam: A History.* New York: The Viking Press, 1988.

Kross, Peter. "John Paul Vann: Man and Legend. HistoryNet. Retrieved March 15, 2021.

Lewy, Guenter. *America in Vietnam.* Oxford, UK: Oxford University Press, 1980.

Sheehan, Neil. *A Bright Shining Lie: John Paul Vann and America in Vietnam.* New York:
Random House, 1988.

———. "An American Soldier in Vietnam." *New Yorker,* July 11, 1988.

Steel, Ronald. "The Man Who Was the War." *New York Times,* September 25, 1988.

Edward Lansdale

Boot, Max. *The Road Not Taken: Edward Lansdale and the American Tragedy in Vietnam.*
New York: Liveright Publishing Corporation, 2018.

Currey, Cecil B. *Edward Lansdale, the Unquiet American.* Boston: Houghton Mifflin,
1988.

Hastings, Max. *Vietnam: An Epic Tragedy, 1945–1975.* New York: HarperCollins, 2018.

Karnow, Stanley. *Vietnam: A History.* New York: The Viking Press, 1988.

Lansdale, Edward G. *In the Midst of Wars: An American's Mission to Southeast Asia.* 2nd ed.
New York: Fordham University Press, 1991.

McAllister, James. "The Lost Revolution: Edward Lansdale and the American Defeat in
Vietnam, 1964–1968." *Small Wars and Insurgencies* 14 (2003).

Millett, Allen R., ed. *A Short History of the Vietnam War.* Bloomington: Indiana University
Press, 1978.

Sheehan, Neil. *A Bright Shining Lie: John Paul Vann and America in Vietnam.* New York:
Random House, 1988.

Victor H. Krulak

Coram, Robert. *Brute: The Life of Victor Krulak, U.S. Marine.* New York: Back Bay Books,
2011.

Hastings, Max. *Vietnam: An Epic Tragedy, 1945–1975.* New York: HarperCollins, 2018.

Karnow, Stanley. *Vietnam: A History.* New York: The Viking Press, 1988.

Krulak, Victor. *First to Fight: An Inside View of the U.S. Marine Corps*. Annapolis, MD: Naval Institute Press, 1984.

Miller, Stephen. "Military Innovator Who Sought New Approach to Battle in Vietnam." *Wall Street Journal*, January 3, 2009. Retrieved March 22, 2021.

Sheehan, Neil. *A Bright Shining Lie: John Paul Vann and America in Vietnam*. New York: Random House, 1988.

GRENADA

Adkin, Major Mark. *Urgent Fury: The Battle for Grenada*. Lexington, MA: Lexington Books, 1989.

Couvillon, Major Michael J. *Grenada Grinder: The Complete Story of AC-130H Spectre Gunships in Operation Urgent Fury*. Marietta, GA: Deeds Publishing Company, 2011.

Harding, Stephen. *Air War Grenada*. Missoula, MT: Pictorial Histories Publishing Company, 1984.

Joint History Office of the Joint Chiefs of Staff. *Operation Urgent Fury*. Washington, DC, 2014.

Kukielski, Philip. *The U.S. Invasion of Grenada: Legacy of a Flawed Victory*. Jefferson, NC: McFarland Publishing, 2020.

Raines, Edgar F., Jr. *The Rucksack War*. Washington, DC: United States Army Center for Military History, 2012.

Russell, Lee E., and M. Albert Mendez. *Grenada 1983*. London: Osprey Publishing Ltd., 1985.

Schwarzkopf, General H. Norman, and Peter Petre. *It Doesn't Take a Hero*. New York: Bantam Books, 1992.

Stewart, Richard W., and Edgar F. Raines. *Operation Urgent Fury: The Invasion of Grenada 1983*. Washington, DC: United States Army Center for Military History, 2012.

George B. Crist

Adkin, Major Mark. *Urgent Fury: The Battle for Grenada*. Lexington, MA: Lexington Books, 1989.

"General George B. Crist, USMC (Retired)." Marine Corps University, Research-Marine Corps History Division. Retrieved March 27, 2021.

Joint History Office of the Joint Chiefs of Staff. *Operation Urgent Fury*. Washington, DC, 2014.

Raines, Edgar F. *The Rucksack War*. Washington, DC: United States Army Center for Military History, 2012.

Stewart, Richard W., and Edgar F. Raines. *Operation Urgent Fury: The Invasion of Grenada, 1983*. Washington, DC: United States Army Center for Military History, 2012.

"Who's Who in Marine Corps History." History Division, United States Marine Corps. Retrieved March 27, 2021.

H. Norman Schwarzkopf

Grossman, Mark. *World Military Leaders: A Biographical Dictionary*. New York: Facts on File, 2007.

Joint History Office of the Joint Chiefs of Staff. *Operation Urgent Fury*. Washington, DC, 2014.

McNeese, Tim. *H. Norman Schwarzkopf*. New York: Chelsea Publishing, 2003.

Schwarzkopf, H. Norman, and Peter Petre. *It Doesn't Take a Hero*. New York: Bantam Books, 1992.

Stewart, Richard W. *Operation Urgent Fury: The Invasion of Grenada, October, 1983*. Washington, DC: United States Army Center for Military History, 2008.

PANAMA

Chen, Edwin. "Panama: The Road to Victory." *Los Angeles Times*, December 26, 1989.

De Young, Karen. *Soldier: The Life of Colin Powell*. New York: Alfred A. Knopf, 2006.

Donnelly, Thomas, Margaret Roth, and Caleb Baker. *Operation Just Cause: The Storming of Panama*. New York: Lexington Books, 1991.

Hook, Franklin. *Yankee Go Home*. Charleston, SC: CreateSpace, 2017.

Joint History Office, Office of the Chairman of the Joint Chiefs of Staff. *Operation Just Cause: Panama*. Washington, DC: Government Printing Office, 2020.

McConnell, Malcolm. *Just Cause*. New York: St. Martin's Press, 1991.

Woodward, Bob. *The Commanders*. New York: Simon & Schuster, 1991.

Maxwell Thurman

Chen, Edwin. "Panama: The Road to Victory." *Los Angeles Times*, December 26, 1989.

De Young, Karen. *Soldier: The Life of Colin Powell*. New York: Alfred A. Knopf. 2006.

Donnelly, Thomas, Margaret Roth, and Caleb Baker. *Operation Just Cause: The Storming of Panama*. New York: Lexington Books. 1991.

Hook, Franklin. *Yankee Go Home*. Charleston, SC: CreateSpace. 2017.

Joint History Office, Office of the Chairman of the Joint Chiefs of Staff. *Operation Just Cause: Panama*. Washington, DC: Government Printing Office, 2020.

"Maxwell Reid Thurman: General—United States Army." Arlington National Cemetery Website. Retrieved September 18, 2020.

McConnell, Malcolm. *Just Cause*. New York: St. Martin's Press, 1991.

Patrick, Bethanne Kelly. "Army General Maxwell Thurman." Military.com. Retrieved September 18, 2020.

Woodward, Bob. *The Commanders*. New York: Simon & Schuster, 1991.

Carl W. Stiner

Chen, Edwin. "Panama: The Road to Victory." *Los Angeles Times*, December 26, 1989.

Clancy, Tom, and Carl W. Stiner. *Shadow Warriors: Inside the Special Forces*. New York: G. P. Putnam's Sons, 2002.

Donnelly, Thomas, Margaret Roth, and Caleb Baker. *Operation Just Cause: The Storming of Panama*. New York: Lexington Books, 1991.

Joint History Office, Office of the Chairman of the Joint Chiefs of Staff. *Operation Just Cause: Panama*. Washington, DC: Government Printing Office, 2020.

McConnell, Malcolm. *Just Cause*. New York: St. Martin's Press, 1991.

United States Army Official Biography—Carl W. Stiner. Retrieved April 26, 2021.

GULF WAR
Books

Atkinson, Rick. *Crusade: The Untold Story of the Persian Gulf War.* New York: Houghton Mifflin Company, 1993.

Halberstam, David. *War in the Time of Peace: Bush, Clinton, and the Generals:* New York: Little, Brown and Company, 2006.

Hallion, Richard P. *Storm over Iraq: Airpower in the Gulf.* Washington, DC: Smithsonian Institute Press, 1992.

Hiro, Dilip. *Desert Shield to Desert Storm.* London: HarperCollins, 1992.

Keegan, John. *The Iraq War.* New York: Alfred A. Knopf, 2004.

Mann, Colonel Edward G., III. *Thunder and Lightning: Desert Storm and the Air Power Debates.* Maxwell Air Force Base, AL: Air University Press, 1995.

Powell, Colin L., and Joseph E. Persico. *My American Journey.* New York: Ballantine Books, 1995.

Reynolds, Colonel Richard T. *Heart of the Storm: The Genesis of the Air Campaign against Iraq.* Maxwell Air Force Base, AL: Air University Press, 1995.

Schwarzkopf, General H. Norman. *It Doesn't Take a Hero.* New York: Bantam Books, 1992.

Woodward, Bob. *The Commanders: The Pentagon and the First Gulf War.* New York: Simon & Schuster, 1991.

United States Department of Defense. *Conduct of the Persian Gulf War: First Report to Congress.* Washington, DC: Government Printing Office, 1992.

Periodicals

Correll, John T. "The Assault on EBO." *Air Force Magazine* (January 2013): pp. 50–54.

———. "The Ups and Downs of Close Air Support." *Air Force Magazine* (December 2019): p. 61.

Grant, Rebecca. "Desert Shield." *Air Force Magazine* (August 2010): pp. 52–57.

———. "Horner's Gulf War." *Air Force Magazine* (March 2016): pp. 22–26.

———. "A Prelude to War." *Air Force Magazine* (August 2015).

Kelly, Michael. "The American War of War." *The Atlantic Monthly* (June 2002).

———. "Slow Squeeze." *The Atlantic Monthly* (May 2002).

Mellinger, Phillip S. "Learning the Not-So-Obvious Lessons." *Air Force Magazine* (March 2017), pp. 71–72.

"War in the Gulf." Special issue, *Time*, January 28, 1991. See especially pages 17, 20–21, 23, 30, 32.

John A. Warden III

Atkinson, Rick. *Crusade: The Untold Story of the Persian Gulf War.* New York: Houghton Mifflin, 1993.

Halberstam, David. *War in the Time of Peace: Bush, Clinton, and the Generals.* New York: Little, Brown and Company, 2002.

Kelly, Michael. "The American Way of War." *Atlantic Monthly* (January 2002).

Mann, Colonel Edward G., III. *Thunder and Lightning: Desert Storm and the Air Power Debates.* Maxwell Air Force Base, AL: Air University Press, 1995.

Olson, John Andrews. *John Warden and the Renaissance of American Air Power.* Washington, DC: Potomac Books, 2007.

Powell, Colin, and Joseph E. Persico. *My American Journey.* New York: Ballantine Books, 1995.

Reynolds, Colonel Richard T. *Heart of the Storm: The Genesis of the Air Campaign against Iraq.* Maxwell Air Force Base, AL: Air University Press, 1995.

United States Air Force Official Biography. "Colonel John A. Warden III."

Woodward, Bob. *The Commanders: The Pentagon and the First Gulf War.* New York: Simon and Schuster, 1991.

David A. Deptula

Atkinson, Rick. *Crusade: The Untold Story of the Persian Gulf War.* New York: Houghton Mifflin Harcourt Publishing Company, 1993.

Correll, John T. "The Assault on EBO." *Air Force Magazine* (January 2013).

Hallion, Richard P. *Storm over Iraq: Airpower in the Gulf.* Washington, DC: Smithsonian Institute Press, 1992.

Lieutenant General David A. Deptula U.S. Air Force Biography. Retrieved April 12, 2021.

Mann, Colonel Edward G., III. *Thunder and Lightning: Desert Storm and the Air Power Debate.* Maxwell Air Force Base, AL: Air University Press, 1995.

Olson, John Andreas. *Strategic Air Power in Desert Storm.* London: Routledge, 2013.

Reynolds, Colonel Richard T. *Heart of the Storm: The Genesis of the Air Campaign against Iraq.* Maxwell Air Force Base, AL: Air University Press, 1995.

William "Gus" Pagonis

Atkinson, Rick. *Crusade: The Untold Story of the Persian Gulf War.* New York: Houghton Mifflin Publishing Company, 1993.

Pagonis, William G., and Jeffrey L. Cruickshank. *Moving Mountains: Leadership and Logistics Lessons from the Gulf War.* Boston: Harvard Business Review Press, 1992.

Pyle, Richard. *Schwarzkopf: The War, the Mission, the Triumph.* New York: Arrow, 1991.

Schwarzkopf, H. Norman, and Peter Petre. *It Doesn't Take a Hero.* New York: Bantam Books, 1992.

United States Army Official Biography. "William G. Pagonis." Retrieved March 31, 2021.

William "Gus" Pagonis Speaker Profile. *AAE Speaker.* Retrieved April 8, 2021.

H. R. McMaster

Atkinson, Rick. *Crusade: The Untold Story of the Persian Gulf War.* New York: Houghton Mifflin Harcourt Publishing Company, 1993.

"Gen McMaster Makes *Time*'s 100 Most Influential." *Military Times,* April 27, 2014.

Gertz, Bill. "Iconoclast Army General to Get Third Star." *Military Times,* April 27, 2014.

Keegan, John. *The Iraq War.* New York: Alfred A. Knopf, 2004.

"Lieutenant General H. R. McMaster: Visiting Fellows Biography." Hoover Institution. Retrieved April 12, 2021.

McMaster, H. R. "The Warriors-Eye View of Afghanistan." Interview. *Wall Street Journal*, May 11, 2017.

Schwarzkopf, General H. Norman, and Peter Petre. *It Doesn't Tale a Hero*. New York: Bantam Books, 1992.

"Why Did Trump Drop National Security Advisor?" *BBC World News*, March 22, 2018.

AFGHANISTAN/IRAQ/GLOBAL WAR ON TERRORISM

Belasco, Mary. *Troop Levels in the Afghanistan and Iraq Wars, FY 2001–2012: Cost and Related Issues*. Washington, DC: Congressional Research Service, July 2, 2009.

Bergan, Peter L. *The Longest War: The Enduring Conflict between America and Al-Qaeda*. New York: Free Press, 2011.

Cloud, David, and Greg Joffe. *The Fourth Star: Four Generals and the Epic Struggle for the Future of the United States Army*. New York: Crown Publishers, 2009.

Filkins, Dexter. *The Forever War*. New York: Alfred A. Knopf, 2008.

Franks, General Tommy. *American Soldier*. New York: Regan Books, 2004.

Gannon, Kathy, and Tameem Akhgar. "Renewed Hope for Peace Talks." Associated Press, May 17, 2021.

George, Susannah, Missy Kane, Tyler Pager, Pamela Constable, John Hudson, and Griff White. "Surprise, Panic, and Fateful Choices: The Day America Lost Its Longest War." *Washington Post*, August 28, 2021.

Gordon, Michael R., and General Bernard E. Trainor. *Cobra II: The Inside Story of the Invasion and Occupation of Iraq*. New York: Pantheon Books, 2006.

———. *The Endgame: The Inside Struggle for Iraq from George W. Bush to Barack Obama*. New York: Pantheon Books, 2012.

Hanson, Victor Davis. *The Savior Generals: How Five Great Commanders Saved Wars That Were Lost—From Ancient Greece to Iraq*. New York: Bloomsbury Press, 2013.

Ignatius, David. "News in a New Afghanistan." *Washington Post*, October 3, 2021.

Jones, Seth. *In the Graveyard of Empires: America's War in Afghanistan*. New York: W. W. Norton & Company, 2009.

Keegan, John. *The Iraq War*. New York: Alfred A. Knopf, 2004.

Kreishner, Otto. "Army General Calls Decision to Invade Iraq an 'Intellectual Failure.'" *Air Force Magazine* (February 2015).

Morell, Michael. *The Great War of Our Time: The CIA's Fight against Terrorism from Al Qa'ida to ISIS*. New York: Twelve, Hachette Book Group, 2015.

Owen, Mark. *No Easy Day: The Autobiography of a Navy Seal*. New York: Dutton, 2012.

Ricks, Thomas E. *Fiasco: The American Military Adventure in Iraq*. New York: Penguin Press, 2006.

———. *The Gamble: General David Petraeus and the American Adventure in Iraq, 2006–2008*. New York: Penguin Press, 2009.

———. *The Generals: American Military Commanders from World War II to Today*. New York: Penguin Books, 2012.

Scahill, Jeremy. *Dirty Wars*. New York: Norton Books, 2013.

Sentiford, Barry M. *Success in the Shadows: Operation Enduring Freedom-Philippines and the Global War on Terrorism*. Fort Leavenworth, KS: Combat Studies Institute Press, 2018.

Sopko, John F. *What We Need to Learn: Lessons from Twenty Years of Afghan Reconstruction.* Special Inspector General for Afghanistan Reconstruction, 11th Report. Arlington, VA, August 16, 2021.
Stern, Jessica, and J. M. Berger. *ISIS: The State of Terror.* New York: HarperCollins, 2015.
Woodward, Bob. *Plan of Attack.* New York: Simon & Schuster, 2004.

Biographies
Academy of Achievement. William McRaven Biography. Washington, D.C.: Museum of Living History, April 26, 2016.
General William Wallace.
Lieutenant General John F. Mulholland Jr.
Lieutenant General Sean MacFarland.
United States Army Official Biographies.

Gary Berntsen
Bergen, Peter L. *The Longest War: The Enduring Conflict between America and Al-Qaeda.* New York: Free Press, 2011.
Berntsen, Gary, and Ralph Pezzullo. *Jawbreaker: The Attack on Bin Laden and Al-Qaeda—A Personal Account by the CIA'S Key Field Commander.* New York: Crown Publications, 2005.
Hirst, Michael. "CIA Commander: U.S. Let Bin Laden Slip Away." *Newsweek,* August 15, 2005.
Jones, Seth G. *In the Graveyard of Empires: America's War in Afghanistan.* New York: W. W. Norton and Company, 2009.
Risen, James. *State of War: The Secret History of the CIA and the Bush Administration.* New York: Simon & Schuster, 2006.
"Senate Report: Bin Laden Was Within Grasp." CBS News. Retrieved November 34, 2016.

David H. Petraeus
Bergen, Peter L. *The Longest War: The Enduring Conflict between America and Al-Qaeda.* New York: Free Press, 2011.
Gordon, Michael R., and General Bernard E. Trainor. *Cobra II: The Inside Story of the Invasion and Occupation of Iraq.* New York: Pantheon Books, 2006.
Petraeus, General David H. "General Petraeus Updates Guidance on Use of Force." Cent com.mil. Retrieved April 13, 2021.
Ricks, Thomas D. *In the Company of Soldiers: A Chronicle of Combat.* New York: Henry Holt and Company, 2007.
Ricks, Thomas E. *The Gamble: General David Petraeus and the American Military Adventure in Iraq 2006–2008.* New York: The Penguin Press, 2009.
———. *The Generals.* New York: The Penguin Press, 2012.
United States Army. *Army Field Manual 3-24 Counterinsurgency.* U.S. Army Combined Warfare Center. Fort Leavenworth, KS: Department of the Army, 2006.

William H. McRaven

Academy of Achievement. *William McRaven Biography.* Washington, DC: Museum of Living History, April 26, 2016.

Caruso, Robert. *Opinion: The Legacy of Adm William McRaven.* Annapolis, MD: United States Naval Institute, 2014.

Gellman, Barton. "The Admiral." *Time,* December 16, 2011–January 2, 2012, p. 100.

McRaven, William (principal author). *The National Strategy for Combating Terrorism.* Washington, DC: The Department of State, 2006.

Morell, Michael. *The Great War of Our Time: The CIA's Fight against Terrorism from Al Qa'ida to ISIS.* New York: Twelve, Hachette Book Group, 2015.

Owen, Mark. *No Easy Day: The Autobiography of a Navy Seal.* New York: Dutton, 2012.

Scahill, Jeremy. *Dirty Wars.* New York: Norton Books, 2013.